Corvette

The Great American Sports Car

D1264033

Published by

Krause Publications, a division of F+W Media, Inc.
700 East State Street • Iola, WI 54990-0001
715-445-2214 • 888-457-2873
www.krausebooks.com

To order books or other products call toll-free 1-800-258-0929
or visit us online at www.krausebooks.com or www.Shop.Collect.com

Library of Congress Control Number: 2010931153

ISBN-13: 978-1-4402-1551-3
ISBN-10: 1-4402-1551-0

Designed by Sharon Bartsch
Edited by Brian Earnest

Printed in the United States of America

CONTENTS

A SINGULAR BREED

Just how unique is the Corvette? Ask yourself this: Regardless of the year, does the Corvette remind you of any other car? Does any other car remind you of a Corvette?

From its most humble beginnings, when Chevrolet produced a mere 300 1953 Polo White, fiberglass-bodied roadsters, the 'Vette has occupied a class of American car all by itself. At the time of its birth, there was nothing even remotely like it built on U.S. soil. Over the years, many challengers have come and gone, but the mighty Corvette is still going strong in its sixth generation.

There have been obstacles, for sure. High-horsepower cars like the 'Vette fell out of favor in the 1970s and '80s, when gas prices and insurance rates soared, and the demand for high performance dwindled. American car buyers began placing more of a premium on practicality, economy, seating space and cargo room — all things the Corvette will never provide.

But somehow, the 'Vette has been above it all. Its appeal is evergreen. The very idea of a sexy, somewhat dangerous, rear-engined rocket never ceases to go out of style. A Corvette on the open road with the top down still seems about as close to flying as most of us will ever get in an automobile.

So here's to the 'Vette. There is nothing else like it. Whether it's a split-window '63, a toothy '57, a shark-bodied '72, an ultra-cool '96 Grand Sport or a mind-numbing 2010 Z06, the Corvette is simply in a league all its own.

1953

The new 1953 Corvette had a fiberglass body, chrome-framed grille with 13 heavy vertical chrome bars, rounded front fenders with recessed headlights with wire screen covers, no side windows or outside door handles, a wraparound windshield and protruding, fender-integrated taillights. The interior featured a floor-mounted shifter for the Powerglide two-speed automatic transmission and oil pressure, battery, water temperature and fuel gauges, plus a tachometer and clock. Each 1953 Corvette was virtually hand-built and a lot of minor changes were made during the production run. All of the first-year cars were Polo White with Sportsman Red interiors. All had black canvas convertible tops which manually folded into a storage space behind the seats. Other 1953-only features included special valve covers, a one-piece carburetor linkage and a small trunk mat. Short exhaust extensions were used on all '53s (and early '54s) because they were prone to drawing exhaust fumes into the car through the vent windows. A black oil-

THE 1953 CORVETTE ROADSTER, ONE OF ONLY 300 BUILT.

Nicky Wright

THE 1953 CORVETTE ROADSTER.

Nicky Wright

Jerry Heasley

A 1953 CORVETTE ROADSTER INTERIOR.

Jerry Heasley

THE 1953 CORVETTE 235.5-CID 150-HP INLINE SIX-CYLINDER ENGINE.

Nicky Wright

A 1953 CORVETTE ROADSTER. NOTE THE FACTORY MESH-COVERED HEADLIGHTS.

cloth window storage bag was provided to protect the 1953 Corvette's removable plastic side windows when stowed in the trunk.

ENGINE

Inline. Six-cylinder. Overhead valve. Cast iron block. Displacement: 235.5 cid. Bore and stroke: 3.56 x 3.96 in. Compression ratio: 8.0:1. Brake hp: 150 at 4200 rpm. Single breaker-point ignition. Carburetor: Three Carter Type YH one-barrel Model 2066S (early models); Model 2055S (later models).

CHASSIS FEATURES

Wheelbase: 102 inches. Overall length: 167 inches. Front tread: 57 inches. Rear tread: 58.8 inches. Steel disk wheels. Tires: 6.70 x 15. Front suspension: Coil springs, tubular shock absorbers and stabilizer bar. Rear suspension: Leaf springs, tube shocks and solid rear axle. Drum brakes. Axle ratio: 3.55:1.

OPTIONS

Signal-seeking AM radio ($145.15). Heater ($91.40). White sidewall tires.

HISTORICAL FOOTNOTES

The first Corvette was built on June 30, 1953, at the Flint, Michigan, assembly plant. In addition to being the first, it is the rarest Corvette. Model year production peaked at 300 units. About 200 of the 300 Corvettes made in 1953 are known to exist today, although the first two cars built are missing. The '53s were constructed in an area at the rear of Chevrolet's customer delivery garage on Van Slyke Ave., in Flint, Michigan. Calendar-year sales of 300 cars was recorded. By early 1954, Chevrolet announced that 315 Corvettes had been built and that production of the model had been shifted to the assembly plant in St. Louis, Missouri. Programming, at that point, called for production of 1,000 Corvettes per month in St. Louis by June 1954. The company predicted that 10,000 per year could be built and sold. Zora Arkus-Duntov joined Chevrolet Motor Division in 1953 and would become chief engineer of the Corvette.

1954

For all practical purposes the 1953 and 1954 Corvettes were the same. Minor changes were made to the window storage bag, air cleaners, starter and locations of the fuel and brake lines. Unlike the previous year's model, 1954s were available in Pennant Blue, Sportsman Red and Black, in addition to Polo White. The soft top was now offered in beige. A new style of valve cover was used. It was held on by four bolts through the outside lip instead of two center studs. The valve cover decals were different with larger lettering. The optional radio had Conelrad National Defense System icons on its face. In early 1954, the original two-handled hood latch was changed to a single-handle design. Six-cylinder Corvettes after serial number E54S003906 had integrated dual-port air cleaners. A clip to hold the ventipanes closed was added in late 1954 and also used on all 1955 models.

ENGINE

Inline. Six-cylinder. Overhead valve. Cast-iron block. Displacement: 235.5 cid. Bore and stroke: 3.56 x 3.96 in. Compression ratio: 8.0:1. Brake hp: 150 at 4200 rpm. Single breaker-point ignition system. Four main bearings. Carburetor: Three Carter Type YH one-barrel Model 2066S.

NOTE: Later in the model year a new camshaft upped horsepower to 155.

CHASSIS FEATURES

Wheelbase: 102 inches. Overall length: 167 inches. Front tread: 57 inches. Rear tread: 58.8 inches. Tires: 6.70 x 15. Front suspension: Coil springs, tube shocks and stabilizer bar. Rear suspension: Leaf springs, tube shocks and solid rear axle. Drum brakes. Steel disk wheels. Axle ratio: 3.55:1.

Jerry Heasley

A 1954 CORVETTE ROADSTER WITH POWERGLIDE TRANSMISSION.

Nicky Wright

**THE 1954 CORVETTE ROADSTER. NOTE THE EXHAUST
EXTENSIONS NOT FOUND ON 1953 MODELS.**

Nicky Wright

1954 CORVETTE DUAL-FIN, BULLET TAIL LIGHTS.

OPTIONS

RPO 102A Signal-seeking AM radio ($145.15). RPO Directional signals ($16.75). RPO 101A Heater ($91.40). RPO 422A windshield washer ($11.85). RPO 420A parking brake alarm ($5.65). RPO 313M Powerglide automatic transmission ($178.35). RPO 290B 6.70 x 15 white sidewall tires. RPO 421A Courtesy light ($4.05)

HISTORICAL FOOTNOTES

Production of 1954 Corvettes began December 23, 1953. Approximately 80 percent of 1954 Corvettes were painted White. About 15 percent had a Pennant Blue exterior with Shoreline Beige interior. About three percent were Red with a Red interior and some Black cars with Red interiors were built. In addition, Metallic Green and Metallic Brown cars are thought to have been built. The 1954 Corvette did not achieve its sales target of 10,000 cars. In fact, over 1,100 were unsold when the year ended. A 1954 Corvette could go from 0 to 60 mph in 11 seconds and from 0 to 100 mph in 41 seconds.

**A 1954 CORVETTE INTERIOR.
THE SPEEDOMETER REACHED 140 MPH.**

**THE 1954 CORVETTE ROADSTER RETAINED THE 1953
GRILLE AND MESH-COVERED HEADLIGHTS.**

1955

Corvette styling remained the same as last year's model. The big news was the availability of a V-8 engine. An enlarged gold "V" within the word "CheVrolet" on the front fenders was a quick way to tell the V-8 powered (12-volt electrical system) cars from those with a six-cylinder engine (and six-volt electrical system). On the 1955 V-8 cars the frame was modified to allow room for the fuel pump.

ENGINES

SIX: Inline. Six-cylinder. Overhead valve. Cast-iron block. Displacement: 235.5 cid. Bore and stroke: 3.75 x 3.00 in. Compression ratio: 8.0:1. Brake hp: 155 at 5000 rpm. Single breaker-point ignition system. Four main bearings. Solid valve lifters. Carburetor: Three Carter one-barrel Model 3706989.

V-8: Inline. Overhead valve. Cast-iron block. Displacement: 265 cid. Bore and stroke: 3.56 x 3.96 in. Compression ratio: 8.0:1. Brake hp: 195 at 4200 rpm. Single breaker-point ignition system. Five main bearings. Solid valve lifters. Carburetor: Rochester four-barrel Model 7008005.

CHASSIS FEATURES

Wheelbase: 102 inches. Overall length: 167 inches. Front tread: 57 inches. Rear tread: 58.8 inches. Tires: 6.70 x 15. Frame: Welded steel box-section type. Front suspension: Coil springs, tube shocks and stabilizer bar. Rear suspension: Leaf springs, tube shocks and solid rear axle. Drum brakes. Steel disk wheels. Axle ratio: 3.55:1.

OPTIONS

RPO Directional signals ($16.75). RPO

Jerry Heasley

A 1955 CORVETTE ROADSTER, ONE OF ONLY 700 BUILT.

Jerry Heasley

A 1955 CORVETTE ROADSTER WITH 265-CID 195-HP V-8 ENGINE.

101A Heater ($91.40). RPO 102A Signal-seeking AM radio ($145.15). RPO 422A windshield washer ($11.85). RPO 420A Parking brake alarm ($5.65). RPO 313M Powerglide automatic transmission ($178.35). RPO 290B 6.70 x 15 White sidewall tires ($26.90). RPO 421A Courtesy light ($4.05).

HISTORICAL FOOTNOTES

Production of 1955 Corvettes began October 28, 1954. New-for-1955 Corvette colors included Copper with a Beige interior and Harvest Gold (yellow) with a Green and Yellow interior. Cars with a Red exterior now featured a Light Beige interior. The interior material was called Elascofab. Soft convertible tops were offered in canvas and vinyl. New top colors included White and Dark Green. A V-8 powered 1955 Corvette could go from 0-to-60 mph in 8.7 seconds; from 0-to-100 mph in 24.7 seconds.

1956

In 1956, the Corvette began to define itself as a true American sports car. A lot of people would have been perfectly content if Chevrolet had frozen Corvette styling with the 1956 model. The same basic grille styling was kept intact, but the grille teeth looked a bit slimmer. Chevrolet styling studio chief Clare MacKichan directed the 1956 redesign, which was somewhat inspired by the thrusting headlamps and twin-bulge hood of the Mercedes-Benz 300SL gullwing coupe. There were new front fenders with chrome-rimmed headlights; glass windows; external door handles; chrome-outlined concave side body coves and sloping, taillight-integrated rear fenders. The dash layout remained the same as in the past. The 1956 rear view mirror, located on the center of the top of the dash, was adjusted by using a

thumbscrew. Improved-fit soft convertible tops were standard and a power top was optional, as was a removable fiberglass hardtop. Upholstery colors were limited to Beige or Red, but seven nitro-cellulose lacquer body colors were available. They were Onyx Black with a Silver panel (Black or White soft top); Polo White with a Silver panel (Black or White soft top); Venetian Red with a Beige panel (Beige or White soft top); Cascade Green with a Beige panel (Beige or White soft

Nicky Wright

THE 1956 CORVETTE.

Jerry Heasley

A 1956 CORVETTE HARDTOP WITH 210-HP STANDARD V-8.

top); Aztec Copper with a Beige panel (Beige or White soft top); Arctic Blue with a Silver panel (Beige or White soft top) and Inca Silver with an Imperial Ivory panel (Black or White soft top).

ENGINES

BASE ENGINE: V-8. Overhead valve. Cast-iron block. Displacement: 265 cid. Bore and stroke: 3.75 x 3.00 inches. Compression ratio: 9.25:1. Brake hp: 210 at 5600 rpm. Five main bearings. Solid valve lifters. Carburetor: Carter Type WCFB four-barrel Model 2419S.

OPTIONAL ENGINE: V-8. Overhead valve. Cast-iron block. Displacement: 265 cid. Bore and stroke: 3.75 x 3.00 inches. Compression ratio: 9.25:1. Brake hp: 225. Five main bearings. Solid valve lifters. Carburetor: Two four-barrel carburetors.

OPTIONAL ENGINE: V-8. Overhead valve. Cast-iron block. Displacement: 265 cid. Bore and stroke: 3.75 x 3.00 inches. Compression ratio: 9.25:1. Brake hp: 240 at 5200 rpm. Five main bearings. Solid valve lifters. High-lift camshaft. Carburetor: Two four-barrel carburetors.

CHASSIS FEATURES

Wheelbase: 102 inches. Overall length: 168 inches. Overall height: 51.9 inches. Overall width: 70.5 inches. Front tread: 57 inches. Rear tread: 59 inches. Ground clearance: Six inches. Tires: 6.70 x 15. Frame: Welded steel box-section, X-braced type. Front suspension: Independent; unequal-length A-arms; coil springs, tube shocks. Steering: Saginaw worm-and-ball, 16:1 ratio, 37-foot turning circle. Rear suspension: Live axle on semi-elliptic leaf springs, anti-roll bar, tubular shock absorbers. Rear axle type: Hypoid semi-floating. Brakes: Four-wheel hydraulic, internal-expanding, 11-inch diameter drums, 157 square inches effective lining area (121 square inches with optional sintered metallic linings). 15-inch steel bolt-on wheels. Standard rear axle ratio with three-speed 3.70:1; with Powerglide: 3.55:1. Optional axle ratios: 3.27:1, 4.11:1 and 4.56:1.

OPTIONS

RPO 101 Heater ($115). RPO 102 Signal-seeking AM radio ($185). RPO 107 Parking brake signal ($5). RPO 108 Courtesy lights ($8). RPO 109 Windshield washer ($11). RPO 290 White sidewall tires 6.70 x 15 ($30). RPO 313 Powerglide automatic transmission ($175). RPO 419 Auxiliary hardtop ($200). RPO 426

A 1956 CORVETTE CONVERTIBLE WITH ONE OF ONLY 887 BEIGE INTERIORS.

Jerry Heasley

Electric power windows ($60). RPO 449 Special high-lift camshaft. ($175). RPO 469 Dual four-barrel carburetor equipment ($160). RPO 473 Hydraulic folding top mechanism ($100).

HISTORICAL FOOTNOTES

Production of 1956 Corvettes began November 4, 1955. Chevrolet general manager Ed Cole and Corvette chief engineer Zora Arkus-Duntov decided it was time for the Corvette to go racing in 1956. Zora drove one car to a two-way average of 150.583 mph at Daytona's Flying Mile. John Fitch also set a record of 90.932 mph for the standing-start mile at Daytona and 145.543 mph in the production sports car class. In the spring of 1956, at Pebble Beach, Calif., dentist Dr. Dick Thompson finished second overall and first in class in a sports car road race. Thompson went on to take the Sports Car Club of America (SCCA) 1956 championship with his Corvette. A 225-hp 1956 Corvette could go from 0-to-60 mph in 7.3 seconds; from 0-to-100 mph in 20.7 seconds.

Jerry Heasley

THE 1956 CORVETTE RAGTOP.

Jerry Heasley

A 1956 CORVETTE CONVERTIBLE – 1,259 OF 3,467 HAD TWO-TONED PAINT.

1957

The 1957 Corvette looked the same as the previous year's model. The thumb-screw-adjusted rearview mirror of 1956 was replaced with a lock-nut type that required a wrench to adjust. The big news was the availability of a 283-cid 283-hp fuel-injected V-8. Among the standard features were: dual exhaust; all-vinyl bucket seats; three-spoke competition-style steering wheel; carpeting; outside rearview mirror; electric clock and tachometer. Corvettes were now available in seven colors: Code 704 Onyx Black (Black, White or Beige top); Code 718 Polo White (Black, White or Beige top); Code 709 Aztec Copper (White or Beige top); Code 713 Arctic Blue (Black, White or Beige top); Code 712 Cascade Green (Black, White or Beige top); Code 714 Venetian Red (Black, White or Beige top) or Code 804 Inca Silver (Black or White top). White, Silver, and Beige were optional color choices for the side cove.

ENGINES

BASE ENGINE: V-8. Overhead valve. Cast iron block. Bore and stroke: 3.87 x 3.00 inch-

Nicky Wright

THE 1957 CORVETTE CONVERTIBLE IN VENETIAN RED.

Jerry Heasley

A 1957 CORVETTE WITH FUEL INJECTION.

Jerry Heasley

THE 1957 CORVETTE "FUELIE." ONYX BLACK WAS 1957'S MOST POPULAR COLOR.

Jerry Heasley

A 1957 CORVETTE WITH 283-CID 283-HP FUEL-INJECTED V-8.

es. Displacement: 283 cid. Compression ratio: 8.50:1. Brake hp: 185 at 4600 rpm. Taxable hp: 48.00. Torque: 275 at 2400. Five main bearings. Crankcase capacity: 4 qt. (Add 1 qt. for filter). Cooling system capacity: 16 qt. (Add 1 qt. for heater). Dual exhaust. Carburetor: Carter Model 3744925 four-barrel.

BASE ENGINE: V-8. Overhead valve. Cast iron block. Displacement: 283 cid. Bore and stroke: 3.87 x 3.00 inches. Compression ratio: 9.50:1. Brake hp: 220 at 4800 rpm. Five main bearings. Carburetor: Carter four-barrel Model 3744925.

OPTIONAL ENGINE: V-8. Overhead valve. Cast iron block. Displacement: 283 cid. Bore and stroke: 3.87 x 3.00 inches. Compression ratio: 9.50:1. Brake hp: 245. Five main bearings. Carburetor: Four-barrel carburetor.

OPTIONAL ENGINE: V-8. Overhead valve. Cast iron block. Displacement: 283 cid. Bore and stroke: 3.87 x 3.00 inches. Compression ratio: 9.50:1. Brake hp: 250. Five main bearings.

Jerry Heasley

A 1957 CORVETTE, ONE OF 1,040 FUEL-INJECTED MODELS.

Induction: Rochester fuel injection.

OPTIONAL ENGINE: V-8. Overhead valve. Cast iron block. Displacement: 283 cid. Bore and stroke: 3.87 x 3.00 inches. Compression ratio: 9.50:1. Brake hp: 270. Five main bearings. Carburetor: Two four-barrel carburetors.

OPTIONAL ENGINE: V-8. Overhead valve. Cast iron block. Displacement: 283 cid. Bore and stroke: 3.87 x 3.00 inches. Compression ratio: 10.50:1. Brake hp: 283. Five main bearings. Induction: Rochester fuel injection.

NOTE: A solid lifter camshaft was used with EL and EG engines; hydraulic lifters with others.

CHASSIS FEATURES

Wheelbase: 102 inches. Overall length: 168 inches. Overall height: 51.9 inches. Overall width: 70.5 inches. Front tread: 57 inches. Rear tread: 59 inches. Ground clearance: Six inches. Tires: 6.70 x 15. Frame: Welded steel box-section, X-braced type. Front suspension: Indepen-dent; unequal-length A-arms; coil springs, tube shocks. Steering: Saginaw worm-and-ball, 16:1 ratio, 37-foot turning circle. Rear suspension: Live axle on semi-elliptic leaf springs, anti-roll bar, tubular shock absorbers. Rear axle type: Hypoid semi-floating. Brakes: Four-wheel hydraulic, internal-expanding, 11-inch diameter drums, 157 square inches effective lining area (121 square inches with optional sintered metallic linings). 15-inch steel bolt-on wheels. Standard rear axle ratio with three-speed 3.70:1; with Powerglide: 3.55:1. Optional axle ratios: 3.27:1, 4.11:1 and 4.56:1.

OPTIONS

RPO 101 Heater ($110). RPO 102 Signal-seeking AM radio ($185). RPO 107 Parking brake alarm ($5). RPO 108 Courtesy Lights ($8). RPO 109 Windshield washer ($11). RPO 276 Five 15 x 5.5-inch wheels ($14). RPO 290 White sidewall tires 6.70 x 15 ($30). RPO 313 Powerglide automatic transmission ($175). RPO

Jerry Heasley

THE 1957 CORVETTE RETAINED THE 1956 BODY STYLE.

419 Auxiliary hardtop ($200). RPO 426 Power windows ($55). RPO 440 Optional cove color ($18). RPO 469A 283-cid 245-hp dual four-barrel carburetor V-8 engine ($140). RPO 469B V-8 283-cid 270-hp dual four-barrel carburetor engine with Duntov competition camshaft ($170). RPO 579A V-8 283-cid 250-hp fuel-injection engine ($450). RPO 579B V-8 283-cid 283-hp fuel-injection engine with Duntov competition camshaft ($450). RPO 579E V-8 283-cid 283-hp fuel-injection engine with cold-air induction system ($675). RPO 473 Power-operated folding top mechanism ($130). RPO 677 Positraction axle with 3.70:1 ratio ($45). RPO Positraction axle with 4.11:1 ratio ($45). RPO Positraction axle with 4.56:1 ratio ($45). RPO 684 Heavy-duty racing suspension ($725). RPO 685 Four-speed manual transmission ($175).

HISTORICAL FOOTNOTES

Production of 1957 Corvettes began October 19, 1956. The fuel-injected 1957 Corvette reached the magical one-horsepower-per-cubic-inch high-performance bracket. The Corvette's continuous-flow fuel-injection system was a joint effort of Zora Arkus-Duntov, John Dolza and General Motor's Rochester Division. Only 1,040 of the 1957 Corvettes were fuel-injected. A 283 hp fuel-injection 1957 Corvette could go from 0-to-60 mph in 5.7 seconds and from 0-to-100 mph in 16.8 seconds. It had a top speed of 132 mph. Another important option was the competition suspension package RPO 684 which included heavy-duty springs, shocks and roll bars, 16.3:1 quick-ratio steering; a Positraction differential; special brake cooling equipment; and Cerametallic brake linings. Dick Thompson and Gaston Audrey won the 12-hour Sebring Race in Corvettes and Thompson took the SCCA B-production championship for the second year in a row.

1958

Corvette styling was jazzed up for 1958. There were now four chrome rimmed headlights with fender length chrome strips running between each pair of lights. As if that weren't enough glitter, fake louvers were placed on the hood. The grille was similar to the previous year, but had four fewer vertical bars. Three horizontal chrome strips were added to the new cove. A couple of vertical chrome bars decorated the trunk. They detracted from an otherwise graceful rear-end treatment. The wraparound front and rear bumpers were larger. The interior changed dramatically. The gauges were clustered together in front of the driver, rather than spread across the dash as before. A center console and passenger assist (sissy) bar were added. Seat belts were made standard equipment. They had been a dealer-installed option in 1956 and 1957. There were six exterior body colors offered: Charcoal (Black or White soft top); Silver Blue (White or Beige soft top); Regal Turquoise (Black or White soft top); Signet Red (Black or White soft top); Panama Yellow (Black or White soft top) and Snowcrest White (Black, White, or Beige soft top).

ENGINES

BASE ENGINE: V-8. Overhead valve. Cast iron block. Displacement: 283 cid. Bore and stroke: 3.87 x 3.00 inches. Compression ratio: 9.50:1. Brake hp: 230 at 4800 rpm. Five main bearings. Carburetor: Carter Type WCFB four-barrel.

OPTIONAL ENGINE: V-8. Overhead valve. Cast iron block. Displacement: 283 cid. Bore

Nicky Wright

1958 CORVETTE DESIGN CHANGES INCLUDED DUAL HEADLIGHTS AND HOOD LOUVERS.

THE 1958 CORVETTE.

Nicky Wright

and stroke: 3.87 x 3.00 inches. Compression ratio: 9.50:1. Brake hp: 245. Five main bearings. Carburetor: Two four-barrel carburetors.

OPTIONAL ENGINE: V-8. Overhead valve. Cast iron block. Displacement: 283 cid. Bore and stroke: 3.87 x 3.00 inches. Compression ratio: 9.50:1. Brake hp: 250. Five main bearings. Induction: Rochester fuel injection.

OPTIONAL ENGINE: V-8. Overhead valve. Cast iron block. Displacement: 283 cid. Bore and stroke: 3.87 x 3.00 inches. Compression ratio: 9.50:1. Brake hp: 270. Five main bearings. Carburetor: Two four-barrel carburetors.

OPTIONAL ENGINE: V-8. Overhead valve. Cast iron block. Displacement: 283 cid. Bore and stroke: 3.87 x 3.00 inches. Compression ratio: 10.50:1. Brake hp: 290. Five main bearings. Induction: Rochester fuel injection.

CHASSIS FEATURES

Wheelbase: 102 inches. Overall length: 177.2 inches. Overall height: 51.6 inches. Overall width: 72.8 inches. Front tread: 57 inches.

Rear tread: 59 inches. Ground clearance: Six inches. Tires: 6.70 x 15. Frame: Welded steel box-section, X-braced type. Front suspension: Independent; upper and lower A-arms, unequal-length wishbones; coil springs; anti-roll bar; tubular shocks. Steering: Saginaw recirculating ball, 17:1 ratio; 3.7 turns lock-to-lock; 38.5-foot turning circle. Rear suspension: Live axle on semi-elliptic leaf springs, tubular shock absorbers. Rear axle type: Hypoid semi-floating. Brakes: Four-wheel hydraulic, internal-expanding, 11-inch diameter drums, 157 square inches effective lining area (121 square inches with optional sintered metallic linings). 15-inch steel bolt-on wheels. Standard rear axle ratio with three-speed 3.70:1; with Powerglide: 3.55:1. Optional axle ratios: 4.11:1 and 4.56:1.

OPTIONS

RPO 101 Heater ($96.85). RPO 102 Signal-seeking AM radio ($144.45). RPO 107 Parking brake alarm ($5.40). RPO 108 Courtesy Lights ($6.50). RPO 109 Windshield washer

Nicky Wright

1958 CORVETTE DESIGN CHANGES INCLUDE DUAL HEADLIGHTS AND HOOD LOUVERS.

($16.15). RPO 276 Five 15 x 5.5-inch wheels (no charge). RPO 290 White sidewall tires 6.70 x 15 ($31.55). RPO 313 Powerglide automatic transmission ($188.30). RPO 419 Auxiliary hardtop ($215.20). RPO 426 Electric power windows ($59.20). RPO 440 Optional cove color ($16.15). RPO 469 283-cid 245-hp dual four-barrel carburetor V-8 engine ($150.65). RPO 469C V-8 283-cid 270-hp dual four-barrel carburetor engine ($182.95). RPO 579 V-8 283-cid 250-hp fuel-injection engine ($484.20). RPO 579D V-8 283-cid 290-hp fuel-injection engine ($484.20). RPO 473 Power-operated folding top mechanism ($139.90). RPO 677 Positraction axle with 3.70:1 ratio ($48.45). RPO 678 Positraction axle with 4.11:1 ratio ($48.45). RPO 679 Positraction axle with 4.56:1 ratio ($45). RPO 684 Heavy-duty racing suspension ($780.10). RPO 685 Four-speed manual transmission ($215.20).

HISTORICAL FOOTNOTES

Production of 1958 Corvettes began October 31, 1957. Almost 11 percent of 1958 Corvettes were powered by the 283-cid 290-hp fuel-injected V-8. A 1958 Corvette with the standard 230-hp V-8 and 4.11:1 rear axle could go from 0-to-60 mph in 9.2 seconds. It did the quarter mile in 17.4 seconds at 83 mph and had a top speed of 103 mph. A 1958 Corvette with the optional 250-hp fuel-injected V-8 and 3.70:1 rear axle could go from 0-to-60 mph in 7.6 seconds and from 0-to-100 mph in 21.4 seconds. It did the quarter mile in 15.7 seconds at 90 mph and had a top speed of 120 mph. A 1959 Corvette with the 290-hp fuel-injected engine took only 6.9 seconds to go from 0-to-60 mph and got slightly better gas mileage.

1959

The 1959 Corvette was basically a cleaned-up 1958. The fake hood louvers and vertical chrome strips on the trunk were removed. Interior changes included redesigned bucket seats and door panels, a fiberglass package tray under the sissy bar and concave gauge lenses. A tachometer, outside rearview mirror, seat belts, dual exhaust and electric clock were among the standard features. Sunvisors became optional. New concave instrument lenses reduced reflections. The optional four-speed manual transmission had a T-shaped reverse-lockout shifter with a white plastic shifter knob. There were seven exterior body colors offered: Tuxedo Black (Black or White soft top); Classic Cream (Black or White soft top); Frost Blue (White or Blue soft top); Crown Sapphire (White or Turquoise soft top); Roman Red (Black or White soft top); Snowcrest White (Black, White, Tan or Blue soft top) and Inca Silver (Black or White soft top). Blue, Red, Turquoise, and (for the first time) Black interiors were available. The armrests and door handles were in a different position, the seats had a new shape and a shelf was added.

ENGINES

BASE ENGINE: V-8. Overhead valve. Cast-iron block. Displacement: 283 cid. Bore and stroke: 3.87 x 3.00 inches. Compression ratio: 9.50:1. Brake hp: 230 at 4800 rpm. Five main bearings. Hydraulic valve lifters. Carburetor: Carter Type WCFB four-barrel Model 2816.

OPTIONAL ENGINE: V-8. Overhead valve. Cast-iron block. Displacement: 283 cid. Bore and stroke: 3.87 x 3.00 inches. Compression ratio: 9.50:1. Brake hp: 245. Five main bearings. Carburetor: Two four-barrel carburetors.

OPTIONAL ENGINE: V-8. Overhead valve. Cast-iron block. Displacement: 283 cid. Bore and stroke: 3.87 x 3.00 inches. Compression ratio: 9.50:1. Brake hp: 250. Five main bearings.

Nicky Wright

THE 1958 CORVETTE WAS SIMILAR IN MANY WAYS TO THE 1958 MODEL.

THE 1959 CORVETTE LISTED AT $3,875.

Nicky Wright

Induction: Rochester fuel injection.

OPTIONAL ENGINE: V-8. Overhead valve. Cast-iron block. Displacement: 283 cid. Bore and stroke: 3.87 x 3.00 inches. Compression ratio: 9.50:1. Brake hp: 270. Five main bearings. Carburetor: Two four-barrel carburetors.

OPTIONAL ENGINE: V-8. Overhead valve. Cast-iron block. Displacement: 283 cid. Bore and stroke: 3.87 x 3.00 inches. Compression ratio: 10.50:1. Brake hp: 290. Five main bearings. Induction: Rochester fuel injection.

TRANSMISSIONS

STANDARD MANUAL TRANSMISSION: A three-speed manual all-synchromesh transmission with floor-mounted gear shifter was standard equipment.

AUTOMATIC TRANSMISSION: A two-speed Powerglide automatic transmission was optional equipment.

OPTIONAL MANUAL TRANSMISSION: A four-speed manual all-synchromesh transmission with floor-mounted gear shifter was optional equipment.

CHASSIS FEATURES

Wheelbase: 102 inches. Overall length: 177.2 inches. Overall height: 51.6 inches. Overall width: 72.8 inches. Front tread: 57 inches. Rear tread: 59 inches. Ground clearance: six inches. Tires: 6.70 x 15. Frame: Welded steel box-section, X-braced type. Front suspension: Independent; upper and lower A-arms, unequal-length wishbones; coil springs; anti-roll bar; tubular shocks. Steering: Saginaw recirculating ball, 17:1 ratio; 3.7 turns lock-to-lock; 38.5-foot turning circle. Rear suspension: Live axle on semi-elliptic leaf springs, tubular shock absorbers. Rear axle type: Hypoid semi-floating. Brakes: Four-wheel hydraulic, internal-expanding, 11-inch diameter drums, 157 square inches effective lining area (121 square inches with optional sintered metallic linings). 15-inch steel bolt-on wheels. Standard rear axle ratio with three-speed 3.70:1; with Powerglide: 3.55:1. Optional axle ratios: 4.11:1 and 4.56:1.

OPTIONS

Additional cove color ($16.15). RPO 101 Heater ($102.25). RPO 102 Signal-seeking AM radio ($149.80). RPO 107 Parking brake alarm ($5.40). RPO 108 Courtesy lights ($6.50). RPO 109 Windshield washer ($16.15). RPO 261 Sunshades ($10.80). 276 Five 15 x 5.5-inch wheels (No charge). RPO 290 White sidewall tires 6.70 x 15 ($31.55). RPO 313 Powerglide automatic transmission ($199.10). RPO 419 Auxiliary hardtop ($236.75). RPO 426 Electric power windows ($59.20). RPO 269 283-cid 245-hp dual four-barrel carburetor V-8 engine ($150.65). RPO 469C V-8 283-cid 270-hp dual four-barrel carburetor engine ($182.95). RPO 579 V-8 283-cid 250-hp fuel-injection engine ($484.20). RPO

A 1959 CORVETTE WITH 283-CID V-8.

Jerry Heasley

THE 1959 CORVETTE IN ROMAN RED.

Jerry Heasley

579D V-8 283-cid 290-hp fuel-injection engine ($484.20). RPO 473 Power-operated folding top mechanism ($139.90). RPO 675 Positraction axle with optional ratio ($48.45). RPO 684 Heavy-duty brakes and suspension ($425.05). RPO 685 Four-speed manual transmission ($188.30). RPO 686 Metallic brakes ($26.90)

HISTORICAL FOOTNOTES

A 250-hp fuel-injected 1959 Corvette with the 3.70:1 rear axle could go from 0-to-60 mph in 7.8 seconds. It did the quarter mile in 15.7 seconds at 90 mph and had a top speed of 120 mph. A 290-hp fuel-injected 1959 Corvette with the 4.11:1 rear axle could go from 0-to-60 mph in 6.8 seconds; from 0-to-100 mph in 15.5 seconds. It did the quarter mile in 14.9 seconds at 96 mph and had a top speed of 124 mph. *Road & Track* described the 1959 Corvette as "a pretty package with all the speed you need and then some."

1960

The 1960 Corvette looked much the same as the previous year's model. A new rear suspension sway bar improved the car's handling. Aluminum cylinder heads and an aluminum radiator were introduced, but later withdrawn. Standard equipment included: tachometer, sun visors, dual exhaust, carpeting, seat belts, outside rearview mirror and electric clock. Buyers could choose from eight exterior finishes: Tuxedo Black (Black, White or Blue soft top); Ermine White (Black, White or Blue soft top); Tasco Turquoise (Black, White or Blue soft top); Horizon Blue (Black, White or Blue soft top); Sateen Silver (Black, White or Blue soft top); Cascade Green (Black, White or Blue soft top); Roman Red (Black or White soft top) and Honduras Maroon (Black soft top). A new aluminum clutch housing cut the Corvette's weight by 18 pounds. A larger-diameter front anti-roll bar and new rear bar enhanced ride and handling characteristics of the 1960 model.

ENGINES

BASE ENGINE: V-8. Overhead valve. Cast-iron block. Displacement: 283 cid. Bore and stroke: 3.87 x 3.00 inches. Compression ratio: 9.50:1. Brake hp: 230 at 4800 rpm. Five main bearings. Hydraulic valve lifters. Carburetor: Carter Type WCFB four-barrel Model 3779178.

OPTIONAL ENGINE: V-8. Overhead valve. Cast-iron block. Displacement: 283 cid. Bore and stroke: 3.87 x 3.00 inches. Compression ratio: 9.50:1. Brake hp: 245. Five main bearings. Hydraulic valve lifters. Carburetor: Two four-barrel carburetors.

OPTIONAL ENGINE: V-8. Overhead valve. Cast-iron block. Displacement: 283 cid. Bore and stroke: 3.87 x 3.00 inches. Compression ratio: 9.50:1. Brake hp: 270. Five main bearings. Hydraulic valve lifters. Carburetor: Two four-barrel carburetors.

OPTIONAL ENGINE: V-8. Overhead valve.

THE 1960 CORVETTE IN HONDURAS MAROON.

Karen O' Brien

THE 1960 CORVETTE INTERIOR WITH A FOUR-SPEED.

THE 1960 CORVETTE, ONE OF 280 PAINTED SATEEN SILVER WITH A WHITE COVE.

Cast-iron block. Displacement: 283 cid. Bore and stroke: 3.87 x 3.00 inches. Compression ratio: 11.00:1. Brake hp: 275. Five main bearings. Hydraulic valve lifters. Induction: Rochester fuel injection.

OPTIONAL ENGINE: V-8. Overhead valve. Cast-iron block. Displacement: 283 cid. Bore and stroke: 3.87 x 3.00 inches. Compression ratio: 11.00:1. Brake hp: 315 at 6200 rpm. Five main bearings. Solid valve lifters. Induction: Rochester fuel injection.

TRANSMISSIONS

STANDARD MANUAL TRANSMISSION: A three-speed manual all-synchromesh transmission with floor-mounted gear shifter was standard equipment.

AUTOMATIC TRANSMISSION: A two-speed Powerglide automatic transmission was optional equipment.

Karen O'Brien

A 1960 CORVETTE CONVERTIBLE, ONE OF 65 IN CASCADE GREEN WITH WHITE COVE.

Karen O'Brien

THE 1960 CORVETTE 283-CID FUEL-INJECTED V-8 ENGINE.

OPTIONAL MANUAL TRANSMISSION: A four-speed manual all-synchromesh transmission with floor-mounted gear shifter was optional equipment.

CHASSIS FEATURES

Wheelbase: 102 inches. Overall length: 177.2 inches. Overall height: 51.6 inches. Overall width: 72.8 inches. Front tread: 57 inches. Rear tread: 59 inches. Ground clearance: Six inches. Tires: 6.70 x 15. Frame: Welded steel box-section, X-braced type. Front suspension: Independent; upper and lower A-arms, unequal-length wishbones; coil springs; anti-roll bar; tubular shocks. Steering: Saginaw recirculating ball, 17:1 ratio; 3.7 turns lock-to-lock; 38.5-foot turning circle. Rear suspension: Live axle on semi-elliptic leaf springs, tubular shock absorbers. Rear axle type: Hypoid semi-floating. Brakes: Four-wheel hydraulic, internal-expanding, 11-inch diameter drums, 157 square inches effective lining area (121 square inches with optional sintered metallic linings). 15-inch steel bolt-on wheels. Standard rear axle ratio with three-speed 3.70:1; with Powerglide: 3.55:1. Optional axle ratios: 4.11:1 and 4.56:1.

OPTIONS

Additional cove color ($16.15). RPO 101 Heater ($102.25). RPO 102 Signal-seeking AM radio ($137.75). RPO 107 Parking brake alarm ($5.40). RPO 108 Courtesy Lights ($6.50). RPO 109 Windshield washer ($16.15). RPO 121 Temperature control radiator fan ($21.55). RPO 261 Sunshades ($10.80). RPO 276 Five 15 x 5.5-inch wheels (No charge). RPO 290 White sidewall tires 6.70 x 15, four-ply ($31.55). RPO 313 Powerglide automatic transmission ($199.10). RPO 419 Auxiliary hardtop ($236.75). RPO 426 Electric power windows ($59.20). RPO 469 283-cid 245-hp dual four-barrel carburetor V-8 engine ($150.65). RPO 469C V-8 283-cid 270-hp dual four-barrel carburetor engine ($182.95). RPO 579 V-8 283-cid 275-hp fuel-injection engine ($484.20). RPO 579D V-8 283-cid 315-hp fuel-injection engine ($484.20). RPO 473 Power-operated folding top mechanism ($139.90). RPO 675 Positraction axle with optional ratio ($43.05). RPO 685 Four-speed manual transmission ($188.30). RPO 686 Metallic brakes ($26.90). RPO 687 Heavy-duty brakes and suspension ($333.60). RPO 1408 Five 6.70 x 15 Nylon tires ($15.75). RPO 1625A 24-gallon fuel tank ($161.40).

HISTORICAL FOOTNOTES

The majority of 1960 Corvettes, 50.1 percent, were sold with a detachable hardtop. Most, 51.9 percent, also had a four-speed manual transmission. A 1960 Corvette with the 283-cid 230-hp V-8 could go from 0-to-60 in 8.4 seconds and did the quarter mile in 16.1 seconds at 89 mph. The Route 66 television series, featuring Martin Milner and George Maharis driving their 1960 Corvette across the country on the "Mother Road" debuted this season.

1961

The badge on the front of the 1961 Corvette was a crossed flag over a "V." A refined, thin, vertical and horizontal bar grille and duck-tail rear end treatment with four cylindrical taillights quickly set the new 1961 Corvette apart from its predecessor. This design was a predecessor to the Sting Ray coming in 1963 and added more space to the Corvette's trunk. The rear emblem had a spun silver background with the crossed flags over a "V" design and the words "Chevrolet Corvette." The exhaust now exited under the car, rather than through bumper ports. Standard equipment included: tachometer; seat belts; sun visors; dual exhaust; carpeting; electric clock, an outside rearview mirror, a lockable rear-seat storage area and a new aluminum radiator. A temperature-controlled radiator fan was also made standard. Seven exterior colors were available: Tuxedo Black (Black or White soft top); Ermine White (Black or White soft top); Roman Red (Black or White soft top); Sateen Silver (Black or White soft top); Jewel Blue (Black or White soft top); Fawn Beige (Black or White soft top); Honduras Maroon (Black or White soft top).

ENGINES

BASE ENGINE: V-8. Overhead valve. Cast-iron block. Displacement: 283 cid. Bore and stroke: 3.87 x 3.00 inches. Compression ratio: 9.50:1. Brake hp: 230 at 4800 rpm. Five main bearings. Hydraulic valve lifters. Carburetor: Carter Type WCFB four-barrel Model 3779178.

OPTIONAL ENGINE: V-8. Overhead valve. Cast-iron block. Displacement: 283 cid. Bore and stroke: 3.87 x 3.00 inches. Compression ratio: 9.50:1. Brake hp: 245. Five main bearings. Hydraulic valve lifters. Carburetor: Two four-barrel carburetors.

OPTIONAL ENGINE: V-8. Overhead valve. Cast-iron block. Displacement: 283 cid. Bore and stroke: 3.87 x 3.00 inches. Compression ratio: 9.50:1. Brake hp: 270. Five main bearings.

Nicky Wright

THE 1961 CORVETTE WITH REDESIGNED GRILLE.

Hydraulic valve lifters. Carburetor: Two four-barrel carburetors.

OPTIONAL ENGINE: V-8. Overhead valve. Cast-iron block. Displacement: 283 cid. Bore and stroke: 3.87 x 3.00 inches. Compression ratio: 11.00:1. Brake hp: 275. Five main bearings. Hydraulic valve lifters. Induction: Rochester fuel injection.

OPTIONAL ENGINE: V-8. Overhead valve. Cast-iron block. Displacement: 283 cid. Bore and stroke: 3.87 x 3.00 inches. Compression ratio: 11.00:1. Brake hp: 315 at 6200 rpm. Five main bearings. Solid valve lifters. Induction: Rochester fuel injection.

TRANSMISSIONS

STANDARD MANUAL TRANSMISSION: A three-speed manual all-synchromesh transmission with floor-mounted gear shifter was standard equipment.

AUTOMATIC TRANSMISSION: A two-speed Powerglide automatic transmission was optional equipment.

OPTIONAL MANUAL TRANSMISSION: A four-speed manual all-synchromesh transmission with floor-mounted gear shifter was optional equipment.

CHASSIS FEATURES

Wheelbase: 102 inches. Overall length: 177.2 inches. Overall height: 51.6 inches. Overall width: 72.8 inches. Front tread: 57 inches. Rear tread: 58.8 inches. Ground clearance: Six inches. Tires: 6.70 x 15. Frame: Welded steel box-section, X-braced type. Front suspension: Independent; upper and lower A-arms, unequal-

Nicky Wright

SUN SHADES WERE STANDARD.

Nicky Wright

THE 1961 CORVETTE IN SATEEN SILVER.

length wishbones; Coil springs; anti-roll bar; tubular shocks. Steering: Saginaw recirculating ball, 17:1 ratio; 3.7 turns lock-to-lock; 38.5-foot turning circle. Rear suspension: Live axle on semi-elliptic leaf springs, tubular shock absorbers. Rear axle type: Hypoid semi-floating. Brakes: Four-wheel hydraulic, internal-expanding, 11-inch diameter drums, 157 square inches effective lining area (121 square inches with optional sintered metallic linings). 15-inch steel bolt-on wheels. Standard rear axle ratio with three-speed 3.36:1.

OPTIONS

Additional cove color ($16.15). RPO 101 Heater ($102.25). RPO 102 Signal-seeking AM radio ($137.75). RPO 276 Five 15 x 5.5-inch wheels (No charge). RPO 290 White sidewall tires 6.70 x 15, four-ply ($31.55). RPO 313 Powerglide automatic transmission ($199.10). RPO 419 Auxiliary hardtop ($236.75). RPO 426 Electric power windows ($59.20). RPO 441 Direct-Flow exhaust system (no charge). RPO 469 283-cid 245-hp dual four-barrel carburetor V-8 engine ($150.65). RPO 468 V-8 283-cid 270-hp dual four-barrel carburetor engine ($182.95).

RPO 353 V-8 283-cid 275-hp fuel-injection engine ($484.20). RPO 354 V-8 283-cid 315-hp fuel-injection engine ($484.20). RPO 473 Power-operated folding top mechanism ($161.40). RPO 675 Positraction axle with optional ratio ($43.05). RPO 685 Four-speed manual transmission ($188.30). RPO 686 Metallic brakes ($37.70). RPO 687 Heavy-duty brakes and suspension ($333.60). RPO 1408 Five 6.70 x 15 Nylon tires ($15.75). RPO 1625A 24-gallon fuel tank ($161.40).

HISTORICAL FOOTNOTES

Most 1961 Corvettes, 51.98 percent, came with a detachable hardtop and 64.1 percent had a four-speed manual transmission. This was the last year wide whitewall tires were available. A 1961 Corvette with a 283-cid 315-hp solid-lifter fuel-injected V-8 and the 3.70:1 rear axle could go from 0-to-30 mph in 2.6 seconds; from 0-to-60 mph in 6.0 seconds and from 0-to-100 mph in 14.2 seconds. It did the quarter mile in 15.5 seconds at 106 mph and had a maximum speed of 140 mph. This was the last year a contrasting color could be ordered from the factory for the side coves.

THE 1961 CORVETTE.

Nicky Wright

1962

The most noticeable changes for 1962 were the removal of the side cove chrome trim, a blacked-out grille and ribbed chrome rocker panel molding. For the first time since 1955, Corvettes were offered in solid colors only. Standard features included: electric clock; dual exhaust; tachometer; heater and defroster; seat belts; outside rearview mirror and windshield washer. The wheels were available in Black, Beige, Red, Silver or Maroon. The last time buyers had a choice of wheel colors was in 1957. In following years, wheels would be offered in only a single color. Seven exterior colors were available: Tuxedo Black (Black or White soft top); Ermine White (Black or White soft top); Roman Red (Black or White soft top); Sateen Silver (Black or White soft top); Fawn Beige (Black or White soft top); Honduras Maroon (Black or White soft top); Almond Beige (Black or White top).

ENGINES

BASE ENGINE: V-8. Overhead valve. Cast-iron block. Displacement: 327 cid. Bore and stroke: 4.00 x 3.25 inches. Compression ratio: 10.5:1. Brake hp: 250 at 4400 rpm. Five main bearings. Hydraulic valve lifters. Carburetor: Carter Type AFB four-barrel Model 3788246.

OPTIONAL ENGINE: V-8. Overhead valve. Cast-iron block. Displacement: 327 cid. Bore and stroke: 4.00 x 3.25 inches. Compression ratio: 10.5:1. Brake hp: 300. Five main bearings. Hydraulic valve lifters. Carburetor: Carter Type AFB four-barrel.

OPTIONAL ENGINE: V-8. Overhead valve. Cast-iron block. Displacement: 327 cid. Bore and stroke: 4.00 x 3.25 inches. Compression ratio: 11.25:1. Brake hp: 340. Five main bearings. Hydraulic valve lifters. Carburetor: Carter Type AFB four-barrel.

OPTIONAL ENGINE: V-8. Overhead valve. Cast-iron block. Displacement: 327 cid. Bore and stroke: 4.00 x 3.25 inches. Compression ratio: 11.25:1. Brake hp: 360. Five main bearings. Hydraulic valve lifters. Induction: Fuel injection.

TRANSMISSIONS

STANDARD MANUAL TRANSMISSION: A three-speed manual all-synchromesh transmission with floor-mounted gear shifter was standard equipment.

AUTOMATIC TRANSMISSION: A two-speed Powerglide automatic transmission was optional equipment.

A 1962 CORVETTE GULF OIL RACE CAR.

Jerry Heasley

THE 1962 CORVETTE.

Jerry Heasley

OPTIONAL MANUAL TRANSMISSION: A four-speed manual all-synchromesh transmission with floor-mounted gear shifter was optional equipment.

CHASSIS FEATURES

Wheelbase: 102 inches. Overall length: 177.2 inches. Overall height: 52.1 inches with hardtop. Overall width: 72.8 inches. Front tread: 57 inches. Rear tread: 58.8 inches. Ground clearance: Six and 7/10 inches. Tires: 6.70 x 15. Hardtop weight: 55 pounds. Interior hip room: 59.6 inches. Hat room: 42.3 inches. Leg room: 46.5 inches. Shoulder room: 49.4 inches. Trunk room: 12.1 cubic feet. Frame: Welded steel box-section, X-braced type. Front suspension: Independent; upper and lower A-arms, unequal-length wishbones; coil springs; anti-roll bar; tubular shocks. Steering: Saginaw recirculating ball, 21:1 ratio; 3.7 turns lock-to-lock; 38.5-foot turning circle. Rear suspension: Live axle on semi-elliptic leaf springs, tubular shock absorbers. Rear axle type: Hypoid semi-floating. Brakes: Four-wheel hydraulic, internal-expanding, 11-inch diameter drums, 327 square inches effective lining area. 15-inch steel bolt-on wheels. Standard rear axle ratio with three-speed 3.36:1.

OPTIONS

RPO 102 Signal-seeking AM radio ($137.75). RPO 276 Five 15 x 5.5-inch wheels (No charge). RPO 313 Powerglide automatic transmission ($199.10). RPO 419 Auxiliary hardtop ($236.75). RPO 426 Electric power windows ($59.20). RPO 441 Direct-Flow exhaust system (no charge). RPO 473 Power-operated folding top mechanism ($161.40). RPO 583 327-cid 300-hp V-8 engine ($53.80). RPO 396 327-cid 340-hp V-8 engine ($107.60). RPO 582 327-cid 370-hp fuel-injected V-8 engine ($484.20). RPO 675 Positraction axle with optional ratio ($43.05). RPO 685 Four-speed manual transmission ($188.30). RPO 686 Metallic brakes ($37.70). RPO 687 Heavy-duty brakes and suspension ($333.60). RPO 1832 Five 6.70 x 15 white sidewall tires ($31.55). RPO 1833 Five 6.70 x 15 Nylon tires ($15.75).

HISTORICAL FOOTNOTES

A 1962 Corvette with a 327-cid 360-hp fuel-injected V-8 and the 3.70:1 rear axle could go from 0-to-30 mph in 2.5 seconds; from 0-to-60 mph in 5.9 seconds and from 0-to-100 mph in 13.5 seconds. It did the quarter mile in 14.5 seconds at 104 mph and had an estimated maximum speed of 150 mph.

A 1962 CORVETTE WITH NARROW WHITEWALL TIRES.

Jerry Heasley

Nicky Wright

THE 1963 CORVETTE SPLIT-WINDOW COUPE WITH STANDARD WHEEL COVERS.

1963

The Corvette received major restyling in 1963, including a divided rear window for a new "split-window" fastback coupe. The sides of the front fenders, behind the wheel openings, were decorated with two long, horizontal "wind split" indentations or louvers that were designed to look like brake cooling ducts, although they were not functional. The rear deck treatment resembled that of the previous year's model, but the rest of the car appeared totally new. The twin side-by-side headlights were hidden in an electrically-operated panel. This was more than a styling gimmick, as it added to the car's basic aerodynamic design. The recessed fake hood louvers were another matter. Front fender louvers, vents on the roof side panels (of the fastback "split-window" sport coupe) and ribbed rocker panel molding were styling features used on the sides of the new Corvette. The interior had circular gauges with black faces. There was storage space under the seats of early models. Among the standard equipment was windshield washer; carpeting; outside rearview mirror; dual exhaust; tachometer; electric clock; heater and defroster; cigarette lighter; and safety belts. Seven interior colors were offered: Black, White, Silver, Silver-Blue, Daytona

blue, Red and Tan. For the first time since 1957, a Beige softtop was available. Seven exterior colors were available: Tuxedo Black; Ermine White; Riverside Red; Silver Blue; Daytona Blue; Saddle Tan and Sebring Silver. All were available with a Black, White, or Beige soft top.

ENGINES

BASE ENGINE: V-8. Overhead valve. Cast-iron block. Displacement: 327 cid. Bore and stroke: 4.00 x 3.25 inches. Compression ratio: 10.5:1. Brake hp: 250 at 4400 rpm. Torque: 350 lbs.-ft. at 2800 rpm. Five main bearings. Hydraulic valve lifters. Carburetor: Carter Type

Nicky Wright

1963 WAS THE FIRST YEAR FOR HIDDEN HEADLIGHTS.

A 1963 CORVETTE CONVERTIBLE.

Nicky Wright

WCFB four-barrel Model 3501S.

OPTIONAL ENGINE: [RPO L75] V-8. Overhead valve. Cast-iron block. Displacement: 327 cid. Bore and stroke: 4.00 x 3.25 inches. Compression ratio: 10.5:1. Brake hp: 300 at 5000 rpm. Torque: 360 lbs.-ft. at 3200 rpm. Five main bearings. Hydraulic valve lifters. Carburetor: Carter aluminum Type AFB four-barrel.

OPTIONAL ENGINE: [RPO L76] V-8. Overhead valve. Cast-iron block. Displacement: 327 cid. Bore and stroke: 4.00 x 3.25 inches. Compression ratio: 11.25:1. Brake hp: 340 at 6000 rpm. Torque: 344 lbs.-ft. at 4000 rpm. Five main bearings. Mechanical valve lifters. Duntov camshaft. Carburetor: Carter aluminum Type AFB four-barrel.

OPTIONAL ENGINE: [RPO L84] V-8. Overhead valve. Cast-iron block. Displacement: 327 cid. Bore and stroke: 4.00 x 3.25 inches. Compression ratio: 11.25:1. Brake hp: 360 at 6000 rpm. Torque: 352 lbs.-ft. at 4000 rpm. Five main bearings. Mechanical valve lifters. Duntov camshaft. Induction: Ram-Jet fuel injection.

TRANSMISSIONS

STANDARD MANUAL TRANSMISSION: A three-speed manual all-synchromesh transmission with floor-mounted gear shifter was standard equipment.

AUTOMATIC TRANSMISSION: A two-speed Powerglide automatic transmission with floor-mounted gear shifter was optional equipment.

OPTIONAL MANUAL TRANSMISSION: A four-speed manual all-synchromesh transmission with floor-mounted gear shifter was optional equipment.

CHASSIS FEATURES: Wheelbase: 98 inches. Overall length: [Convertible] 175.2 inches [Coupe] 175.3 inches. Overall height: [Coupe] 49.8 inches. Overall width: 69.6 inches. Front tread: 56.3 inches. Rear tread: 57.0 inches. Ground clearance: Five inches. Tires: 6.70 x 15. Frame: Full-length ladder type with five cross members and separate body. Front suspension: Independent; upper and lower A-arms, unequal-length wishbones; coil springs; anti-roll bar; tubular shocks. Steering: Saginaw recirculating ball, 17:1 ratio; 3.4 turns lock-to-lock. Rear suspension: Independent with fixed differential; nine leaf springs; lateral struts and universally-jointed axle shafts; radius arms and direct-acting shock absorbers. Rear axle type: Hypoid semi-floating. Brakes: Hydraulic, duo-servo, self-adjusting with sintered iron linings and cast-iron drums. Drum diameter [Front]: 11 x 2.75 inches; [Rear]: 11 x 2.0 inches. Total swept area: 134.9 square inches. 15-inch five-lug steel disc wheels. Standard rear axle ratio 3.70:1.

OPTIONS

RPO 898 Genuine leather seat trim ($80).

Jerry Heasley

THE 1963 CORVETTE COUPE.

RPO 941 Sebring Silver exterior paint ($80.70). RPO A01 Soft-Ray tinted glass, all windows ($16.15). RPO A02 Soft-Ray tinted glass, windshield ($10). RPO 431 Electric power windows ($59.20). RPO C07 Auxiliary hardtop for convertible ($236.75). RPO C48 Heater and defroster deletion ($100 credit). RPO C60 Air conditioning ($421.80). RPO G81 Positraction rear axle, all ratios ($43.05). RPO G91 Special 3.08:1 "highway" ratio rear axle ($2.20). RPO J50 Power brakes ($43.05). RPO J65 Sintered metallic brakes ($37.70). RPO L75 327-cid 300-hp V-8 ($53.80). RPO L76 327-cid 340-hp V-8 ($107.60). RPO L84 327-cid 370-hp fuel-injected V-8 ($430.40). RPO M20 Four-speed manual transmission ($188.30). RPO M35 Powerglide automatic transmission ($199.10). RPO N03 36-gallon fuel tank for "split-window" coupe only ($202.30). RPO N11 Off-road exhaust system ($37.70). RPO N34 Woodgrained plastic steering wheel ($16.15). RPO N40 Power steering ($75.35). RPO P48 Special cast-aluminum knock-off wheels ($322.80). RPO P91 Nylon tires, 6.70 x 15 black sidewall ($15.70). RPO P92 Rayon tires, 6.70 x 15, white sidewall ($31.55). RPO T86 Back-up lamps ($10.80). RPO U65 Signal-seeking AM radio ($137.75). RPO U69 AM-FM radio ($174.35). RPO Z06 Special performance equipment for "split-window" coupe ($1,818.45).

HISTORICAL FOOTNOTES

The Corvette Sting Ray evolved from a racing car called the Mitchell Sting Ray. William L. Mitchell had replaced Harley Earl as head of General Motors styling in 1958. Mitchell thought it was important for the Corvette to be associated with racing, so he persuaded Chevrolet general manager Ed Cole to sell him the chassis of the 1957 Corvette SS "mule" for $1 (to get around the corporate racing ban) so he could build a race car. Mitchell had designer Larry Shinoda create a body for the Sting Ray race car inspired by the sea creature of the same name. Shinoda came up with the "split-window" coupe design, which Mitchell loved although Zora Arkus-Duntov was against its vision-blocking look. The "split-window" was offered only one year and has become a very collectible item. Corvette "firsts" for 1963 included optional knock-off wheels, air conditioning and leather upholstery. Air conditioning was a rare option in 1963 because it was introduced late in the year. Only 1.3 percent of the 1963 Corvettes were so-equipped. However, 83.5 percent came with four-speed manual transmission. The L84-powered Corvette could go from 0-to-60 mph in 5.9 seconds and from 0-to-100 mph in 16.5 seconds. Five historic Corvette Grand Sports were constructed in 1963 before all GM racing programs were canceled. Grand Sports weighed 1,908 pounds and had a 377-cid version of the small-block Chevy V-8 equipped with an aluminum cylinder block and aluminum hemi-head cylinder heads. They also featured a twin ignition system and port fuel injection.

1964

Styling was cleaned up a bit for 1964. The previous year's distinctive rear window divider was replaced by a solid piece of glass. The fake hood vents were eliminated and the roof vents were restyled. A three-speed fan was available in the coupe to aid in ventilation. Seven exterior colors were available: Tuxedo Black; Ermine White; Riverside Red; Satin Silver; Silver Blue; Daytona Blue and Saddle Tan. All were available with a Black, White or Beige soft top.

ENGINES

BASE ENGINE: V-8. Overhead valve. Cast-iron block. Displacement: 327 cid. Bore and stroke: 4.00 x 3.25 inches. Compression ratio: 10.5:1. Brake hp: 250 at 4400 rpm. Torque: 350 lbs.-ft. at 2800 rpm. Five main bearings. Hydraulic valve lifters. Carburetor: Carter Type WCFB four-barrel Model 3501S.

OPTIONAL ENGINE: [RPO L75] V-8. Overhead valve. Cast-iron block. Displacement: 327 cid. Bore and stroke: 4.00 x 3.25 inches. Compression ratio: 10.5:1. Brake hp: 300 at 5000 rpm. Torque: 360 lbs.-ft. at 3200 rpm. Five main bearings. Hydraulic valve lifters. Carburetor: Carter aluminum Type AFB four-barrel.

OPTIONAL ENGINE: [RPO L76] V-8. Overhead valve. Cast-iron block. Displacement: 327 cid. Bore and stroke: 4.00 x 3.25 inches. Compression ratio: 11.00:1. Brake hp: 365 at 6200 rpm. Torque: 350 lbs.-ft. at 4000 rpm. Five main bearings. Mechanical valve lifters. High-lift camshaft. Carburetor: Holley four-barrel Model 4150.

OPTIONAL ENGINE: [RPO L84] V-8. Overhead valve. Cast-iron block. Displacement: 327 cid. Bore and stroke: 4.00 x 3.25 inches. Compression ratio: 11.00:1. Brake hp: 375 at 6200 rpm. Torque: 350 lbs.-ft. at 4400 rpm. Five main bearings. Mechanical valve lifters. High-lift camshaft. Induction: Ram-Jet fuel injection.

TRANSMISSIONS

STANDARD MANUAL TRANSMISSION: A three-speed manual all-synchromesh trans-

A 1964 CORVETTE COUPE WITH OPTIONAL CAST-ALUMINUM WHEELS.

THE 1964 CORVETTE CONVERTIBLE, ONE OF 13,925 PRODUCED.

Nicky Wright

mission with floor-mounted gear shifter was standard equipment.

AUTOMATIC TRANSMISSION: A two-speed Powerglide automatic transmission with floor-mounted gear shifter was optional equipment.

OPTIONAL MANUAL TRANSMISSION: A four-speed manual all-synchromesh transmission with floor-mounted gear shifter was optional equipment.

CHASSIS FEATURES

Wheelbase: 98 inches. Overall length: [Convertible] 175.2 inches [Coupe] 175.3 inches. Overall height: [Coupe] 49.8 inches. Overall width: 69.6 inches. Front tread: 56.8 inches. Rear tread: 57.6 inches. Ground clearance: Five inches. Tires: 6.70 x 15. Frame: Full-length ladder type with five cross members and separate body. Front suspension: Independent; upper and lower A-arms, unequal-length wishbones; Coil springs; anti-roll bar; tubular shocks. Steering: Saginaw recirculating ball, 17:1 ratio; 3.4 turns lock-to-lock. Rear suspension: Independent with fixed differential; nine leaf spirings; lateral struts and universally-jointed axle shafts; radius

A 1964 CORVETTE CONVERTIBLE WITH STANDARD WHEEL COVERS.

Nicky Wright

arms and direct-acting shock absorbers. Rear axle type: Hypoid semi-floating. Brakes: Hydraulic, duo-servo, self-adjusting with sintered iron linings and cast-iron drums. Drum diameter [Front]: 11 x 2.75 inches; [Rear]: 11 x 2.0 inches. Total swept area: 134.9 square inches. 15-inch five-lug steel disc wheels. Standard rear axle ratio 3.70:1. Available rear axle gear ratios: 4.11:1; 4.56:1; 3.08:1; 3.36:1; 3.55:1; 3.70:1.

OPTIONS

RPO 898 Genuine leather seat trim ($80.70). RPO A01 Soft-Ray tinted glass, all windows ($16.15). RPO A02 Soft-Ray tinted glass, windshield ($10). RPO 431 Electric power windows ($59.20). RPO C07 Auxiliary hardtop for convertible ($236.75). RPO C48 Heater and defroster deletion ($100 credit). RPO C60 Air conditioning ($421.80). RPO F40 Special front and rear suspension ($37.70). RPO G81 Positraction rear axle, all ratios ($43.05) RPO G91 Special 3.08:1 "highway" ratio rear axle ($2.20). RPO J50 Power brakes ($43.05). RPO J56 Sintered metallic brakes ($37.70). RPO K66 Transistor ignition system ($65.35). RPO L75 327-cid 300-hp V-8 ($53.80). RPO L76 327-cid 365-hp V-8 ($107.60). RPO L84 327-cid 375-hp fuel-injected V-8 ($538.40). RPO M20 Four-speed manual transmission ($188.30). RPO M35 Powerglide automatic transmission ($199.10). RPO N03 36-gallon fuel tank for coupe only ($202.30). RPO N11 Off-road exhaust system ($37.70). RPO N40 Power steering ($75.35). RPO P48 Special cast-aluminum knock-off

Nicky Wright

THE 1964 CORVETTE CONVERTIBLE IN SILVER BLUE.

wheels ($322.80). RPO P91 Nylon tires, 6.70 x 15 black sidewall ($15.70). RPO P92 Rayon tires, 6.70 x 15, white sidewall ($31.85). RPO T86 Back-up lamps ($10.80). RPO U69 AM-FM radio ($174.35).

HISTORICAL FOOTNOTES

Only 3.2 percent of 1964 Corvettes were sold with the standard three-speed manual transmission. Most, 85.7 percent, were equipped with a four-speed manual transmission. An L84-powered 1964 Corvette could go from 0-to-60 mph in 6.3 seconds and from 0-to-100 mph in 14.7 seconds. It had a top speed of 138 mph.

Jerry Heasley

**THE 1964 CORVETTE COUPE FEATURED FUNCTIONAL
AIR-EXHAUST VENTS ON THE LEFT REAR PILLAR.**

1965

Three functional, vertical front, slanting louvers on the sides of the front fenders; a blacked-out, horizontal-bars grille and different rocker panel moldings were the main styling changes for 1965 Corvettes. A new hood without indentations was standard, but Corvettes with a newly optional 396-cid "big-block" V-8 used a special hood with a funnel-shaped "power blister" air scoop. Inside the car the instruments were changed to a flat-dial, straight-needle design with an aircraft-type influence. The seats had improved support and one-piece molded inside door panels were introduced. Standard equipment included: tachometer; safety belts; heater and defroster; windshield washer; outside rearview mirror; dual exhaust; electric clock; carpeting; manually-operated top (convertible) and sun visors. A four-wheel disc-brake system was standard, although drum brakes could be substituted for a $64.50 credit. Fuel injection was phased out at the end of the 1965 model year. New options included a nasty-looking side exhaust system and telescoping steering wheel. Eight exterior colors were available: Tuxedo Black; Ermine White; Nassau Blue; Glen Green; Milano Maroon; Silver Pearl; Rally Red and Goldwood Yellow. All convertibles came with a choice of a Black, White or Beige soft top. Interior colors were Black, Red, Blue, Saddle, Silver, White, Green, and Maroon.

ENGINES

BASE ENGINE: V-8. Overhead valve. Cast-iron block. Displacement: 327 cid. Bore and stroke: 4.00 x 3.25 inches. Compression ratio: 10.5:1. Brake hp: 250 at 4400 rpm. Torque: 350 lbs.-ft. at 2800 rpm. Five main bearings. Hydraulic valve lifters. Carburetor: Carter Type WCFB four-barrel Model 3846247.

OPTIONAL ENGINE: [RPO L75] V-8. Overhead valve. Cast-iron block. Displacement: 327 cid. Bore and stroke: 4.00 x 3.25 inches. Compression ratio: 10.5:1. Brake hp: 300 at 5000 rpm. Torque: 360 lbs.-ft. at 3200 rpm. Five main bearings. Hydraulic valve lifters. Carburetor: Carter Type AFB four-barrel.

Jerry Heasley

ONLY 168 1965 CORVETTE COUPES CAME WITH BLACKWALL TIRES.

FOUR-WHEEL DISC BRAKES WERE STANDARD ON THE 1965 CORVETTE.

Jerry Heasley

OPTIONAL ENGINE: [RPO L79] V-8. Overhead valve. Cast-iron block. Displacement: 327 cid. Bore and stroke: 4.00 x 3.25 inches. Compression ratio: 11.00:1. Brake hp: 350 at 5800 rpm. Torque: 360 lbs.-ft. at 3600 rpm. Five main bearings. Hydraulic valve lifters. High-lift camshaft. Carburetor: Holley 4150 four-barrel.

OPTIONAL ENGINE: [RPO L76] V-8. Overhead valve. Cast-iron block. Displacement: 327 cid. Bore and stroke: 4.00 x 3.25 inches. Compression ratio: 11.00:1. Brake hp: 365 at 6200 rpm. Torque: 350 lbs.-ft. at 4000 rpm. Five main bearings. Mechanical valve lifters. High-lift camshaft. Carburetor: Holley 4150 four-barrel.

OPTIONAL ENGINE: [RPO L84] V-8. Overhead valve. Cast-iron block. Displacement: 327 cid. Bore and stroke: 4.00 x 3.25 inches. Compression ratio: 11.00:1. Brake hp: 375 at 6200 rpm. Torque: 350 lbs.-ft. at 4400 rpm. Five main bearings. Mechanical valve lifters. High-lift camshaft. Induction: Ram-Jet fuel injection.

1965 1/2 ENGINE

OPTIONAL ENGINE: [RPO L78] V-8. Overhead valve. Cast-iron block. Displacement: 396 cid. Bore and stroke: 4.094 x 3.76 inches. Compression ratio: 11.00:1. Brake hp: 425 at 6400 rpm. Torque: 415 lbs.-ft. at 4000 rpm. Five main bearings. Mechanical valve lifters. High-lift camshaft. Carburetor: Holley 4150 four-barrel.

TRANSMISSIONS

STANDARD MANUAL TRANSMISSION: A three-speed manual all-synchromesh transmission with floor-mounted gear shifter was standard equipment.

AUTOMATIC TRANSMISSION: A two-speed Powerglide automatic transmission with floor-mounted gear shifter was optional equipment.

OPTIONAL MANUAL TRANSMISSION: A high-performance all-synchromesh four-speed manual transmission with floor-mounted

Jerry Healsey

**THE 1965 CORVETTE CONVERTIBLE —
15,376 WERE BUILT.**

gear shifter was optional equipment.

OPTIONAL MANUAL TRANSMISSION: A special high-performance four-speed manual all-synchromesh close-ratio transmission with floor-mounted gear shifter was optional equipment.

CHASSIS FEATURES

Wheelbase: 98 inches. Overall length: [Convertible] 175.2 inches [Coupe] 175.3 inches. Overall height: [Coupe] 49.8 inches. Overall width: 69.6 inches. Front tread: 56.8 inches. Rear tread: 57.6 inches. Ground clearance: Five inches. Tires: 7.75 x 15. Frame: Full-length ladder type with five cross members and separate body. Front suspension: Independent; upper and lower A-arms, unequal-length wishbones; coil springs; anti-roll bar; tubular shocks. Steering: Saginaw recirculating ball, 17:1 ratio; 3.4 turns lock-to-lock. Rear suspension: Independent with fixed differential; nine leaf springs; lateral struts and universally-jointed axle shafts; radius arms and direct-acting shock absorbers. Rear axle type: Hypoid semi-floating. Brakes: Hydraulic, four-wheel discs. Steel disc wheels. Standard rear axle ratio 3.36:1. Available rear axle gear ratios: 4.11:1; 4.56:1; 3.08:1; 3.55:1; 3.70:1.

OPTIONS

RPO 898 Genuine leather seat trim ($80.70). RPO A01 Soft-Ray tinted glass, all windows ($16.15). RPO A02 Soft-Ray tinted glass, windshield ($10.80). RPO 431 Electric power windows ($59.20). RPO C07 Auxiliary hardtop for convertible ($236.75). RPO C48 Heater and defroster deletion ($100 credit). RPO C60 Air conditioning ($421.80). RPO F40 Special front and rear suspension ($37.70). RPO G81 Positraction rear axle, all ratios ($43.05). RPO G91 Special 3.08:1 "highway" ratio rear axle ($2.20). RPO J50 Power brakes ($43.05). RPO J61 Drum brake substitution ($64.50 credit). RPO K66 Transistor ignition system ($75.35). RPO L75 327-cid 300-hp V-8 ($53.80). RPO L76 327-cid 365-hp V-8 ($129.15). RPO L78 396-cid 425-hp V-8 ($292.70). RPO L79 327-cid 350-hp V-8 ($107.60). RPO L84 327-cid 375-hp fuel-injected V-8 ($538.00). RPO M20 Four-speed manual transmission ($188.30). RPO M22 Close-ratio four-speed manual transmission ($236.95). RPO M35 Powerglide automatic transmission ($199.10). RPO N03 36-gallon fuel tank for coupe only ($202.30). RPO N11 Off-road exhaust system ($37.70). RPO N14 Side Mount exhaust system ($134.50). RPO N32 Teakwood steering wheel ($48.45). RPO N36 Telescopic steering wheel ($43.05). RPO N40 Power steering ($96.85). RPO P48 Special cast-aluminum knock-off wheels ($322.80). RPO P92 7.75 x 15, white sidewall tires ($31.85). RPO T01 7.75 x 15 gold sidewall tires ($50.05). RPO U69 AM-FM radio ($203.40). RPO Z01 Back-up lamps and inside Day/Night mirror ($16.15).

HISTORICAL FOOTNOTES

Most 1965 Corvettes (89.6 percent) were sold with a four-speed manual transmission; 8.6 percent had Powerglide automatic transmission; 69.5 percent had tinted glass; 10.3 percent had air conditioning and 13.7 percent had power steering. An L78-powered 1965 Corvette could go from 0-to-60 mph in 5.7 seconds; from 0-to-100 mph in 13.4 seconds.

1966

A plated, cast-metal grille with an "egg crate" insert; ribbed rocker panel moldings; chrome-plated exhaust bezels; spoke-style wheel covers; a vinyl covered headliner and the elimination of roof vents helped set the 1966 Corvette apart from the previous year's model. The front fender sides again had thee slanting vertical air louvers. Inside, the seats had an extra amount of pleats. Corvettes equipped with the new 427-cid V-8 came with a power-bulge hood. The 10 lacquer exterior finishes offered were Tuxedo Black; Ermine White; Nassau Blue; Mosport Green; Milano Maroon; Silver Pearl; Rally Red; Sunfire Yellow; Laguna Blue and Trophy Blue. All convertibles came with a choice of a Black, White or Beige soft top. Interior colors were Black; Red; Bright Blue; White-Blue; Saddle; Silver; Green and Blue.

ENGINES

BASE ENGINE: [RPO L75] V-8. Overhead valve. Cast-iron block. Displacement: 327 cid. Bore and stroke: 4.00 x 3.25 inches. Compression ratio: 10.5:1. Brake hp: 300 at 5000 rpm. Torque: 350 lbs.-ft. at 2800 rpm. Five main bearings. Hydraulic valve lifters. Carburetor: Holley four-barrel.

OPTIONAL ENGINE: [RPO L79] V-8. Overhead valve. Cast-iron block. Displacement: 327 cid. Bore and stroke: 4.00 x 3.25 inches. Compression ratio: 11.00:1. Brake hp: 350 at 5800 rpm. Torque: 360 lbs.-ft. at 3000 rpm. Five main bearings. Hydraulic valve lifters. High-performance camshaft. Carburetor: Holley four-barrel.

OPTIONAL ENGINE: [RPO L30] V-8. Overhead valve. Cast-iron block. Displacement: 427 cid. Bore and stroke: 4.251 x 3.76 inches. Compression ratio: 10.25:1. Brake hp: 390 at 5200 rpm. Torque: 460 lbs.-ft. at 3600 rpm. Five main bearings. Hydraulic valve lifters. High-performance camshaft. Carburetor: Holley four-barrel.

OPTIONAL ENGINE: [RPO L72] V-8. Overhead valve. Cast-iron block. Displacement: 427 cid. Bore and stroke: 4.251 x 3.76 inches. Compression ratio: 11.00:1. Brake hp: 425 at 5000 rpm. Torque: 460 lbs.-ft. at 4000 rpm. Five main bearings. Mechanical valve lifters. Special-performance camshaft. Carbu-

Jerry Heasley

THE 1966 CORVETTE CONVERTIBLE WITH NEW "EGG-CRATE" GRILLE.

Jerry Heasley

THE 1966 CORVETTE COUPE.

retor: Large Holley four-barrel.

TRANSMISSIONS

STANDARD MANUAL TRANSMISSION: A three-speed manual all-synchromesh transmission with floor-mounted gear shifter was standard equipment.

AUTOMATIC TRANSMISSION: An automatic transmission with floor-mounted gear shifter was optional equipment.

OPTIONAL MANUAL TRANSMISSION: A high-performance all-synchromesh four-speed manual transmission with floor-mounted gear shifter was optional equipment.

OPTIONAL MANUAL TRANSMISSION: A special high-performance four-speed manual all-synchromesh close-ratio transmission with floor-mounted gear shifter was optional equipment.

CHASSIS FEATURES: Wheelbase: 98 inches. Overall length: [Convertible] 175.2 inches. Overall height: [Coupe] 49.6 inches. Overall width: 69.6 inches. Front tread: 57.6 inches. Rear tread: 58.3 inches. Ground clearance: Five inches. Tires: 7.75 x 15 redwall or whitewall. Frame: Full-length steel ladder type with five cross members and separate body.

Front suspension: Independent; unequal-length A-arms, coil springs; tubular shocks and anti-roll bar. Steering: Saginaw recirculating ball, 17.6:1 ratio; 2.9 turns lock-to-lock; turning circle 41.6 feet. Rear suspension: Independent; transverse leaf springs; transverse struts; half shafts with universal-joints; trailing arms and tubular shock absorbers. Rear axle type: Hypoid semi-floating. Brakes: Hydraulic, vented four-wheel discs; 11.75-inch diameter; single calipers; total swept area 461 sq. in. Six-inch wide pressed steel disc wheels. Standard rear axle ratio 3.55:1. Available rear axle gear ratios: 3.08:1; 3.36:1; 3.55:1; 3.70:1; 4.11:1; 4.56:1.

OPTIONS

RPO 898 Genuine leather seat trim ($79). RPO A01 Soft-Ray tinted glass, all windows ($15.80). RPO A02 Soft-Ray tinted glass, windshield ($10.55). RPO 431 Electric power windows ($59.20). RPO A82 Headrests ($42.15). RPO A85 Shoulder harness ($26.35). RPO C07 Auxiliary hardtop for convertible ($231.75). RPO C48 Heater and defroster deletion ($97.85 credit). RPO C60 Air conditioning ($412.90). RPO F41 Special front and rear suspension ($36.90). RPO G81 Positraction rear axle, all ra-

THE 1966 CORVETTE COUPE.

Jerry Heasley

THIS 1966 CORVETTE CONVERTIBLE CAME WITH THE 427-CID V-8.

Jerry Heasley

tios ($42.15). RPO J50 Power brakes ($43.05). RPO J56 Special heavy-duty brakes ($342.30). RPO K66 Transistor ignition system ($73.75). RPO L79 327-cid 350-hp V-8 ($105.35). RPO L36 427-cid 390-hp V-8 ($181.20). RPO L72 427-cid 427-hp V-8 ($312.85). RPO M20 Four-speed manual transmission ($184.30). RPO M21 Four-speed close-ratio manual transmission ($184.30). RPO M22 Heavy-duty close-ratio four-speed manual transmission ($237). RPO M35 Powerglide automatic transmission ($194.85). RPO N03 36-gallon fuel tank for coupe ($198.05). RPO N11 Off-road exhaust system ($36.90). RPO N14 Side Mount exhaust system ($131.65). RPO N32 Teakwood steering wheel ($48.45). RPO N36 Telescopic steering wheel ($42.15). RPO N40 Power steering ($94.80). RPO P48 Special cast-aluminum knock-off wheels ($326.00). RPO P92 7.75 x 15, white sidewall tires ($31.30). RPO T01 7.75 x 15 gold sidewall tires ($46.55). RPO U69 AM-FM radio ($199.10). RPO V74 Traffic hazard lamp switch ($11.60).

HISTORICAL FOOTNOTES

Only two percent of all 1966 Corvettes had a three-speed manual transmission; 89.3 percent came with a four-speed manual gearbox; 13.2 percent had a tilting steering wheel and 20.2 percent had power steering.

1967

Some consider the 1967 the best looking of the early Sting Rays. Its styling, although basically the same as in 1966, was a bit cleaner. The same egg-crate style grille with Argent Silver finish was carried over. The same smooth hood seen in 1966 was re-used. Big-block cars had a large front-opening air scoop over the center bulge instead of the previous power blister. The crossed flags badge on the nose of the 1967 Corvette had a widened "V" at its top. On the sides of the front fenders were five vertical and functional louvers that slanted towards the front of the car. Minor changes were made to the interior. The most noticeable was the relocation of the parking brake from under the dash to the center console. The new headliner was cushioned with foam and fiber material. Four-way flashers, directional signals with a lane-change function, larger interior vent ports and folding seat-back latches were all new. At the rear there were now dual round taillights on each side (instead of a taillight and optional back-up light). The twin back-up lights were now mounted in the center of the rear panel, above the license plate. Standard equipment included: a new dual-chamber brake master cylinder; six-inch wide slotted rally wheels with trim rings; an odometer; a clock; carpeting and a tachometer. The optional finned aluminum wheels were changed in design and had a one-year-only, non-knock-off center. The 10 lacquer exterior finishes offered were: Tuxedo Black; Ermine White; Elkhart Blue; Lyndale Blue; Marina Blue; Goodwood Green; Rally Red; Silver Pearl; Sunfire Yellow and Marlboro Maroon. All convertibles came with a choice of a Black, White or Teal Blue soft top. The all-vinyl foam-cushioned bucket seats came in Black, Red, Bright Blue, Saddle, White and Blue, White and Black, Teal Blue and Green.

ENGINES

BASE ENGINE: [RPO L75] V-8. Overhead valve. Cast-iron block. Displacement: 327 cid. Bore and stroke: 4.00 x 3.25 inches. Compression ratio: 10.0:1. Brake hp: 300 at 5000 rpm. Torque: 360 lbs.-ft. at 3400 rpm. Five main bearings. Hydraulic valve lifters. Holley four-barrel Model R3810A or R3814A.

OPTIONAL ENGINE: [RPO L79] V-8. Overhead valve. Cast-iron block. Displacement: 327 cid. Bore and stroke: 4.00 x 3.25

A 1967 CORVETTE CONVERTIBLE.

Jerry Heasley

Nicky Wright

A 1967 CORVETTE STING RAY COUPE WITH FUNCTIONAL, FIVE-SLOT FENDER LOUVERS.

inches. Compression ratio: 11.0:1. Brake hp: 350 at 5800 rpm. Torque: 360 lbs.-ft. at 3600 rpm. Five main bearings. Hydraulic valve lifters. High-performance camshaft. Carburetor: Holley four-barrel.

OPTIONAL ENGINE: [RPO L36] V-8. Overhead valve. Cast-iron block. Displacement: 427 cid. Bore and stroke: 4.251 x 3.76 inches. Compression ratio: 10:25:1. Brake hp: 390 at 5400 rpm. Torque: 460 lbs.-ft. at 3600 rpm. Five main bearings. Hydraulic valve lifters. High-performance camshaft. Carburetor: Holley four-barrel.

OPTIONAL ENGINE: [RPO L68] V-8. Overhead valve. Cast iron block. Displacement: 427 cid. Bore and stroke: 4.251 x 3.76 inches. Compression ratio: 10.25:1. Brake hp: 400 at 5400 rpm. Taxable hp: 57.80. Torque: 460 at 3600 rpm. Five main bearings. Hydraulic valve lifters. Special-performance camshaft. Crankcase capacity: 5 qt. (Add 1 qt. for filter). Cooling system capacity: 21 qt. (Add 1 qt. for heater). Carburetor: Three Holley two-barrel. Sales code: L68.

OPTIONAL ENGINE: [RPO L71] V-8. Overhead valve. Cast-iron block. Displacement: 427 cid. Bore and stroke: 4.251 x 3.76 inches. Compression ratio: 11.0:1. Brake hp: 435 at 5800 rpm. Five main bearings. Mechanical valve lifters. Special-performance camshaft. Carburetor:

Nicky Wright

THE 1967 CORVETTE STING RAY COUPE.

Three Holley two-barrels.

OPTIONAL ENGINE [RPO L72]: V-8. Overhead valve. Cast iron block. Displacement: 427 cid. Bore and stroke: 4.251 x 3.76 inches. Compression ratio: 11.0:1. Brake hp: 425 at 5600 rpm. Taxable hp: 57.80. Torque: 460 at 3800 rpm. Five main bearings. Mechanical valve lifters. Special-performance camshaft. Crankcase capacity: 5 qt. (Add 1 qt. for filter). Cooling system capacity: 21 qt. (Add 1 qt. for heater). Carburetor: Four-barrel. Sales code: L72.

OPTIONAL ENGINE: [RPO L89] V-8. Overhead valve. Cast-iron block. Displacement: 427 cid. Bore and stroke: 4.251 x 3.76 inches. Compression ratio: 11.0:1. Brake hp: 435 at 5800 rpm. Torque: 460 lbs.-ft. at 4000 rpm. Five main bearings. Mechanical valve lifters. Aluminum cylinder heads. Extra-large exhaust valves. Special-performance camshaft. Carburetor: Three Holley two-barrels.

Jerry Heasley

A 1967 CORVETTE CONVERTIBLE.

1967 1/2 ENGINE

OPTIONAL ENGINE: [RPO L88] V-8. Overhead valve. Displacement: 427 cid. Bore and stroke: 4.251 x 3.76 inches. Compression ratio: 12.50:1. Brake hp: 560 at 6400 rpm. Five main bearings. Mechanical valve lifters. Special ultra-high-performance camshaft with .5365-inch intakes. Carburetor: Single Holley 850CFM four-barrel.

TRANSMISSIONS

STANDARD MANUAL TRANSMISSION: A three-speed manual all-synchromesh transmission with floor-mounted gear shifter was standard equipment.

AUTOMATIC TRANSMISSION: An automatic transmission with floor-mounted gear shifter was optional equipment.

OPTIONAL MANUAL TRANSMISSION: A high-performance all-synchromesh four-speed manual transmission with floor-mounted gear shifter was optional equipment.

OPTIONAL MANUAL TRANSMISSION: A special high-performance four-speed manual all-synchromesh close-ratio transmission with floor-mounted gear shifter was optional equipment.

OPTIONAL MANUAL TRANSMISSION: A special heavy-duty four-speed manual all-synchromesh close-ratio transmission with floor-mounted gear shifter was optional.

CHASSIS FEATURES

Wheelbase: 98 inches. Overall length: [Convertible] 175.2 inches. Overall height: [Coupe] 49.6 inches. Overall width: 69.6 inches. Front tread: 57.6 inches. Rear tread: 58.3 inches. Ground clearance: Five inches. Tires: 7.75 x 15 red sidewall or whitewall. Frame: Full-length steel ladder type with five cross members and separate body. Front suspension: Independent; unequal-length A-arms, coil springs; tubular shocks and anti-roll bar. Steering: Saginaw recirculating ball, 17.6:1 ratio; 2.9 turns lock-to-lock; turning circle 41.6 feet. Rear suspension: Independent; transverse leaf springs; transverse struts; half shafts with universal-joints; trailing arms and tubular shock absorbers. Rear axle type: Hypoid semi-floating. Brakes: Hydraulic, vented four-wheel discs; 11.75-inch diameter; single calipers; total swept area 461 sq. in. Six-inch wide pressed steel disc wheels. Standard rear axle ratio 3.55:1. Available rear axle gear ratios: 3.08:1; 3.36:1; 3.55:1; 3.70:1; 4.11:1; 4.56:1.

Nicky Wright

THE 1967 CORVETTE COUPE WITH 427-CID V-8.

OPTIONS

RPO 898 Genuine leather seat trim ($79). RPO A01 Soft-Ray tinted glass, all windows ($15.80). RPO A02 Soft-Ray tinted glass, windshield ($10.55). RPO A31 Electric power windows ($57.95). RPO A82 Headrests ($42.15). RPO A85 Shoulder harness for coupe only ($26.35). RPO C07 Auxiliary hardtop for convertible ($231.75). RPO C48 Heater and defroster deletion ($97.85 credit). RPO C60 Air conditioning ($412.90). RPO F41 Special front and rear suspension ($36.90). RPO J50 Power brakes ($42.15). RPO J56 Special heavy-duty brakes ($342.30). RPO K66 Transistor ignition system ($73.75). RPO L36 427-cid 390-hp V-8 ($200.15). RPO L68 427-cid 400-hp V-8 ($305.50). RPO L71 427-cid 435-hp V-8 ($437.10). RPO L79 327-cid 350-hp V-8 ($105.35). RPO L88 427-cid 560-hp V-8 ($947.90). RPO L89 Aluminum cylinder heads for RPO L71 V-8 ($368.65). RPO M20 Four-speed manual transmission ($184.30). RPO M21 Four-speed close-ratio manual transmission ($184.30). RPO M22 Heavy-duty close-ratio four-speed manual transmission ($237.00).

RPO M35 Powerglide automatic transmission ($194.85). RPO N03 36-gallon fuel tank for coupe only ($198.05). RPO N11 Off-road exhaust system ($36.90). RPO N14 Side mount exhaust system ($131.65). RPO N36 Telescopic steering wheel ($42.15). RPO N40 Power steering ($94.80). RPO P48 Special cast-aluminum knock-off wheels ($263.30). RPO P92 7.75 x 15, white sidewall tires ($31.35). RPO QB1 7.75 x 15 red sidewall tires ($46.65). RPO U15 Speed-warning indicator ($10.55). RPO U69 AM-FM radio ($199.10).

HISTORICAL FOOTNOTES

Eighty-eight percent of 1967 Corvettes came with a four-speed manual transmission; 10.1 percent had Powerglide automatic transmission; 20.8 percent had power brakes; 16.5 percent had air conditioning; 10.5 percent had a telescoping steering wheel and 25.1 percent came with power steering. A 327-cid 300 hp V-8-powered Corvette of this vintage would go from 0-to-60 mph in 7.8 seconds; from 0-to-100 mph in 23.1 seconds. The 1967 Corvette is considered the most refined of the original Sting Ray models of 1963-1967.

THE STING RAY NAME WAS NOT USED IN 1968.

1968

The Corvette's first major restyling since 1963 occurred in this year. As the sales brochure read, "Corvette '68 . . . all different all over." The fastback was replaced by a tunneled-roof coupe. It featured a removable back window and a two-piece detachable roof section or T-top. The convertible's optional hardtop had a glass rear window. The front end was more aerodynamic than those on previous Corvettes. As before, the headlights were hidden. Now they were vacuum-operated, rather than electrical. The wipers also disappeared when not in use. Except for the rocker panels, the sides were devoid of chrome. Conventional door handles were eliminated and in their place were push buttons. The blunt rear deck contained four round taillights with the word Corvette printed in chrome in the space between them. The wraparound, wing-like rear bumper and license plate holder treatment resembled that used on the 1967 models. Buyers had their choice of 10 exterior colors: Tuxedo Black, Polar White, Corvette Bronze, LeMans Blue, International Blue, Cordovan Maroon, Rally Red, Silverstone Silver, British Green and Safari Yellow. All convertibles came with a choice of Black, White or Beige soft tops. Interior colors were: Black, Red, Medium Blue, Dark Blue, Dark Orange, Tobacco, and Gunmetal.

ENGINES

BASE ENGINE: [RPO L75] V-8. Overhead valve. Cast-iron block. Displacement: 327 cid. Bore and stroke: 4.00 x 3.25 inches. Compression ratio: 10.25:1. Brake hp: 300. Five main bearings. Hydraulic valve lifters. Carburetor: Rochester Type 4MV four-barrel Model 7028207.

OPTIONAL ENGINE: [RPO L79] V-8. Overhead valve. Cast-iron block. Displacement: 327 cid. Bore and stroke: 4.00 x 3.25 inches. Compression ratio: 11.0:1. Brake hp: 350 at 5800 rpm. Torque: 360 lbs.-ft. at 3600 rpm. Five main bearings. Hydraulic valve lifters. High-performance camshaft. Carburetor: Holley four-barrel.

OPTIONAL ENGINE: [RPO L36] V-8. Overhead valve. Cast-iron block. Displacement: 427 cid. Bore and stroke: 4.251 x 3.76 inches. Compression ratio: 10:25:1. Brake hp: 390 at 5400 rpm. Torque: 460 lbs.-ft. at 3600 rpm. Five main bearings. Hydraulic valve lift-

THE 1968 CORVETTE T-TOP COUPE.

ers. High-performance camshaft. Carburetor: Holley four-barrel.

OPTIONAL ENGINE: [RPO L71] V-8. Overhead valve. Cast-iron block. Displacement: 427 cid. Bore and stroke: 4.251 x 3.76 inches. Compression ratio: 11.0:1. Brake hp: 435 at 5800 rpm. Torque: 460 lbs.-ft. at 4000 rpm. Five main bearings. Mechanical valve lifters. Special-performance camshaft. Carburetor: Three Holley two-barrels.

OPTIONAL ENGINE [RPO L71/L89] V-8. Overhead valve. Cast iron block. Bore and stroke: 4.251 x 3.76 inches. Displacement: 427 cid. Compression ratio: 11.0:1. Brake hp: 435 at 5800 rpm. Taxable hp: 57.80. Torque: 460 at 4000 rpm. Five main bearings. Mechanical valve lifters. Aluminum cylinder heads. Extra-large exhaust valves. Special-performance camshaft. Crankcase capacity: 5 qt. (Add 1 qt. for filter). Cooling system capacity: 21 qt. (Add 1 qt. for heater). Carburetor: Three Holley two-barrels. Sales code: L71/L89.

OPTIONAL ENGINE: [RPO L88] V-8. Overhead valve. Displacement: 427 cid. Bore and stroke: 4.251 x 3.76 inches. Compression ratio: 12.50:1. Brake hp: 560 at 6400 rpm. Five main bearings. Mechanical valve lifters. Special-ultra-high-performance camshaft with

.5365-in. intakes. Carburetor: Single Holley 850CFM four-barrel.

TRANSMISSIONS

STANDARD MANUAL TRANSMISSION: A three-speed manual all-synchromesh transmission with floor-mounted gear shifter was standard equipment.

AUTOMATIC TRANSMISSION: An Turbo Hydra-Matic automatic transmission with floor-mounted gear shifter was optional equipment.

OPTIONAL MANUAL TRANSMISSION: A high-performance all-synchromesh four-speed manual transmission with floor-mounted gear shifter was optional equipment.

OPTIONAL MANUAL TRANSMISSION: A special high-performance four-speed manual all-synchromesh close-ratio transmission with floor-mounted gear shifter was optional equipment.

OPTIONAL MANUAL TRANSMISSION: A special heavy-duty four-speed manual all-synchromesh close-ratio transmission with floor-mounted gear shifter was optional.

CHASSIS FEATURES

Wheelbase: 98 inches. Overall length: 182.1 inches. Overall height: 48.6 inches. Overall width: 69.2 inches. Front tread: 58.3 inches.

Nicky Wright

1968 CORVETTE CONVERTIBLE WITH NON-STOCK WHEELS AND PAINT.

Rear tread: 59.0 inches. Tires: F70-15. Frame: Full-length ladder type with five cross members. Steel box sections, welded. Front suspension: Unequal-length A-arms with coil springs; tube shocks and stabilizer bar. Steering: Saginaw recirculating ball. Turns lock-to-lock: 2.9. Turning radius: 39.9 feet. Rear suspension: Trailing arms, toe links, transverse chromium-carbon steel leaf spring, tube shocks and anti-roll bar. Rear axle type: Sprung differential, hypoid gear. Brakes: Four-wheel disc brakes. Vented discs front and rear. Optional power assist. Diameter: 11.8 inches front and 11.8 inches rear. Total swept area: 259 sq. in. per ton 461.2 in. total. Wheels: Slotted steel discs. Standard rear axle ratio: 3.36:1. Available rear axle gear ratios: 3.08:1; 3.36:1; 3.55:1; 3.70:1; 4.11:1; 4.56:1.

OPTIONS

RPO 898 Genuine leather seat trim ($79). RPO A01 Soft-Ray tinted glass, all windows ($15.80). RPO A31 Electric power windows ($57.95). RPO A82 Restraints ($42.15). RPO A85 Custom shoulder belts ($26.35). RPO C07 Auxiliary hardtop for convertible ($231.75). RPO C08 Vinyl cover for auxiliary hardtop ($52.70). RPO C50 Rear window defroster ($31.60). RPO C60 Air conditioning ($412.90). RPO F41 Special front and rear suspension ($36.90). RPO G81 Positraction rear axle, all ratios ($46.35). RPO J50 Power brakes ($42.15). RPO J56 Special heavy-duty brakes ($384.45). RPO K66 Transistor ignition system ($73.75).

RPO L36 427-cid 390-hp V-8 ($200.15). RPO L68 427-cid 400-hp V-8 ($305.50). RPO L71/81 427-cid 435-hp ($437.10). RPO L79 327-cid 350-hp V-8 ($105.35). RPO L88 427-cid 560-hp V-8 ($947.90). RPO M20 Four-speed manual transmission ($184.30). RPO M21 Four-speed close-ratio manual transmission ($184.30). RPO M22 Heavy-duty close-ratio four-speed manual transmission ($263.30). RPO M35 Turbo Hydra-Matic automatic transmission ($226.45). RPO N11 Off-road exhaust system ($36.90). RPO N36 Telescopic steering wheel ($42.15). RPO N40 Power steering ($94.80). RPO P01 Bright metal wheel cover ($57.95). RPO PT6 Red stripe nylon tires F70 x 15 ($31.30). RPO PT7 F70 x 15 white stripe tires ($31.35). RPO UA6 Alarm system ($26.35). RPO U15 Speed-warning indicator ($10.55). RPO U69 AM-FM radio ($172.75). RPO U79 Stereo radio ($278.10).

HISTORICAL FOOTNOTES

Just over 80 percent of 1968 Corvettes were equipped with four-speed manual transmission; 81 percent had tinted glass; 36.3 percent had power steering; 19.8 percent had air conditioning and 33.7 percent had power brakes. The L79-powered Corvette of this year could go from 0-to-60 mph in 7.7 seconds and from 0-to-100 mph in 20.7 seconds. The L71-powered Corvette of this year could go from 0-to-30 in 3.0 seconds; from 0-to-50 in 5.3 seconds and from 0-to-60 in 6.5 seconds. It did the quarter mile in 13.41 seconds at 109.5 mph. Top speed (L71) was 142 mph.

1969

After a year's absence, the Stingray name (now spelled as one word) re-appeared on the front fenders. The back-up lights were integrated into the center taillights. The ignition was now on the steering column and the door depression button used in 1968 was eliminated. (A key lock was put in its place.) Front and rear disc brakes, headlight washers, center console, wheel trim rings, carpeting, and all-vinyl upholstery were standard.

Buyers had their choice of 10 exterior colors: Tuxedo Black, Can-Am White, Monza Red, LeMans Blue, Monaco Orange, Fathom Green, Daytona Yellow, Cortez Silver, Burgundy and Riverside Gold. All convertibles came with a choice of Black, White or Beige soft tops. Interior colors were: Black, Bright Blue, Green, Red, Gunmetal, and Saddle.

ENGINES

BASE ENGINE: Overhead valve V-8. Cast-iron block. Displacement: 350 cid. Bore and stroke: 4.00 x 3.48 inches. Compression ratio: 10.25:1. Brake hp: 300 at 4800 rpm. Five main bearings. Hydraulic valve lifters. Carburetor: Rochester four-barrel Model 7029203.

OPTIONAL ENGINE: [RPO L46] V-8. Overhead valve. Cast-iron block. Displacement: 350 cid. Bore and stroke: 4.00 x 3.48 inches. Compression ratio: 11.0:1. Brake hp: 350. Five main bearings. Hydraulic valve lifters. Carburetor: Rochester four-barrel.

OPTIONAL ENGINE: [RPO L36] V-8. Overhead valve. Cast-iron block. Displacement: 427 cid. Bore and stroke: 4.251 x 3.76 inches. Compression ratio: 10:25:1. Brake hp: 390 at 5400 rpm. Torque: 460 lbs.-ft. at 3600 rpm. Five main bearings. Hydraulic valve lifters. High-performance camshaft. Carburetor: Holley four-barrel.

OPTIONAL ENGINE: [RPO L68] V-8. Overhead valve. Cast-iron block. Displacement: 427 cid. Bore and stroke: 4.251 x 3.76 inches. Compression ratio: 10.25:1. Brake hp:

Nicky Wright

THE 1969 CORVETTE STINGRAY WITH DELUXE WHEEL COVERS.

Nicky Wright

THE 1969 CORVETTE CONVERTIBLE FEATURED HEADLIGHT WASHERS.

400. Five main bearings. Three Holley two-barrel carburetors.

OPTIONAL ENGINE: [RPO L71] V-8. Overhead valve. Cast-iron block. Displacement: 427 cid. Bore and stroke: 4.251 x 3.76 inches. Compression ratio: 11.0:1. Brake hp: 435 @ 5800 rpm. Torque: 460 lbs.-ft. at 4000 rpm. Five main bearings. Mechanical valve lifters. Special-performance camshaft. Carburetor: Three Holley two-barrels.

OPTIONAL ENGINE: [RPO L88] V-8. Overhead valve. Displacement: 427 cid. Bore and stroke: 4.251 x 3.76 inches. Compression ratio: 12.0:1. Brake hp: 430 (actually about 560 @ 6400 rpm). Five main bearings. Mechanical valve lifters. Special-ultra-high-performance camshaft with .5365-inch intakes. Carburetor: Holley four-barrel.

OPTIONAL ENGINE: [RPO L89] V-8. Overhead valve. Displacement: 427 cid. Bore and stroke: 4.251 x 3.76 inches. Compression ratio: 12.0:1. Brake hp: 435. Five main bearings. Mechanical valve lifters. Carburetor: Holley four-barrel.

OPTIONAL ENGINE: [RPO ZL1] V-8. Overhead valve. Displacement: 427 cid. Bore and stroke: 4.251 x 3.76 inches. Compression ratio: 12.5:1. Brake hp: 430 at 5200 rpm (actually over 500). Torque: 450 lbs.-ft. at 4400 rpm. Aluminum block. Five main bearings. Mechanical valve lifters. Special-ultra-high-performance camshaft. Carburetor: Single Holley 850CFM four-barrel on aluminum manifold.

TRANSMISSIONS

STANDARD MANUAL TRANSMISSION: A three-speed manual all-synchromesh transmission with floor-mounted gear shifter was standard equipment.

AUTOMATIC TRANSMISSION: A Turbo Hydra-Matic automatic transmission with floor-mounted gear shifter was optional equipment.

OPTIONAL MANUAL TRANSMISSION: A high-performance all-synchromesh four-

Jerry Heasley

A 1969 CORVETTE STINGRAY CONVERTIBLE WITH SIDE-MOUNT EXHAUST SYSTEM.

speed manual transmission with floor-mounted gear shifter was optional equipment.

OPTIONAL MANUAL TRANSMISSION: A special high-performance four-speed manual all-synchromesh close-ratio transmission with floor-mounted gear shifter was optional equipment.

OPTIONAL MANUAL TRANSMISSION: A special heavy-duty four-speed manual all-synchromesh close-ratio transmission with floor-mounted gear shifter was optional.

CHASSIS FEATURES

Wheelbase: 98 inches. Overall length: 182.5 inches. Overall height: 47.9 inches. Overall width: 69.0 inches. Front tread: 58.7 inches. Rear tread: 59.4 inches. Tires: F70-15. Frame: Full-length welded-steel ladder type with five cross members. steel box sections, welded. Front suspension: Unequal-length A-arms with coil springs; tube shocks and stabilizer bar. Steering: Saginaw recirculating ball; ratio 17.6:1; turns lock-to-lock: 2.9; turning radius: 39.0 feet. Rear suspension: Trailing arms, toe links, transverse chromium-carbon steel leaf spring, tube shocks and anti-roll bar. Rear axle type: Sprung differential, hypoid gear. Brakes: Four-wheel disc brakes. Vented discs front and rear. optional power assist; diameter: 11.75 inches front and 11.75 inches rear; total swept area: 461 sq. in. 15 x 8-inch slotted steel disc wheels. Standard rear axle ratio 3.36:1. Available rear axle gear ratios:

3.08:1; 3.36:1; 3.55:1; 3.70:1; 4.11:1; 4.56:1.

OPTIONS

RPO 898 Genuine leather seat trim ($79). RPO A01 Soft-Ray tinted glass, all windows ($16.90). RPO A31 Electric power windows ($63.20). RPO A85 Custom shoulder belts ($42.15). RPO C07 Auxiliary hardtop for convertible ($252.80). RPO C08 Vinyl cover for auxiliary hardtop ($57.95). RPO C50 Rear window defroster ($32.65). RPO C60 Air conditioning ($428.70). RPO F41 Special front and rear suspension ($36.90). RPO G81 Positraction rear axle, all ratios ($46.35). RPO J50 Power brakes ($42.15). RPO K05 Engine block heater ($10.55). RPO K66 Transistor ignition system ($81.10). RPO L36 427-cid 390-hp V-8 ($221.20). RPO L46 350-cid 350-hp V-8 ($131.65). RPO L68 427-cid 400-hp V-8 ($326.55). RPO L71 427-cid 435-hp V-8 ($437.10). RPO L88 427-cid 435-hp V-8 ($1032.15). RPO L89 427-cid 435-hp V-8 ($832.05). RPO ZL1 Optional special 427-cid aluminum V-8 ($3,000). RPO M20 Four-speed manual transmission ($184.80). RPO M21 Four-speed close-ratio manual transmission ($184.80). RPO M22 Heavy-duty close-ratio four-speed manual transmission ($290.40). RPO M40 Turbo Hydra-Matic automatic transmission ($221.80). RPO N14 Side mount exhaust system ($147.45). RPO N37 Tilt-tele-

Jerry Heasley

THE 1969 CORVETTE STINGRAY L89 CONVERTIBLE.

Nicky Wright

BACKUP LIGHTS WERE MOVED INSIDE THE TAIL LIGHTS ON THE 1969 CORVETTE.

scopic steering wheel ($84.30). RPO N40 Power steering ($105.35). RPO P02 Wheel covers ($57.95). RPO PT6 Red stripe nylon tires, F70 x 15 ($31.30). RPO PT7 F70 x 15, white stripe tires ($31.30). TJ2 Front fender louver trim ($21.10). RPO UA6 Alarm system ($26.35). RPO U15 Speed-warning indicator ($11.60). RPO U69 AM-FM radio ($172.45). RPO U79 Stereo radio ($278.10).

HISTORICAL FOOTNOTES

The majority of 1969 Corvettes, 59.2 percent, came with power steering; 78.4 percent had four-speed manual transmissions and one-in-four had power windows. A 350-cid 300-hp V-8 was available this season. Cars with this powerplant and automatic transmission were capable of 0-to-60 mph speeds in the 8.4 second bracket and could move from 0-to-100 mph in approximately 21.7 seconds.

1970

Refinements were made to the basic styling used since 1968. A new ice-cube-tray design grille and matching side fender louvers; rectangular, amber front signal lights; fender flares; and square exhaust exits were exterior changes. The bucket seats and safety belt retractor containers were also improved. Standard equipment included: Front and rear disc brakes; headlight washers; wheel trim rings; carpeting; center console and all-vinyl upholstery (in either Black; Blue; Green; Saddle; or Red). Buyers had their choice of 10 exterior colors: Mulsanne Blue; Bridgehampton Blue; Donnybrooke Green; Laguna Gray; Marlboro Maroon; Corvette Bronze; Monza Red; Cortez Silver; Classic White; and Daytona Yellow. All convertibles came with a choice of Black or White soft tops. Interior colors were: Black; Blue; Green; Red; Brown; and Saddle.

ENGINES

BASE ENGINE: [RPO ZQ3] Overhead valve. Cast-iron block. Displacement: 350 cid. Bore and stroke: 4.00 x 3.48 inches. Compression ratio: 10.25:1. Brake hp: 300 at 4800 rpm. Five main bearings. Hydraulic valve lifters. Carburetor: Rochester Type Quadra-Jet four-barrel Model 4MV.

OPTIONAL ENGINE: [RPO L46] V-8. Overhead valve V-8. Cast-iron block. Displacement: 350 cid. Bore and stroke: 4.00 x 3.48 inches. Compression ratio: 11.0:1. Brake hp: 350 at 5600 rpm. Torque: 380 lb.-ft. at 3800 rpm. Five main bearings. Hydraulic valve lifters. Carburetor: Rochester Quadra-Jet four-barrel.

OPTIONAL ENGINE: [RPO LS5] V-8. Overhead valve. Cast-iron block. Displacement: 454 cid. Bore and stroke: 4.251 x 4.00

THE 1970 CORVETTE LT1 T-TOP COUPE

Jerry Heasley

Nicky Wright

A 1970 CORVETTE STINGRAY LT1 WITH T-TOPS.

inches. Compression ratio: 10.25:1. Brake hp: 390 at 4800 rpm. Torque: 500 lbs.-ft. at 3400 rpm. Five main bearings. Hydraulic valve lifters. High-performance camshaft. Carburetor: Rochester 750CFM Quadra-Jet four-barrel.

OPTIONAL ENGINE: [RPO LT1] V-8. Overhead valve. Cast-iron block. Displacement: 350 cid. Bore and stroke: 4.00 x 3.48 inches. Compression ratio: 11.0:1. Brake hp: 370 at 6000 rpm. Torque: 380 lbs.-ft. at 4000 rpm. Five main bearings. Solid valve lifters. High-performance camshaft. Carburetor: Holley four-barrel on aluminum intake manifold.

PROPOSED OPTIONAL ENGINE: [RPO LS7] V-8. Overhead valve. Cast-iron block. Displacement: 454 cid. Bore and stroke: 4.251 x 4.00 inches. Compression ratio: 11.25:1. Brake hp: 465 at 5200 rpm. Torque: 490 lbs.-ft. at 3400 rpm. Five main bearings. Solid valve lifters. High-performance camshaft. Carburetor: Holley 800CFM four-barrel.

(NOTE: Only one car with the LS7 engine was built. Sports Car Graphic editor Paul Van Valkenburgh drove it 2,500 miles from a press conference at Riverside, Calif., to Detroit and raved about it. The car did the quarter mile in 13.8 seconds at 108 mph. However, GM's policies against ultra-high-performance cars at this time led to the option being stillborn. The LS7 option is listed in some early 1970 sales literature but none were ever sold.)

TRANSMISSION

AUTOMATIC TRANSMISSION: A Turbo Hydra-Matic automatic transmission with floor-mounted gear shifter was standard equipment.

OPTIONAL MANUAL TRANSMISSION: A close-ratio four-speed manual transmission with floor-mounted gear shifter was a no-cost option.

OPTIONAL MANUAL TRANSMISSION: A heavy-duty close-ratio four-speed manual transmission with floor-mounted gear shifter was optional equipment.

CHASSIS FEATURES

Wheelbase: 98 inches. Overall length: 182.5 inches. Overall height: 47.4 inches. Overall width: 69.0 inches. Ground clearance: 4.5 inches. Front tread: 58.7 inches. Rear tread: 59.4

Nicky Wright

A 1970 CORVETTE STINGRAY LT1 COUPE. FENDER LOUVERS ARE NOW A SINGLE GRATE.

THE 1970 CORVETTE LT1 T-TOP COUPE.

inches. Tires: F70-15. Frame: Full-length welded-steel ladder type with five cross members. Steel box sections, welded. Front suspension: Unequal-length A-arms with coil springs, tube shocks, and stabilizer bar. Steering: Saginaw recirculating ball; ratio 17.6:1; turns lock-to-lock 2.9; turning radius 39.0 feet. Rear suspension: Trailing arms; toe links; transverse chromium-carbon steel leaf springs; tube shocks; and anti-roll bar. Rear axle type: Sprung differential, hypoid gear. Brakes: Four-wheel disc brakes; vented discs front and rear; optional power assist; diameter 11.75 inches front and 11.75 inches rear; total swept area 461 sq. in.; 15 x 8-inch slotted steel disc wheels. Standard rear axle ratio: 3.36:1. Available rear axle gear ratios: 2.73:1; 3.08:1; 3.36:1; 3.55:1; 4.11:1; 4.56:1.

OPTIONS

RPO Custom interior trim ($158). RPO A31 Electric power windows ($63.20). RPO A85 Custom shoulder belts ($42.15). RPO C07 Auxiliary hardtop for convertible ($273.85). RPO C08 Vinyl cover for auxiliary hardtop ($63.20). RPO C50 Rear window defroster ($36.90). RPO C60 Air conditioning ($447.65). RPO G81 Positraction rear axle, all ratios ($12.65). RPO J50 Power brakes ($47.40). RPO L46 350-cid 350-hp V-8 ($158.). RPO LS5 454-cid 390-hp V-8 ($289.65). RPO LT1 350-cid 370-hp V-8 ($447.60). RPO M21 Four-speed close-ratio

Nicky Wright

THE 1970 CORVETTE LT1 COUPE.

THE 1970 CORVETTE CONVERTIBLE.

John Gunnell

1970 CORVETTE STINGRAY CONVERTIBLE.

manual transmission (no-cost option). RPO M22 Heavy-duty close-ratio four-speed manual transmission ($95.). RPO M40 Turbo Hydra-Matic automatic transmission (no cost option). RPO N37 Tilt-telescopic steering wheel ($84.30). RPO N40 Power steering ($105.35). RPO P01 Custom wheel covers ($57.95). RPO PT7 White stripe nylon tires, F70 x 15 ($31.30). RPO PU9 F70 x 15 raised-white-letter tires ($33.15). RPO T60 Heavy-duty battery ($15.80). RPO UA6 Alarm system ($31.60). RPO U69 AM-FM radio ($172.75). RPO U79 Stereo radio ($278.10). Beginning in April 1970, the LT1 engine was made available as part of a ZR1 option. The "Z" meant it was part of Chevrolet's "Special Items" group. The ZR1 package included the LT1 engine; M22 heavy-duty four-speed manual transmission; J50/J56 dual-pin brakes with heavy-duty front pads and power assist; and F41 suspension consisting of special 89 lb./in. ride rate front springs and 121 lb./in. ride rate rear springs, matching shock absorbers, and a 0.75-inch front stabilizer bar.

HISTORICAL FOOTNOTES

Most 1970 Corvettes, 70.5 percent, came with four-speed manual transmission; 33.5 percent had tilting steering wheels; 27.9 percent power windows; 38.5 percent air-conditioning; and 68.8 percent power steering. An L56-powered 1970 Corvette would do 0-to-60 mph in seven seconds and go from 0-to-100 mph in 14 seconds. An LT1-powered 1970 Corvette could do 0-30 mph in 2.5 seconds, 0-60 mph in 5.7 seconds and 0-to-100 mph in 13.5 seconds. The LT1 Corvette did the quarter mile in 14.17 seconds at 102.15 mph and had a top speed of 122 mph.

1971

If you liked the 1970 Corvette, you'd like the 1971 version. They were virtually the same car. A new resin process (that supposedly improved the body) and a different interior were the major changes. Under the hood, the compression ratios were dropped a bit to enable Corvette engines to run on lower octane fuel. Standard equipment included: All-vinyl upholstery; dual exhaust; outside rearview mirror; carpeting; center console; wheel trim rings; electric clock; tachometer; heavy-duty battery; front and rear disc brakes with warning light; and tinted glass. Buyers had their choice of 10 exterior colors: Mulsanne Blue; Bridgehampton Blue; Brands Hatch Green; Steel Cities Gray; Ontario Orange; Mille Miglia Red; Nevada Silver; Classic White; Sunflower Yellow; and War Bonnet Yellow. All convertibles came with a choice of Black or White soft tops. Interior colors were: Black; Dark Blue; Dark Green; Red; and Saddle.

ENGINES

BASE ENGINE: [RPO ZQ3] V-8. Overhead valve. Cast-iron block. Bore and stroke: 4.00 x 3.48 inches. Displacement: 350 cid. Compression ratio: 10.25:1. Brake hp: 300 at 4800 rpm. Taxable hp: 51.20. Torque: 380 at 3200 rpm. Five main bearings. Hydraulic valve lifters. Crankcase capacity: 4 qt. (Add 1 qt. for filter). Cooling system capacity: 14 qt. (Add 1 qt. for heater). Carburetor: Rochester 7029203 four-barrel.

OPTIONAL ENGINE: [RPO LT1] V-8. Overhead valve. Cast-iron block. Bore and stroke: 4.00 x 3.48 inches. Displacement: 350 cid. Compression ratio: 9.00:1. Brake hp: 330 at 5600 rpm. Net brake hp: 275 at 5600 rpm. Taxable hp: 51.20. Torque: 360 at 4000 rpm. Net torque: 300 at 4000 rpm. Five main bearings. Hydraulic valve lifters. Crankcase capacity: 4 qt. (Add 1 qt. for filter). Cooling system capacity: 14 qt. (Add 1 qt. for heater). Carburetor:

Jerry Heasley

THE 1971 CORVETTE STINGRAY LT1 COUPE IN MILLE MIGLIA RED.

A 1971 CORVETTE STINGRAY LT1 WITH T-TOPS.

Nicky Wright

THE 1971 CORVETTE STINGRAY LT1.

Nicky Wright

Rochester Rochester Type Quadra-Jet four-barrel Model 4MV. .

OPTIONAL ENGINE: [RPO LT1/ZR1] V-8. Overhead valve. Cast-iron block. Bore and stroke: 4.00 x 3.48 inches. Displacement: 350 cid. Compression ratio: 9.00:1. Brake hp: 330 at unknown rpm. Net brake hp: unknown at unknown rpm. Taxable hp: 51.20. Torque: unknown at unknown rpm. Net torque: unknown at unknown rpm. Five main bearings. Hydraulic valve lifters. Crankcase capacity: 4 qt. (Add 1 qt. for filter). Cooling system capacity: 14 qt. (Add 1 qt. for heater). Carburetor: Rochester Rochester Type Quadra-Jet four-barrel Model 4MV.

NOTE: Competition engine; only eight assembled.

OPTIONAL ENGINE: [RPO LS5]. V-8. Overhead valve. Cast iron block. Bore and stroke: 4.251 x 4.00 inches. Displacement: 454 cid. Compression ratio: 8.50:1. Brake hp: 365 at 4800 rpm. Net brake hp: 285 at 4000 rpm. Torque: 465 at 3200 rpm. Net torque: 390 at 3200 rpm. Five main bearings. Hydraulic valve lifters. High-performance camshaft. Crankcase capacity: 5 qt. (Add 1 qt. for filter). Cooling system capacity: 21 qt. (Add 1 qt. for heater). Carburetor: Rochester 750CFM Quadra-Jet four-barrel.

OPTIONAL ENGINE: [RPO LS6] V-8. Overhead valve. Cast-iron block. Bore and

Jerry Heasley

THE 1971 CORVETTE STINGRAY L86 COUPE IN ONTARIO ORANGE.

THE 1971 CORVETTE CONVERTIBLE.

stroke: 4.251 x 4.00 inches. Displacement: 454 cid. Compression ratio: 8.5:1. Brake hp: 425 at 5600 rpm. Net brake hp: 325 at 6500 rpm. Torque: 475 at 4000 rpm. Net torque: 390 at 3600 rpm. Five main bearings. Hydraulic valve lifters. High-performance camshaft. Crankcase capacity: 5 qt. (Add 1 qt. for filter). Cooling system capacity: 21 qt. (Add 1 qt. for heater). Carburetor: Holley 880CFM four-barrel.

TRANSMISSION

AUTOMATIC TRANSMISSION: A Turbo Hydra-Matic automatic transmission with floor-mounted gear shifter was standard equipment.

OPTIONAL MANUAL TRANSMISSION: A close-ratio four-speed manual transmission with floor-mounted gear shifter was a no-cost option.

OPTIONAL MANUAL TRANSMISSION:

Jerry Heasley

A 1971 CORVETTE STINGRAY ZR2 CONVERTIBLE WITH THE 454-CID 425-HP LS6 V-8 AND FOUR-SPEED MANUAL TRANSMISSION.

A heavy-duty close-ratio four-speed manual transmission with floor-mounted gear shifter was optional equipment.

CHASSIS FEATURES

Wheelbase: 98 inches. Overall length: 182.5 inches. Overall height: 47.4 inches. Overall width: 69.0 inches. Ground clearance: 4.5 inches. Front tread: 58.7 inches. Rear tread: 59.4 inches. Tires: F70-15. Frame: Full-length welded-steel ladder type with five cross members. Steel box sections, welded. Front suspension: Unequal-length A-arms with coil springs, tube shocks, and stabilizer bar. Steering: Saginaw recirculating ball; ratio 17.6:1; turns lock-to-lock 2.9; turning radius 39.0 feet. Rear suspension: Trailing arms; toe links; transverse chromium-carbon steel leaf springs; tube shocks; and anti-roll bar. Rear axle type: Sprung differential, hypoid gear. Brakes: Four-wheel disc brakes; vented discs front and rear; optional power assist; diameter: 11.75 inches front and 11.75 inches rear; total swept area: 461 sq. in.; 15 x 8-inch slotted steel disc wheels. Standard rear axle ratio 3.36:1. Available rear axle gear ratios: 2.73:1; 3.08:1; 3.36:1; 3.55:1; 4.11:1; 4.56:1.

OPTIONS

RPO Custom interior trim ($158). RPO A31 Electric power windows ($79). RPO A85 Custom shoulder belts ($42). RPO C07 Auxiliary hardtop for convertible ($274). RPO C08 Vinyl cover for auxiliary hardtop ($63). RPO C50 Rear window defroster ($42). RPO C60 Air conditioning ($459). RPO G81 Positraction rear axle, all ratios ($13). RPO J50 Power brakes ($47). RPO LS5 454-cid 365-hp V-8 ($295). RPO LS6 454-cid 425-hp V-8 ($1221). RPO LT1 350-cid 330-hp V-8 ($483). RPO ZR1 350-cid 330-hp V-8 ($1010). RPO ZR2 454-cid 425-hp V-8 ($1747). RPO M21 Four-speed close-ratio manual transmission (no-cost option). RPO M22 Heavy-duty close-ratio four-speed manual transmission ($100). RPO M40 Turbo Hydra-Matic automatic transmission (no-cost option). RPO N37 Tilt-Telescopic steering wheel ($84.30). RPO N40 Power steering ($115.90). RPO P02 Custom wheel covers ($63). RPO PT7 White stripe

THE 1971 CORVETTE COUPE

nylon tires, F70 x 15 ($28). RPO PU9 F70 x 15 raised-white-letter tires ($42). RPO T60 Heavy-duty battery ($15.80). RPO U69 AM-FM radio ($178). RPO U79 Stereo radio ($283). The LT1 engine was again available as part of the ZR1 option. The "Z" meant it was part of Chevrolet's "Special Items" group. The ZR1 package included the LT1 engine, M22 heavy-duty four-speed manual transmission, J50/J56 dual-pin brakes with heavy-duty front pads and power assist and F41 suspension consisting of special 89 lb./in. ride rate front springs and 121 lb./in. ride rate rear springs, matching shock absorbers and a 0.75-inch front stabilizer bar.

HISTORICAL FOOTNOTES

Slightly over one-third of 1971 Corvettes had a tilting steering wheel; 53.9 percent had a four-speed manual transmission; 82.1 percent had power steering; 52.7 percent had air conditioning; and 28.4 percent had power windows. A 1971 Corvette with the base L48 engine could go 0-to-60 mph in 7.1 seconds, 0-to-100 mph in 19.8 seconds and do the standing-start quarter mile in 15.5 seconds at 90.36 mph. A 1971 Corvette with the LS5 engine could go 0-to-60 mph in 5.7 seconds, 0-to-100 mph in 14.1 seconds and do the standing-start quarter mile in 14.2 seconds at 100.33 mph. A 1971 Corvette with the LS6 engine and 3.36:1 rear axle was tested by Car and Driver magazine in June 1971. It moved from 0-to-60 mph in 5.3 seconds, from 0-to-80 mph in 8.5 seconds and from 0-to-100 mph in 12.7 seconds. The same car did the quarter mile in 13.8 seconds at 104.65 mph. A 1971 Corvette with the LT1 engine, M-21 transmission, and 3.70:1 rear axle was tested by Car and Driver magazine in June 1971. It moved from 0-to-40 mph in 3.4 seconds, from 0-to-60 mph in 6.0 seconds, and from 0-to-100 mph in 14.5 seconds. The same car did the quarter mile in 14.57 seconds at 100.55 mph and its speed was 137 mph.

1972

The 1972 Corvette was basically the same as the 1971. Among the standard equipment was a Positraction rear axle; outside rearview mirror; tinted glass; flo-thru ventilation system; front and rear disc brakes; electric clock; carpeting; wheel trim rings; all-vinyl upholstery; and anti-theft alarm system. Buyers had their choice of 10 exterior colors: Sunflower Yellow; Pewter Silver; Bryar Blue; Elkhart Green; Classic White; Mille Miglia Red; Targa Blue; Ontario Orange; Steel Cities Gray and War Bonnet Yellow. All convertibles came with a choice of Black or White soft tops. Interior colors were: Black; Blue; Red; and Saddle.

ENGINES

BASE ENGINE: [RPO ZQ3] V-8. Overhead valve. Cast iron block. Displacement: 350 cid. Bore and stroke: 4.00 x 3.48 inches. Compression ratio: 8.5:1. Brake hp: 200 at 4400 rpm. Torque: 300 lbs.-ft. at 2800 rpm. Five main bearings. Hydraulic valve lifters. Carburetor: Rochester Type Quadra-Jet four-barrel Model 4MV.

OPTIONAL ENGINE: [RPO LS5] V-8. Overhead valve. Cast iron block. Displacement: 454 cid. Bore and stroke: 4.251 x 4.00 inches. Compression ratio: 8.5:1. Brake hp: 270 at 4000 rpm. Torque: 390 lbs.-ft. at 3200 rpm. Five main bearings. Hydraulic valve lifters. High-performance camshaft. Carburetor: Rochester 750CFM Quadra-Jet four-barrel.

OPTIONAL ENGINE: [RPO LT1] V-8. Overhead valve. Cast iron block. Displacement: 350 cid. Bore and stroke: 4.00 x 3.48 inches. Compression ratio: 9.0:1. Brake hp: 255 at 5600 rpm. Torque: 280 lbs.-ft. at 4000 rpm. Five main bearings. Forged steel crankshaft. Solid valve lifters. High-performance camshaft. Carburetor: Holley four-barrel on aluminum intake manifold. 2.50-inch diameter dual exhaust system.

TRANSMISSION

AUTOMATIC TRANSMISSION: A Turbo Hydra-Matic automatic transmission with floor-mounted gear shifter was standard equipment.

OPTIONAL MANUAL TRANSMISSION: A close-ratio four-speed manual transmission

Nicky Wright

THE 1972 CORVETTE STINGRAY LT1 CONVERTIBLE WITH 350-CID 225-HP V-8 ENGINE.

THE 1972 CORVETTE STINGRAY WITH T-TOPS.

with floor-mounted gear shifter was a no-cost option.

CHASSIS FEATURES

Wheelbase: 98 inches. Overall length: 182.5 inches. Overall height: 47.4 inches. Overall width: 69.0 inches. Ground clearance: 4.5 inches. Front tread: 58.7 inches. Rear tread: 59.4 inches. Tires: F70-15. Frame: Full-length welded-steel ladder type with five cross members; steel box sections; welded. Front suspension: Unequal-length A-arms with coil springs, tube shocks, and stabilizer bar. Steering: Saginaw recirculating ball; ratio 17.6:1; turns lock-to-lock 2.9; turning radius 39.0 feet. Rear suspension: Trailing arms, toe links, transverse chromium-carbon steel leaf springs; tube shocks; and anti-roll bar. Rear axle type: Sprung differential, hypoid gear. Brakes: Four-wheel disc brakes; vented discs front and rear; optional power assist; diameter: 11.75 inches front and 11.75 inches rear; total swept area: 461 sq. in.; 15 x 8-inch slotted steel disc wheels. Standard rear axle ratio 3.36:1. Available rear axle gear ratios: 3.70:1; 3.08:1; 3.36:1; 3.55:1; 4.11:1.

OPTIONS

RPO Custom interior trim ($158). RPO A31 Electric power windows ($85.35). RPO A85 Custom shoulder belts ($26.35). RPO C07 Aux-iliary hardtop for convertible ($273.85). RPO C08 Vinyl roof covering for auxiliary hard-top ($158). RPO C50 Rear window defroster ($42.15). RPO C60 Air conditioning ($464.50). RPO G81 Positraction rear axle, all ratios ($12.65). RPO J50 Power brakes ($47.40). RPO LS5 454-cid 270-hp V-8 ($294.90). RPO LT1 350-cid 255-hp V-8 ($483.45). RPO ZR1 350-cid 255-hp V-8 ($1,010.05). RPO M21 Four-speed close-ratio manual transmission (no-cost option). RPO M40 Turbo Hydra-Matic automatic transmission (no-cost option). RPO N37 Tilt-telescopic steering wheel ($84.30). RPO N40 Power steering ($115.90). RPO P02 Custom wheel covers ($63.20). RPO PT7 White stripe nylon tires F70 x 15 ($30.35). RPO PU9 F70 x 15, raised-white-letter tires ($43.65). RPO T60 Heavy-duty battery ($15.80). RPO U69 AM-FM radio ($178). RPO U79 Stereo radio ($283.35).

HISTORICAL FOOTNOTES

Over one-third, 35.1 percent, of 1972 Corvettes came with power windows; 35.1 percent had power windows; 88.2 percent had power steering; 63 percent had air conditioning; 48.1 percent had a tilting steering wheel; six percent had a close-ratio four-speed manual transmission; 7 percent had a heavy-duty four-speed manual transmission and 6.4 percent were

Nicky Wright

1972 WAS THE LAST YEAR FOR CHROME BUMPERS.

1972 CORVETTE STINGRAY WITH T-TOPS AND STANDARD WHEEL COVERS.

powered by the LT1 engine. A 1972 Corvette with the base V-8 could do 0-to-30 mph in 3.1 seconds, 0-60 mph in 8.5 seconds and the quarter mile in 15.2 seconds at 83 mph. A 1972 Corvette with the optional LT1 V-8 could do 0-to-30 mph in 2.9 seconds, 0-60 mph in 6.9 seconds and the quarter mile in 14.3 seconds at 92 mph. A 1972 Corvette with the optional LS5 V-8 could do 0-to-30 mph in 3.8 seconds, 0-60 mph in 6.8 seconds and the quarter mile in

14.1 seconds at 93 mph. *Motor Trend* magazine tested a 1972 LT1 coupe with the M21 transmission and 3.70:1 axle in June 1972. The car did 0-to-30 mph in 2.9 seconds, 0-to-45 mph in 4.8 seconds, 0-to-60 mph in 6.9 seconds, 0-to-75 mph in 10.2 seconds and the quarter mile in 14.3 seconds at 92 mph. In its October/November 1971 edition, Corvette News said that "the engines in most cases still give about the same performance level in 1972 as they did in 1971."

1973

There were predictions in the automotive press that Chevrolet would introduce a mid-engine Corvette this year. However, nothing as radical as that came to be. Major changes for 1973 were a new domed hood, body-color urethane plastic front bumper, and a fixed rear window (which added a little extra trunk space). Corvettes also had a new coolant-recovery system, new chassis mounts, a non-removable rear window, and steel-guard-beam doors. The "egg-crate" front fender side vents of 1971-1972 models were replaced with non-trimmed air-duct types. Radial tires became standard and an effort was made to reduce noise. It was generally effective, but a Road & Track report found the 1973 to be louder than a 1971 in certain circumstances. Buyers who wanted a leather interior could select from Black; Medium Saddle; and Dark Saddle. Buyers had their choice of 10 exterior colors: Classic White; Silver; Medium Blue; Dark Blue; Blue-Green; Elkhart Green; Yellow; Yellow Metallic; Mille Miglia Red; and Orange. All convertibles came with a choice of Black or White soft tops. Interior colors were: Black; Midnight Blue; Dark Red; Dark Saddle; and Medium Saddle.

ENGINES

BASE ENGINE: [RPO ZQ3] V-8. Overhead valve. Cast-iron block. Displacement: 350 cid. Bore and stroke: 4.00 x 3.48 inches. Compression ratio: 8.5:1. Brake hp: 190 at 4400 rpm. Five main bearings. Hydraulic valve lifters. Carburetor: Rochester Type Quadra-Jet four-barrel Model 4MV.

OPTIONAL ENGINE: [RPO LS4] V-8. Overhead valve. Cast-iron block. Displacement: 454 cid. Bore and stroke: 4.251 x 4.00 inches. Compression ratio: 8.5:1. Brake hp: 275 at 4000

Jerry Heasley

THE 1973 CORVETTE FROM THE MOVIE CORVETTE SUMMER.

ON THE 1973 CORVETTE STINGRAY, THE REDESIGNED NOSE WAS A URETHANE PLASTIC.

rpm. Five main bearings. Hydraulic valve lifters. High-performance camshaft. Carburetor: Rochester Quadra-Jet four-barrel.

OPTIONAL ENGINE: [RPO L82] V-8. Overhead valve. Cast-iron block. Displacement: 350 cid. Bore and stroke: 4.00 x 3.48 inches. Compression ratio: 9.0:1. Brake hp: 250 at 5200 rpm. Torque: 285 lbs.-ft. at 4000 rpm. Five main bearings. Forged steel crankshaft. Hydraulic valve lifters. High-performance camshaft. Carburetor: Rochester four-barrel. 2.50-inch diameter dual exhaust system.

TRANSMISSION

AUTOMATIC TRANSMISSION: A Turbo Hydra-Matic automatic transmission with floor-mounted gear shifter was standard equipment.

OPTIONAL MANUAL TRANSMISSION: A close-ratio four-speed manual transmission with floor-mounted gear shifter was a no-cost option.

CHASSIS FEATURES

Wheelbase: 98 inches. Overall length: 182.5 inches. Overall height: 47.4 inches. Overall width: 69.0 inches. Ground clearance: 4.5 inches. Front tread: 58.7 inches. Rear tread: 59.4 inches. Tires: F70-15. Frame: Full-length welded-steel ladder type with five cross members; steel box sections, welded. Front suspension: Unequal-length A-arms with coil springs, tube shocks, and stabilizer bar. Steering: Saginaw recirculating ball; ratio 17.6:1; turns lock-to-lock 2.9; turning radius 39.0 feet. Rear suspension: Trailing arms, toe links, transverse chromium-carbon steel leaf springs; tube shocks; and anti-roll bar. Rear axle type: Sprung differential, hypoid gear. Brakes: Four-wheel disc brakes; vented discs front and rear; optional power assist; diameter: 11.75 inches front and 11.75 inches rear; total swept area: 461 sq. in.; 15 x 8-inch slotted steel disc wheels. Standard rear axle ratio 3.36:1. Available rear axle gear ratios: 3.70:1; 3.08:1; 3.36:1; 3.55:1; 4.11:1.

OPTIONS

RPO Custom interior trim ($154). RPO A31 Electric power windows ($83). RPO A85 Custom shoulder belts ($41). RPO C07 Auxiliary hardtop for convertible ($267). RPO C08 Vinyl roof covering for auxiliary hardtop ($62). RPO C50 Rear window defroster ($41). RPO C60 Air conditioning ($452). RPO G81 Positrac-

Nicky Wright

THE 1973 CORVETTE STINGRAY COUPE.

tion rear axle, all ratios ($12). RPO J50 Power brakes ($46). RPO L82 350-cid 250-hp V-8 ($299). RPO LS4 454-cid 275-hp V-8 ($250). RPO M21 Four-speed close-ratio manual transmission (no-cost option). RPO M40 Turbo Hydra-Matic automatic transmission (no-cost option). RPO N37 Tilt-telescopic steering wheel ($82). RPO N40 Power steering ($113). RPO P02 Custom wheel covers ($62). RPO QRM White stripe nylon steel-belted radial tires GR70 x 15 ($32). RPO QRZ GR70 x 15 raised-white-letter steel-belted radial tires ($43.65). RPO T60 Heavy-duty battery ($15). RPO U58 AM-FM stereo radio ($276). RPO U69 AM-FM radio ($173). RPO UF1 Map light ($5). YJ8 Cast aluminum wheels ($175). RPO Z07 Off-road suspension and brake package ($369).

HISTORICAL FOOTNOTES

The majority of 1973 Corvettes, 70.8 percent, were sold with air conditioning; 41.2 percent had a four-speed manual transmission; 91.5 percent had power steering; 79.3 percent had power brakes and 46 percent had power windows. A 1973 L82-powered Corvette tested by *Road & Track* magazine went from 0-to-30 mph in 3.1 seconds, from 0-to-40 mph in 4.3 seconds, from 0-to-50 mph in 5.6 seconds, from 0-to-60 mph in 7.2 seconds, from 0-to-70 mph in 9.1 seconds, from 0-to-80 mph in 11.7 seconds, from 0-to-100 mph in 17.9 seconds and from 0-to-110 mph in 21.9 seconds. It did the standing-start quarter mile in 15.5 seconds at 94 mph and had a top speed of 124 mph. A 1973 L82-powered Corvette tested by *Car and Driver* magazine went from 0-to-40 mph in 3.5 seconds, from 0-to-60 mph in 6.7 seconds, from 0-to-80 mph in 10.8 seconds and from 0-to-100 mph in 17.1 seconds. It did the standing-start quarter mile in 15.1 seconds at 95.4 mph and had a top speed of 117 mph. The 1973 Corvette was the only one that combined the new soft body-color front end with chrome rear bumpers. The late Larry Shinoda once said that the 1973 model was his favorite Stingray model because its front and rear styling were the closest to what designers had originally hoped for in this series.

1974

A restyled, sloping rear end and the elimination of the conventional rear bumper with a body-color urethane bumper substituted were two noticeable changes for 1974 Corvettes. The new rear end eliminated the last vestiges of the long-lived rear-deck-lid spoiler and replaced it with a smooth-surfaced rear deck and a body-colored resilient urethane extension covering the actual rear bumper and including the circular taillights. The new rear end met federal energy-absorbing standards. It added 30 pounds to the weight of the Corvette. The rear cap section was of a two-piece design for 1974, but was changed to a one-piece design with a pair of fake bumperettes molded in for 1975. The increased weight of the rear end cap necessitated minor suspension changes such as revised front and rear spring rates. A new optional "Gymkhana" suspension featured a 0.9375-inch diameter front stabilizer bar; heavier-duty front suspension bushings; front springs with a 550 lb./in. rating and rear springs with a 304 lbs./in. rating. The power steering, seat belts, and radiator were improved. The alarm system activator was relocated. Buyers once again had their choice of 10 exterior finishes: Classic White; Silver Mist; Corvette Gray; Corvette Medium Blue; Mille Miglia Red; Bright Yellow; Dark Green; Dark Brown; Medium Red; and Corvette Orange. All convertibles came with a choice of Black or White soft tops. Interior

ENGINES

BASE ENGINE: [RPO ZQ3] V-8. Overhead valve. Cast iron block. Displacement: 350 cid. Bore and stroke: 4.00 x 3.48 inches. Compression ratio: 9.0:1. Brake hp: 195 at 4400 rpm. Torque: 275 lbs.-ft at 2800 rpm. Five main bearings. Hydraulic valve lifters. Carburetor: Rochester Type Quadra-Jet four-barrel Model 4MV.

1974 CORVETTE STINGRAY COUPE WITH STANDARD WHEEL COVERS.

THE REAR RACK IS DESIGNED TO HOLD THE T-TOP PIECES ON THE 1974 CORVETTE.

Jerry Heasley

OPTIONAL ENGINE: [RPO LS4] V-8. Overhead valve. Cast iron block. Displacement: 454 cid. Bore and stroke: 4.251 x 4.00 inches. Compression ratio: 8.25:1. Brake hp: 270 at 4400 rpm. Torque: 380 lbs.-ft. at 2800 rpm. Five main bearings. Hydraulic valve lifters. High-performance camshaft. Carburetor: Rochester Quadra-jet four-barrel.

OPTIONAL ENGINE: [RPO L82] V-8. Overhead valve. Cast iron block. Displacement: 350 cid. Bore and stroke: 4.00 x 3.48 inches. Compression ratio: 9.0:1. Brake hp: 250 at 5200 rpm. Torque: 285 lbs.-ft. at 4000 rpm. Five main bearings. Forged steel crankshaft. Hydraulic valve lifters. High-performance camshaft. Carburetor: Rochester four-barrel. 2.50-inch diameter dual exhaust system.

TRANSMISSION

AUTOMATIC TRANSMISSION: A Turbo Hydra-Matic automatic transmission with floor-mounted gear shifter was standard equipment.

OPTIONAL MANUAL TRANSMISSION: A close-ratio four-speed manual transmission with floor-mounted gear shifter was a no cost option.

CHASSIS FEATURES

Wheelbase: 98 inches. Overall length: 185.5 inches. Overall height: 47.4 inches. Overall width: 69.0 inches. Ground clearance: 4.5 inches. Front tread: 58.7 inches. Rear tread: 59.5 inches. Tires: F70-15. Frame: Full-length welded-steel ladder type with five cross members; steel box sections, welded. Front suspension: Unequal-length A-arms with coil springs, tube shocks, and stabilizer bar. Steering: Saginaw recirculating ball; ratio 17.6:1; turns lock-to-lock 2.9; turning radius 39.0 feet. Rear suspension: Trailing arms, toe links, transverse chromium-carbon steel leaf springs, tube shocks, and anti-roll bar. Rear axle type: Sprung differential, hypoid gear. Brakes: Four-wheel disc brakes; vented discs front and rear; optional power

THE 1974 CORVETTE STINGRAY CONVERTIBLE IN SILVER MIST.

assist; diameter: 11.75 inches front and 11.75 inches rear; total swept area: 461 sq. in.; 15 x 8-inch slotted steel disc wheels. Standard rear axle ratio 3.36:1. Available rear axle gear ratios: 3.70:1; 3.08:1; 3.36:1; 3.55:1; and 4.11:1.

OPTIONS

RPO Custom interior trim ($154). RPO A31 Electric power windows ($86). RPO A85 Custom shoulder belts ($41). RPO C07 Auxiliary hardtop for convertible ($267). RPO C08 Vinyl covered auxiliary hardtop ($329). RPO C50 Rear window defroster ($43). RPO C60 Air conditioning ($467). RPO FE7G81 Gymkhana suspension ($7). RPO Positraction rear axle, all ratios ($12). RPO J50 Power brakes ($49). RPO L82 350-cid 250-hp V-8 ($299). LS4 454-cid 270-hp V-8 ($250). RPO M21 Four-speed close-ratio manual transmission (no-cost option). RPO M40 Turbo Hydra-Matic automatic transmission (no-cost option). RPO N37 Tilt-Telescopic steering wheel ($82). RPO N40 Power steering ($117). RPO QRM White stripe nylon steel-belted radial tires GR70 x 15 ($32). RPO QRZ GR70 x 15 raised-white-letter steel-belted radial tires ($45). RPO U05 Dual horns ($4). RPO U58 AM-FM stereo radio ($276). RPO U69 AM-FM radio ($173). RPO UA1 Heavy-duty battery ($15). RPO UF1 Map light ($5). RPO Z07 Off-road suspension and brake package ($369).

HISTORICAL FOOTNOTES

Most 1974 Corvettes, 95.6 percent, had power steering; 88.3 percent had power brakes; 63.1 percent had power windows; 72.9 percent had tilting steering wheel; 77.7 percent had air conditioning and 33.7 percent had a four-speed manual transmission.

1975

Most of the changes on the Corvette for 1975 were hidden. The bumpers were improved (but looked the same). Under the hood were a catalytic converter and a new High-Energy ignition. On the inside, the speedometer included kilometers-per-hour for the first time. This was the last year for the Corvette convertible. For awhile, buyers once again had their choice of 10 exterior finishes: Classic White; Silver; Bright Blue; Steel Blue; Bright Green; Bright Yellow; Medium Saddle; Orange Flame; Dark Red; and Mille Miglia Red. All convertibles came with a choice of Black or White soft tops. Interior colors were: Black; Dark Blue; Neutral; Dark Red; Medium Saddle; and Silver.

ENGINES

BASE ENGINE: [RPO L48] V-8. Overhead valve. Cast iron block. Displacement: 350 cid. Bore and stroke: 4.00 x 3.48 inches. Compression ratio: 8.5:1. Brake hp: 165 at 3800 rpm. Torque: 255 lbs.-ft. at 2400 rpm. Five main bearings. Hydraulic valve lifters. Carburetor: Rochester Type Quadra-Jet four-barrel Model 4MV.

OPTIONAL ENGINE: [RPO L82] V-8. Overhead valve. Cast iron block. Displacement: 350 cid. Bore and stroke: 4.00 x 3.48 inches. Compression ratio: 9.0:1. Brake hp: 205 at 4800 rpm. Torque: 255 lbs.-ft. at 3600 rpm. Five main bearings. Forged steel crankshaft. Hydraulic valve lifters. High-performance camshaft. Carburetor: Rochester Quadra-Jet four-barrel.

TRANSMISSION

AUTOMATIC TRANSMISSION: A Turbo Hydra-Matic automatic transmission with floor-

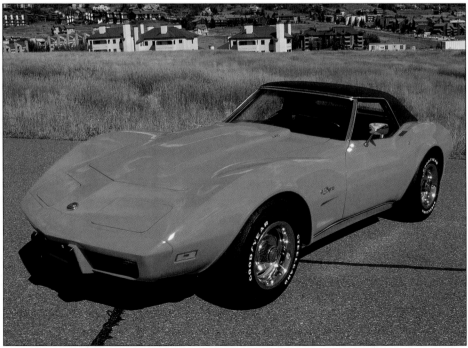

THE 1975 CORVETTE STINGRAY COUPE IN ORANGE FLAME.

Jerry Heasley

THE 1975 CORVETTE STINGRAY COUPE.

mounted gear shifter was standard equipment.

OPTIONAL MANUAL TRANSMISSION: A close-ratio four-speed manual transmission with floor-mounted gear shifter was a no-cost option.

CHASSIS FEATURES

Wheelbase: 98 inches. Overall length: 185.5 inches. Overall height: 47.4 inches. Overall width: 69.0 inches. Ground clearance: 4.5 inches. Front tread: 58.7 inches. Rear tread: 59.5 inches. Tires: F70-15. Frame: Full-length welded-steel ladder type with five cross members; steel box sections, welded. Front suspension: Unequal-length A-arms with coil springs, tube shocks, and stabilizer bar. Steering: Saginaw recirculating ball; ratio 17.6:1; turns lock-to-lock 2.9; turning radius 39 feet. Rear suspension: Trailing arms, toe links, transverse chromium-carbon steel leaf springs, tube shocks, and anti-roll bar. Rear axle type: Sprung differential, hypoid gear. Brakes: Four-wheel disc

brakes; vented discs front and rear; optional power assist; diameter 11.75 inches front and 11.75 inches rear; total swept area 461 sq. in.; 15 x 8-inch slotted steel disc wheels. Standard rear axle ratio 3.36:1. Available rear axle gear ratios: 3.70:1; 3.08:1; 3.36:1; 3.55:1.

OPTIONS

RPO Custom interior trim ($154). RPO A31 Electric power windows ($93). RPO A85 Custom shoulder belts ($41). RPO C07 Auxiliary

1975 WAS THE LAST YEAR FOR THE CONVERTIBLE OPTION.

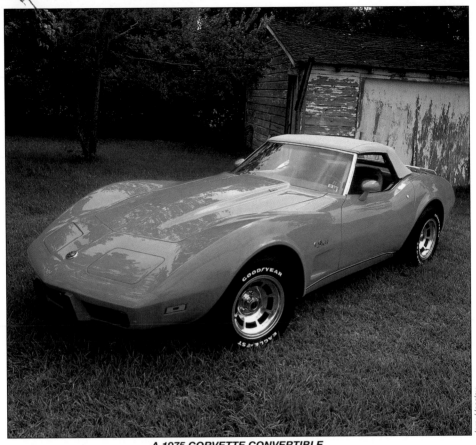

Jerry Heasley

A 1975 CORVETTE CONVERTIBLE.

hardtop for convertible ($267). RPO C08 Vinyl-covered auxiliary hardtop ($350). RPO C50 Rear window defroster ($46). RPO C60 Air conditioning ($490). RPO FE7G81 Gymkhana suspension ($7). RPO Positraction rear axle, all ratios ($12). RPO J50 Power brakes ($50). RPO L82 350-cid 205-hp V-8 ($336). RPO M21 Four-speed close-ratio manual transmission (no-cost option). RPO M40 Turbo Hydra-Matic automatic transmission (no-cost option). RPO N37 Tilt-telescopic steering wheel ($82). RPO N40 Power steering ($129). RPO QRM White stripe nylon steel-belted radial tires GR70 x 15 ($35). RPO QRZ GR70 x 15 raised-white-letter steel-belted radial tires ($48). RPO U05 Dual horns ($4). RPO U58 AM-FM stereo radio ($284). RPO U69 AM-FM radio ($178). RPO UA1 Heavy-duty battery. ($15). RPO UF1 Map light ($5). RPO Z07 Off-road suspension and brake package ($400).

HISTORICAL FOOTNOTES

The 454-cid Corvette engine was dropped this year, as was the convertible style. *Car and Driver* tested a 1975 model and covered the quarter-mile in 16.1 seconds. The magazine timed the car at 0-to-60 mph in 7.7 seconds and found it to have a top speed of 129 mph. Robert D. Lund became Chevrolet general manager. Zora Arkus-Duntov retired as the division's chief engineer. He was replaced by David R. McLellan.

1976

Unlike some advertisers, Chevrolet was correct in billing the fiberglass-bodied Corvette as "America's only true production sports car." The big-block V-8 disappeared after 1974, leaving a 350-cid (5.7-liter) small-block as the power plant for all Corvettes in the next decade. Two V-8s were offered this year, both with a four-barrel carburetor. The base L48 version now developed 180 hp (15 more than in 1975). An optional L82 V-8 produced 210 hp. The L82 had special heads with larger valves, impact-extruded pistons and finned aluminum rocker covers. The standard V-8 drove a new, slightly lighter weight automatic transmission: the Turbo Hydra-Matic 350, which was supposed to improve shifting at wide-open throttle. Optional engines kept the prior Turbo Hydra-Matic 400, but with a revised torque converter. A wide-range four-speed manual gearbox (with 2.64:1 first gear ratio) was standard and a close-ratio version was available at no extra cost. A new Carburetor Outside Air Induction system moved intake from the cowl to above the radiator. The convertible was dropped this year, so only the Stingray coupe remained. It had twin removable roof panels. A partial steel underbody replaced the customary fiberglass, to add strength and improve shielding from exhaust system heat. A new one-piece bar Corvette nameplate was on the rear, between twin-unit tail lamps (which were inset in the bumper cover). Of the 10 body colors, eight were Corvette exclusives. This year's colors were Classic White; Silver; Bright Blue; Dark Green; Mahogany; Bright Yellow; Buckskin; Dark Brown; Orange Flame; and Red. Corvettes had side marker lights with reflectors, parking lamps that went on with the headlamps, lane-change turn signals and two-speed wiper/washers. Inside was a new, smaller-diameter four-spoke sport steering wheel with crossed-flags medallion, which actually came from the Chevrolet Vega subcompact. Not everyone appreciated its lowly origin, so it lasted only this year. A grained vinyl-trimmed instrument panel (with stitched seams) held a 160-mph speedometer with trip odometer and 7,000-rpm electronic tachometer. A key lock in the left front fender set the anti-theft alarm. Corvettes had fully-independent suspension and four-wheel disc brakes. Wide GR70 SBR

Nicky Wright

A 1976 CHEVROLET CORVETTE STINGRAY T-TOP COUPE.

Nicky Wright

THE 1976 CORVETTE COUPE.

tires rode 15 x 8-inch wheels. A total of 5,368 Corvettes had the FE7 Gymkhana suspension installed, 5,720 came with the L82 V-8 and 2,088 had the M21 four-speed close-ratio manual gearbox. Cast-aluminum wheels were a new option, and were installed on 6,253 cars. Standard equipment included bumper guards; flush retracting headlamps; Soft-Ray tinted glass; Hide-A-Way wipers; wide-view day/night mirror; and center console with lighter and ashtray. Behind the seatbacks were three carpeted storage compartments. Bucket seats had textured-vinyl or leather upholstery and deep-pleated saddle-stitching. Interior leather trim was now available in seven colors, while vinyl was available in four colors.

ENGINES

BASE ENGINE: [RPO L48] V-8. 90-degree overhead valve. Cast iron block and head. Displacement: 350 cid (5.7 liters). Bore and stroke: 4.00 x 3.48 inches. Compression ratio: 8.5:1.

Brake hp: 180 at 4000 rpm. Torque: 270 lbs.-ft. at 2400 rpm. Five main bearings. Hydraulic valve lifters. Carburetor: Rochester M4MC.

OPTIONAL ENGINE: [RPO L82] V-8. 90-degree overhead valve. Cast iron block and head. Displacement: 350 cid (5.7 liters). Bore and stroke: 4.00 x 3.48 inches. Compression ratio: 9.0:1. Brake hp: 210 at 5200 rpm. Torque: 255 lbs.-ft. at 3600 rpm. Five main bearings. Hydraulic valve lifters. Carburetor: Rochester M4MC.

TECHNICAL FEATURES

Transmission: Four-speed fully-synchronized manual transmission (floor shift) standard. Gear ratios: (1st) 2.64:1; (2nd) 1.75:1; (3rd) 1.34:1; (4th) 1.00:1; (Rev) 2.55:1. Close-ratio four-speed fully-synchronized manual transmission optional: (1st) 2.43:1; (2nd) 1.61:1; (3rd) 1.23:1; (4th) 1.00:1; (Rev) 2.35:1. Three-speed automatic optional: (1st) 2.52:1; (2nd) 1.52:1; (3rd) 1.00:1; (Rev) 1.94:1. Three-speed automatic ratios with L82 engine: (1st) 2.48:1; (2nd) 1.48:1; (3rd) 1.00:1; (Rev) 2.08:1. Standard final drive ratio: 3.36:1 w/4-spd, 3.08:1 w/auto, except with optional L82 engine 3.55:1 w/4-spd, 3.55:1 or 3.70:1 with close-ratio four-speed, or 3.36:1 w/auto. Positraction standard. Steering: Recirculating ball. Front suspension: Unequal-length control arms with ball joints, coil springs, and stabilizer bar. Rear suspension: Independent with trailing-link, transverse semi-elliptic leaf springs. Brakes: Four-wheel disc (11.75 inch disc diameter). Ignition: HEI electronic. Body construction: Separate fiberglass body and box-type ladder frame with cross-members. Fuel tank: 18 gallons.

A 1976 CHEVROLET CORVETTE STINGRAY T-TOP COUPE.

OPTIONS

RPO Custom interior trim ($164). RPO A31 Electric power windows ($107). RPO C49 Rear window defogger ($78). RPO C08 Vinyl covered auxiliary hardtop ($350). RPO C60 Air conditioning ($523). RPO FE7 Gymkhana suspension ($35). Positraction rear axle, all ratios ($13). RPO J50 Power brakes ($59). RPO L82 350-cid 210-hp V-8 ($481). RPO M21 Four-speed close-ratio manual transmission (no-cost option). RPO M40 Turbo Hydra-Matic automatic transmission (no-cost option). RPO N37 Tilt-telescopic steering wheel ($95). RPO N40 Power steering ($151). RPO QRM White stripe nylon steel-belted radial tires GR70 x 15 ($37). RPO QRZ GR70 x 15 raised-white-letter steel-belted radial tires ($51). RPO U58 AM-FM stereo radio ($281). RPO U69 AM-FM radio ($187). RPO UA1 Heavy-duty battery ($16). RPO UF1 Map light ($10). RPO YJ8 Aluminum wheels ($299).

HISTORICAL FOOTNOTES

Introduced October 2, 1975. Model-year production: 46,558. Calendar-year production: 47,425. Calendar-year sales by U.S. dealers: 41,673. Model-year sales by U.S. dealers: 41,027. Though largely a carry-over from 1975, Corvette set a new sales record. The basic design dated back to 1968. *Car and Driver* (March 1976) tested the L48 and L82 Corvettes. The L48 had the M21 transmission and a 3.36:1 rear axle. It went from 0-to-30 mph in 2.7 seconds, 0-to-60 mph in 6.8 seconds and 0-to-100 mph in 20.2 seconds. It did the standing start quarter mile in 15.4 seconds at 91.5 mph. It had a top speed of 121 mph. The L82 had the M40 transmission and a 3.70:1 rear axle. It went from 0-to-30 mph in 2.8 seconds, 0-to-60 mph in 6.8 seconds and 0-to-100 mph in 19.5 seconds. It did the standing start quarter mile in 15.3 seconds at 92.1 mph. It had a top speed of 121 mph. *Car and Driver* (April 1976) also tested an L82 Corvette with the M40 transmission and 3.36:1 rear axle. It went from 0-to-30 mph in 2.8 seconds, 0-to-60 mph in 7.1 seconds and 0-to-100 mph in 19.5 seconds. It did the standing start quarter mile in 15.3 seconds at 91.9 mph. It had a top speed of 124.5 mph.

1977

Since the Stingray front fender nameplate departed this year, Chevrolet's sports car technically no longer had a secondary title. Changes were fairly modest this year and mainly hidden (such as a steel hood reinforcement) or inside. New crossed-flags emblems stood between the headlamps and on the fuel filler door. A thinner blacked-out pillar gave the windshield and side glass a more integrated look. The Corvette's console was restyled in an aircraft-type cluster design, with individual-look gauges. A voltmeter replaced the former ampmeter. "Door ajar" and "headlamp up" warning lights were abandoned. New heater/air conditioning controls, an ashtray, and a lighter were on the horizontal surface. A recessed pocket was now seen behind the shift lever. Power window switches moved to the new console. The manual shift lever was almost an inch higher, with shorter travel. Automatic transmission levers added a

pointer and both manual and automatic shifters added a new black leather boot. A shorter steering column held a multi-function control lever. This year's steering wheel had a leather-wrapped rim. This year's colors were Classic White; Silver; Black; Corvette Light Blue; Corvette Dark Blue; Corvette Chartreuse (used on one car); Corvette Yellow; Corvette Orange; Medium Red; Corvette Tan; and Corvette Dark Red. The Custom interior, formerly an extra-cost option, was now standard. "Dynasty" horizontal-ribbed cloth upholstery was framed with leather (the first cloth trim offered on a Corvette), or buyers could have the customary all-leather seat panels. Leather came in ten colors, cloth in six. Two new trim colors were available: Red and Blue. Door panel inserts were satin finish Black instead of the prior wood grain. Both the instrument panel and door trim panels lost their embossed stitch

THE 1977 CORVETTE T-TOP COUPE.

Nicky Wright

Jerry Heasley

THE 1977 CORVETTE T-TOP COUPE.

lines. New padded sunshades could swivel to side windows. Passenger-side roof pillars held a soft vinyl coat hook. Power trains were the same as in 1976, but power brakes and steering were now standard. A total of 6,148 Corvettes came with the special L82 V-8 engine under the hood, while 7,269 had the optional Gymkhana suspension. Only 5,743 Corvettes had the M20 four-speed manual gearbox and 2,060 used the M26 close-ratio four-speed. A mere 289 Corvettes came with trailering equipment. New options included an AM/FM stereo radio with tape player, cruise control (for cars with automatic transmission only,) and a luggage carrier that could hold the roof panels. Glass roof panels were announced, but delayed for another year.

ENGINES

BASE ENGINE: [RPO L48] V-8. 90-degree overhead valve. Cast iron block and head. Displacement: 350 cid (5.7 liters). Bore and stroke: 4.00 x 3.48 inches. Compression ratio: 8.5:1. Brake hp: 180 at 4000 rpm. Torque: 270 lbs.-ft. at 2400 rpm. Five main bearings. Hydraulic valve lifters. Carburetor: Rochester M4MC.

OPTIONAL ENGINE: [RPO L82] V-8. 90-degree overhead valve. Cast iron block and head. Displacement: 350 cid (5.7 liters). Bore and stroke: 4.00 x 3.48 inches. Compression ratio: 9.0:1. Brake hp: 210 at 5200 rpm. Torque: 255 lbs.-ft. at 3600 rpm. Five main bearings. Hydraulic valve lifters. Carburetor: Rochester M4MC.

TRANSMISSION

AUTOMATIC TRANSMISSION: A Turbo Hydra-Matic automatic transmission with floor-mounted gear shifter was standard equipment.

OPTIONAL MANUAL TRANSMISSION: A four-speed manual transmission with floor-mounted gear shifter was a no-cost option.

CHASSIS FEATURES

Wheelbase: 98 inches. Overall length: 185.2 inches. Height: 48 inches. Width: 69 inches. Front tread: 58.7 inches. Rear tread: 59.5 inches. Standard tires: GR70 x 15.

Nicky Wright

THE 1977 CORVETTE T-TOP COUPE.

TECHNICAL FEATURES

Transmission: Four-speed manual transmission (floor shift) standard. Gear ratios: (1st) 2.64:1; (2nd) 1.75:1; (3rd) 1.34:1; (4th) 1.00:1; (Rev) 2.55:1. Close-ratio four-speed manual transmission optional: (1st) 2.43:1; (2nd) 1.61:1; (3rd) 1.23:1; (4th) 1.00:1; (Rev) 2.35:1. Three-speed automatic optional: (1st) 2.48:1; (2nd) 1.48:1; (3rd) 1.00:1; (Rev) 2.08:1. Standard final drive ratio: 3.36:1. Steering/Suspension/Body: Same as 1976. Brakes: Four-wheel disc. Ignition: Electronic. Fuel tank: 17 gallon.

OPTIONS

RPO A31 Electric power windows ($116). RPO B32 Color-keyed floor mats ($22). RPO C49 Rear window defogger ($84). RPO C60 Air conditioning ($553). RPO D35 Sport mirrors ($36). RPO FE7 Gymkhana suspension ($38). RPO L82 350-cid 210-hp V-8 ($495). RPO M21 Four-speed close-ratio manual transmission (no-cost option). RPO M40 Turbo Hydra-Matic automatic transmission (no-cost option). RPO N37 Tilt-telescopic steering column ($165). RPO N40 Power steering ($151). RPO QRZ White letter steel-belted radial tires GR70 x 15 ($57). RPO UA1 Heavy-duty battery ($17). RPO U58 AM-FM stereo radio ($281). RPO U69 AM-FM radio ($187). RPO UM2 AM-FM stereo radio with tape system ($414). RPO V54 Luggage rack and roof panel rack ($73). RPO YJ8 Aluminum wheels ($321). RPO ZN1 Trailering package ($83). RPO ZX2 Convenience group ($22).

HISTORICAL FOOTNOTES

Introduced: September 30, 1976. Model-year production: 49,213 (Chevrolet initially reported 49,034 units). Calendar-year production: 46,345. Calendar-year sales by U.S. dealers: 42,571. Model-year sales by U.S. dealers: 40,764.

1978

To mark Corvette's 25th anniversary, the 1978 model received a major aerodynamic restyling with large wraparound back window and a fastback roofline. This was the Corvette's first restyling since 1968. Two special editions were produced, one well known and the other little more than an optional paint job. New tinted glass lift-out roof panels were wired into the standard anti-theft system. A 24-gallon fuel cell replaced the former 17-gallon tank, filling space made available by a new temporary spare tire. Inside was a restyled, padded instrument panel with face-mounted round instruments and a new locking glove box that replaced the former map pocket. The restyled interior had more accessible rear storage area with a roll shade to hide luggage. The wiper-washer control was moved from the steering column back to the instrument panel, but turn signal and headlight-dimmer controls remained on the steering column. Door

trim was now of a cut-and-sew design with soft expanded vinyl or cloth. As in 1977, the seats had leather side bolsters, with either leather or cloth seating areas in a fine rib pattern. Corvette's optional L82 high-performance 350-cid V-8 reached 220 hp as a result of a new dual-snorkel cold-air intake system, larger-diameter exhaust and tailpipes and lower-restriction mufflers. The automatic transmission used with the optional V-8 lost weight and had a low-inertia, high-stall torque converter. Base engines used a Muncie four-speed manual gear box with higher first-second gear ratios than before; the performance V-8 used a close-ratio Borg-Warner. The axle ratios used in cars sold in California and high-altitude counties were switched from 3.08:1 to 3.55:1. A total of 12,739 had the optional L82 engines, 3,385 Corvettes had the M21 four-speed close-ratio gearbox, and 38,614 had automatic transmission. Glass roof

THE 1978 INDIANAPOLIS 500 PACE CAR.

THE 1978 INDIANAPOLIS 500 PACE CAR.

panels, which had been promised earlier, actually became available this year. What Chevrolet described as "aggressive" 60-series white-letter tires also joined the option list for the first time. An optional AM/FM-CB stereo radio used a tri-band power antenna on the rear deck. Each of this year's Corvettes could have Silver Anniversary emblems on the nose and rear deck. A total of 15,283 displayed the $399 special two-tone "Silver Anniversary" paint combination with silver metallic on top and charcoal silver on the lower body. Pinstripes accentuated the fender's upper profiles, wheel openings, front fender vents, hood, and rear license cavity. Interiors were also silver. Various other options were required, including aluminum wheels. For a considerably higher price, buyers could have the Limited Edition replica of the Indy Pace Car with distinctive black-over-silver paint and red accent striping. Equipment in this "Indy Package" (RPO code Z78) included a special silver interior with new lightweight high-back seats, special front and rear spoilers, P255/60R15 white-letter tires on alloy wheels and lift-off glass canopy roof panels. The Indy Pace Car package's content included nearly all Corvette options, plus special decals (unless the customer specified that they

be omitted). Upholstery was silver leather or leather with smoke gray cloth inserts. The year's 11 Corvette colors were Classic White; Silver; Silver Anniversary; Black; Corvette Light Blue; Corvette Yellow; Corvette Light Beige; Corvette Red; Corvette Mahogany; Corvette Dark Blue; and Corvette Dark Brown.

ENGINES

BASE ENGINE: [RPO L48] V-8. 90-degree overhead valve. Cast iron block and head. Displacement: 350 cid (5.7 liters). Bore and stroke: 4.00 x 3.48 inches. Compression ratio: 8.2:1. Brake hp: 185 at 4000 rpm. Torque: 280 lbs.-ft. at 2400 rpm. Five main bearings. Hydraulic valve lifters. Carburetor: Rochester M4MC.

BASE ENGINE: [RPO L48] V-8. 90-degree overhead valve. Cast iron block and head. Displacement: 350 cid (5.7 liters). Bore and stroke: 4.00 x 3.48 inches. Compression ratio: 8.2:1. Brake hp: 175 at 4000 rpm. Torque: 270 lbs.-ft. at 2400 rpm. Five main bearings. Hydraulic valve lifters. Carburetor: Rochester M4MC. California emissions and high-altitude emissions.

OPTIONAL ENGINE: [RPO L82] V-8. 90-degree overhead valve. Cast iron block and head. Displacement: 350 cid (5.7 liters). Bore and stroke: 4.00 x 3.48 inches. Compression ratio: 8.9:1. Brake hp: 220 at 5200 rpm. Torque: 260 lbs.-ft. at 3600 rpm. Five main bearings. Hydraulic valve lifters. Carburetor: Rochester M4MC.

TRANSMISSION

AUTOMATIC TRANSMISSION: A Turbo Hydra-Matic automatic transmission with floor-mounted gear shifter was standard equipment.

OPTIONAL MANUAL TRANSMISSION: A four-speed manual transmission with floor-mounted gear shifter was a no-cost option.

CHASSIS FEATURES

Wheelbase: 98 inches. Overall length: 185.2 inches. Height: 48 inches. Width: 69 inches. Front tread: 58.7 inches. Rear tread: 59.5 inches. Standard tires: P277/70R-15 steel-belted radial.

TECHNICAL FEATURES

Transmission: Four-speed manual transmission (floor shift) standard. Gear ratios: (1st) 2.85:1; (2nd) 2.02:1; (3rd) 1.35:1; (4th) 1.00:1; (Rev) 2.85:1. Close-ratio four-speed manual available at no extra charge: (1st) 2.43:1; (2nd) 1.61:1; (3rd) 1.23:1; (4th) 1.00:1; (Rev) 2.35:1. Three-speed automatic optional: (1st) 2.52:1; (2nd) 1.52:1; (3rd) 1.00:1; (Rev) 1.94:1. Standard final drive ratio: 3.36:1 with four-speed, 3.08:1 w/auto. except L82 V-8, 3.70:1 with four-speed and 3.55:1 w/auto. Steering/Suspension/Body: Same as 1976-77. Brakes: Four-wheel disc (11.75-inch disc diameter). Ignition: Electronic. Fuel tank: 24 gallons.

OPTIONS

RPO A31 Electric power windows ($130). RPO AU3 Power door locks ($120). RPO B2Z Silver Anniversary Paint ($399). RPO CC1 Removable glass roof panels ($349). RPO C60 Air conditioning ($605). RPO D35 Sport mirrors ($40). RPO FE7 Gymkhana suspension ($41). RPO G95 Positraction axle, optional highway ratio ($15). RPO K30 Cruise Control ($99). RPO L82 350-cid 210-hp V-8 ($525). RPO M21 Four-speed close-ratio manual transmission (no cost option). RPO MX1 Turbo Hydra-Matic automatic transmission (no cost option). RPO N37 Tilt-telescopic steering column ($175). RPO QBS P255/60R-15 White-letter steel-belted radial tires ($216.32). RPO QGR P255/70R-15 White-letter steel-belted radial tires ($51). RPO UA1 Heavy-duty battery ($18). RPO UM2 AM-FM stereo radio with tape system ($419). RPO UP6 AM-FM stereo radio with CB system ($638). RPO U58 AM-FM stereo radio ($286). RPO U69 AM-FM radio ($199). RPO U75 Power antenna ($49). RPO U81 Dual rear speakers ($49). RPO YJ8 Aluminum wheels ($340). RPO ZN1 Trailering package ($89). RPO ZX2 Convenience group ($84).

HISTORICAL FOOTNOTES

Introduced: October 6, 1977. Model-year production: 46,772 (but some industry sources have reported a total of 47,667). Calendar-year production: 48,522. Calendar-year sales by U.S. dealers: 42,247. Model year sales by U.S. dealers: 43,106. The limited-edition Indianapolis 500 Pace Car replica was created to commemorate the selection of Corvette as the pace car for the 62nd Indianapolis 500 race on May 28, 1978. A production run of 2,500 was planned, but so many potential buyers who saw it at the New York Auto Show in February wanted one that the goal quickly expanded to 6,500 or roughly one for every Chevrolet dealer. Buyers also had to endure a selection of "forced RPOs" (items installed at the factory whether wanted or not). The mandatory extras included power windows, air conditioning, sport mirrors, a tilt-telescope steering wheel, a rear defogger, an AM/FM stereo with either an 8-track tape player or CB radio, plus power door locks, and a heavy-duty battery. Before long, the original $13,653 list price meant little, as speculators eagerly paid double that amount and more. Later the price retreated to around the original list. Even though so many were built, the Indy Pace Car is still a desirable model. Dave McLellan became head of engineering for Corvettes and worked on the next-generation models.

1979

"The Corvette evolution continues," declared the 1979 Corvette sales catalog. Not much of that evolution was visible, however, after the prior year's massive restyle. Under the hood, the base engine received the dual-snorkel air intake introduced in 1978 for the optional L82 V-8, which added 10 horsepower. The L82 V-8 had a higher-lift cam, special heads with larger valves and higher compression, impact-extruded pistons, a forged steel crankshaft, and finned aluminum rocker covers. The "Y" pipe exhaust system had new open-flow mufflers, while the automatic transmission received a higher numerical (3.55:1) rear axle ratio. All Corvettes now had the high-back bucket seats introduced on the 1978 limited-edition Indianapolis 500 Pace Car. A high pivot point let the seat backrest fold flat on the passenger side, level with the luggage area floor. An AM/FM radio was now standard. Corvettes had black roof panel and window moldings. Bolt-on front and rear spoilers (also from the Indianapolis 500 Pace Car) became available. Buyers who didn't want the full Gymkhana suspension could now order heavy-duty shocks alone. Standard equipment included the L48 V-8 with four-barrel carburetor, either automatic transmission or a four-speed manual gear box (close-ratio version available), power four-wheel disc brakes and limited-slip differential. Other standard items included tinted glass; a front stabilizer bar; concealed windshield wipers and washers; a day/night inside mirror; a wide outside mirror; an anti-theft alarm system; a four-spoke sport steering wheel; an electric clock; a trip odometer; a heater and de-

Nicky Wright

THE 1979 CORVETTE WITH T-TOPS AND THE L48 195-HP V-8.

CORVETTE RED WAS ONE OF TEN BODY COLORS OFFERED FOR 1979.

froster; bumper guards, and a luggage security shade. The standard tires were P225/70R15 steel-belted radial blackwalls on 15 x 8-inch wheels. Corvettes had a four-wheel independent suspension. The bucket seats came with cloth-and-leather or all-leather trim. The aircraft-type console held a 7,000-rpm tachometer, a voltmeter and oil-pressure, temperature and fuel gauges. Seat inserts could have either leather or cloth trim. The ten body colors were Classic White; Silver; Black; Corvette Light Blue; Corvette Yellow; Corvette Dark Green; Corvette Light Beige; Corvette Red; Corvette Dark Brown; and Corvette Dark Blue. Interiors came in Black; Dark Blue; Dark Brown; Light Beige; Red; Dark Green; and Oyster.

ENGINES

BASE ENGINE: [RPO L48] V-8. 90-degree overhead valve. Cast iron block and head. Displacement: 350 cid (5.7 liters). Bore and stroke: 4.00 x 3.48 inches. Compression ratio: 8.2:1. Brake hp: 195 at 4000 rpm. Torque: 285 lbs.-ft. at 3200 rpm. Five main bearings. Hydraulic valve lifters. Carburetor: Rochester M4MC.

OPTIONAL ENGINE: [RPO L82] V-8. 90-degree overhead valve. Cast iron block and head. Displacement: 350 cid (5.7 liters). Bore and stroke: 4.00 x 3.48 inches. Compression ratio: 8.9:1. Brake hp: 225 at 5200 rpm. Torque: 270 lbs.-ft. at 3600 rpm. Five main bearings. Hydraulic valve lifters. Carburetor: Rochester M4MC.

TRANSMISSION

AUTOMATIC TRANSMISSION: A Turbo Hydra-Matic automatic transmission with floor-mounted gear shifter was standard equipment.

OPTIONAL MANUAL TRANSMISSION: A four-speed manual transmission with floor-mounted gear shifter was a no-cost option.

CHASSIS FEATURES

Wheelbase: 98 inches. Overall length: 185.2 inches. Height: 48 inches. Width: 69 inches. Front tread: 58.7 inches. Rear tread: 59.5 inches. Wheel size: 15 x 8 inches. Standard tires: P225/70R-15 SBR.

TECHNICAL FEATURES

Transmission: Four-speed manual transmission (floor shift) standard. Gear ratios: (1st) 2.85:1; (2nd) 2.02:1; (3rd) 1.35:1; (4th) 1.00:1; (Rev) 2.85:1. Close-ratio four-speed manual transmission optional: (1st) 2.43:1; (2nd) 1.61:1; (3rd) 1.23:1; (4th) 1.00:1; (Rev) 2.35:1. Three-speed automatic optional: (1st) 2.52:1; (2nd) 1.52:1; (3rd) 1.00:1; (Rev) 1.93:1. Standard final drive ratio: 3.36:1 with four-speed manual transmission, 3.55:1 with automatic transmission. Steering: Recirculating ball. Front suspension: Control arms, coil springs and stabilizer bar. Rear suspension: Independent, with single transverse leaf spring and lateral struts. Brakes: Four-wheel disc (11.75-inch disc diameter). Ignition: Electronic. Body construction: Fiberglass, on separate frame. Fuel tank: 24 gallons.

OPTIONS

RPO A31 Electric power windows ($141). RPO CC1 Removable glass roof panels ($365). RPO C49 Rear window defogger ($102). RPO C60 Air conditioning ($635). RPO D35 Sport mirrors ($45). RPO FE7 Gymkhana suspension ($49). RPO F51 Heavy-duty shock absorbers ($33). RPO G95 Highway ratio rear axle ($19). RPO K30 Cruise Control ($113). RPO L82 350-cid 225-hp V-8 ($565). RPO MM4 Four-speed manual transmission (no-cost option). RPO M21 Four-speed manual close-ratio transmission (no-cost option). RPO MX1 Turbo Hydra-Matic automatic transmission (no-cost option). RPO N37 Tilt-telescopic steering column ($190). RPO QGR P255/70R-15 Raised-white-letter steel-belted radial tires ($54). RPO QBS P255/60R-15 White Aramid BR tires ($226.20). RPO U58 AM-FM stereo radio ($90). RPO UM2 AM-FM stereo radio with 8-track tape system ($228). RPO UN3 AM-FM stereo radio with cassette ($234). RPO UP6 AM-FM stereo radio with CB system and power antenna ($439). RPO U75 Power antenna ($52). RPO U81 Dual rear speakers ($52). RPO UA1 Heavy-duty battery ($21). RPO ZN1 Trailering package ($98). RPO ZQ2 Power windows and door locks ($272). RPO ZX2 Convenience group ($84).

HISTORICAL FOOTNOTES

Introduced: September 25, 1978. Model-year production: 53,807 (Chevrolet initially reported a total of 49,901 units). Calendar-year production: 48,568. Calendar-year sales by U.S. dealers: 38,631. Model-year sales by U.S. dealers: 39,816. For what it's worth, 7,949 Corvettes were painted this year in Classic White, while 6,960 carried Silver paint. Only 4,385 Corvettes had the MM4 four-speed manual gearbox, while 4,062 ran with the close-ratio M21 version.

1980

The 1980 Corvette was more streamlined and lost close to 250 pounds. The hood and doors were lighter with thinner door glass. Corvette bodies held new fiberglass bumper structures. The lift-off roof panels were made of lightweight, low-density microscopic glass beads. The body panels were urethane-coated. Weight cuts also hit the power train. The differential housing and supports were made of aluminum. The 350-cid (5.7-liter) V-8 had a new aluminum intake manifold, while the 305-cid (5.0-liter) V-8 used in cars sold in California had a stainless exhaust manifold. The Corvette hoods had a new low profile. The front bumper had an integrated lower air dam and the bumper cover now extended to the wheel openings. New two-piece front cornering lamps worked whenever the lights were switched on. A deep-recessed split grille held integral parking lamps. Front fender air vents contained functional black louvers. New front and rear spoilers were molded in and integrated with the bumper caps and were no longer of a bolt-on type. New emblems included an engine identifier for the optional L82 V-8. The dashboard carried a new 85-mph speedometer. Only two storage bins stood behind the seat, where three used to be. Turbo Hydra-Matic transmissions added a lock-up torque converter that engaged at about 30 mph, while the four-speed manual transmission got new gear ratios. In California, Corvette buyers could only get the 305-cid V-8 with automatic transmission this year. The base V-8 lost five horsepower, while the optional version gained five. New standard equipment this year included formerly-optional power windows, a tilt-telescopic steering wheel, and Four Season air conditioning. Rally wheels held P225/70R-15/B blackwall SBR tires with trim rings and center caps. Body colors were: White; Silver; Black; Dark Blue; Dark Brown; Yellow; Dark Green; Frost Beige; Dark Claret; and Red. Interiors came in Black; Claret; Dark Blue; Doeskin; Oyster; and Red.

Nicky Wright

THE 1980 CORVETTE WITH CUSTOM PINSTRIPES AND ALUMINUM WHEELS.

Nicky Wright

THE 1980 CORVETTE IN BLACK.

ENGINES

BASE ENGINE: [RPO L48] V-8. 90-degree overhead valve. Cast-iron block and head. Displacement: 350 cid (5.7 liters). Bore and stroke: 4.00 x 3.48 inches. Compression ratio: 8.2:1. Brake hp: 190 at 4200 rpm. Torque: 280 lbs.-ft. at 2400 rpm. Five main bearings. Hydraulic valve lifters. Carburetor: Rochester Quadrajet.

BASE CALIFORNIA ENGINE: [RPO LG4] V-8. 90-degree overhead valve. Cast-iron block and head. Displacement: 305 cid (5.0 liters). Bore and stroke: 3.74 x 3.48 inches. Compression ratio: 8.5:1. Brake hp: 180 at 4200 rpm. Torque: 255 lbs.-ft. at 2000 rpm. Five main bearings. Hydraulic valve lifters. Carburetor: Rochester Quadrajet.

OPTIONAL ENGINE: [RPO L82] V-8. 90-degree overhead valve. Cast-iron block and head. Displacement: 350 cid (5.7 liters). Bore and stroke: 4.00 x 3.48 inches. Compression ratio: 9.0:1. Brake hp: 230 at 5200 rpm. Torque: 275 lbs.-ft. at 3600 rpm. Five main bearings. Hydraulic valve lifters. Carburetor: Rochester Quadrajet.

Nicky Wright

THE L48 350-CID V-8 PRODUCED 190 HP.

TRANSMISSION

AUTOMATIC TRANSMISSION: A Turbo Hydra-Matic automatic transmission with floor-mounted gear shifter was standard equipment.

OPTIONAL MANUAL TRANSMISSION: A four-speed manual transmission with floor-mounted gear shifter was a no-cost option.

Nicky Wright

THE 1980 CORVETTE WAS MORE THAN 250 LBS. LIGHTER THAN IN 1979.

Nicky Wright

THE 1980 CORVETTE ECKLER CONVERSION.

CHASSIS FEATURES

Wheelbase: 98 inches. Overall length: 185.3 inches. Height: 48.1 inches. Width: 69 inches. Front tread: 58.7 inches. Rear tread: 59.5 inches. Wheel size: 15 x 8 inches. Standard tires: P225/70R-15/B SBR. Optional tires: P255/60R-15/B.

TECHNICAL FEATURES

Transmission: Four-speed manual transmission (floor shift) standard. Gear ratios: (1st) 2.88:1; (2nd) 1.91:1; (3rd) 1.33:1; (4th) 1.00:1; (Rev) 2.78:1. Three-speed Turbo Hydra-Matic optional: (1st) 2.52:1; (2nd) 1.52:1; (3rd) 1.00:1; (Rev) 1.93:1. Standard final drive ratio: 3.07:1 with four-speed manual transmission, 3.55:1 with automatic transmission. Steering: Recirculating ball. Front suspension: Control arms, coil springs and stabilizer bar. Rear suspension: Independent, with single transverse leaf spring and lateral struts. Brakes: Four-wheel disc (11.75-inch disc diameter). Ignition: Electronic. Body construction: Fiberglass, on separate frame. Fuel tank: 24 gallons.

OPTIONS

RPO AU3 Power door locks ($140). RPO CC1 Removable glass roof panels ($391). RPO

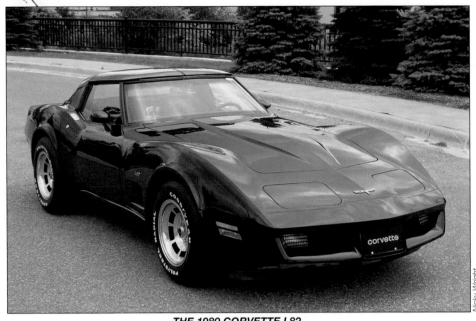

Nicky Wright

THE 1980 CORVETTE L82.

C49 Rear window defogger ($109). RPO FE7 Gymkhana suspension ($55). RPO F51 Heavy-duty shock absorbers ($35). RPO K30 Cruise control ($123). RPO LG4 305-cid 180-hp V-8 mandatory in cars sold in California ($55 credit). RPO L82 350-cid 230-hp V-8 ($595). RPO MM4 Four-speed manual transmission (no-cost option). RPO MX1 Turbo Hydra-Matic automatic transmission (no-cost option). RPO N90 Four aluminum wheels ($407). RPO QGB P255/70R-15 Raised-white-letter steel-belted radial tires ($62). RPO QXH P255/60R-15 Raised white-letter steel-belted radial tires ($426.16). RPO UA1 Heavy-duty battery ($21). RPO U58 AM-FM stereo radio ($46). RPO UM2 AM-FM stereo radio with 8-track tape system ($155). RPO UN3 AM-FM stereo radio with cassette ($168). RPO UP6 AM-FM stereo radio with CB system and power antenna ($391). RPO U75 Power antenna ($56). RPO U81 Dual rear speakers ($52). RPO V54 Roof panel carrier ($125). RPO YF5 California emissions certification ($250). RPO ZN1 Trailering package ($105).

HISTORICAL FOOTNOTES

Introduced: October 25, 1979. Model-year production: 40,614 (but Chevrolet reported a total of 40,564 units). Calendar-year production: 44,190. Model-year sales by U.S. dealers: 37,471. Production continued at the St. Louis, Missouri, plant but a new GMAD operation at Bowling Green, Kentucky, was planned to begin production of the next-generation Corvettes. Chevrolet engineers released a TurboVette that used a Garrette AiResearch turbocharger and fuel injection, but press people who drove it discovered performance more sluggish than a regular L82 V-8 could dish out. Only 5,726 Corvettes had the MM4 four-speed manual gearbox. And only 5,069 carried the special L82 engine. A total of 9,907 had the Gymkhana suspension.

1981

Probably the most significant change this year was hidden from view. Corvettes with Turbo Hydra-Matic had a new fiberglass-reinforced monoleaf rear spring that weighed just eight pounds (33 pounds less than the multileaf steel spring it replaced). The new spring eliminated interleaf friction. Manual-shift models kept the old spring, as did those with optional Gymkhana suspension. Side door glass was made even thinner again, in a further attempt to cut overall car weight. A new L81 version of the 350-cid V-8 arrived this year. It was rated for 190 hp, with lightweight magnesium rocker arm covers. New stainless-steel free-flowing exhaust manifolds weighed 14 pounds less than the previous cast-iron manifolds. A new thermostatically-controlled auxiliary elec-

tric fan boosted cooling and allowed use of a smaller main fan. The engine air cleaner had a new chromed cover. A new Computer Command Control system controlled fuel metering, as well as the torque converter lock-up clutch that operated in second and third gears. Manual transmission was available in all 50 states. It was the first time in several years that buyers of Corvettes sold in California could order a stick shift. A quartz crystal clock was now standard. The Corvette's standard anti-theft alarm added a starter-interrupt device. Joining the option list was a six-way power seat. Electronic-tuning radios could have built-in cassette or 8-track tape players or a CB transceiver. The Corvette's ample standard equipment list included either four-speed manual or automatic

MORE THAN 40,000 1980 CORVETTE COUPES WERE BUILT.

1981 CORVETTE COUPE FACTORY ILLUSTRATIONS.

transmission (same price); four-wheel power disc brakes; limited-slip differential; power steering; tinted glass; twin remote-control sport mirrors; and concealed two-speed wipers. Also standard were halogen high-beam retractable headlamps; air conditioning; power windows; a tilt-telescope leather-wrapped steering wheel; a tachometer; an AM/FM radio; a trip odometer; courtesy lights; and a luggage compartment security shade. Corvette buyers had a choice of cloth-and-vinyl or leather-and-vinyl upholstery. Corvettes rode on P225/70R-15 steel-belted radial blackwall tires on 15 x 8 inch wheels. The optional Gymkhana suspension (price $54) was also included with the trailer towing package. Body colors this year were Mahogany Metallic; White; Silver Metallic; Black; Bright Blue Metallic; Dark Blue Metallic; Yellow; Beige; Red; Maroon Metallic; and Charcoal Metallic. Four two-tone combinations were available: Silver and Dark Blue; Silver and Charcoal; Beige and Dark Bronze; and Autumn Red and Dark Claret. (All two-tone cars were painted at the new plant in Bowling Green, Kentucky). Interiors came in Silver Gray; Charcoal; Dark Blue; Camel; Dark Red; and Medium Red.

ENGINE

BASE ENGINE: [RPO L81] V-8. 90-degree overhead valve. Cast-iron block and head. Displacement: 350 cid (5.7 liters). Bore and stroke: 4.00 x 3.48 inches. Compression ratio: 8.2:1. Brake hp: 190 at 4200 rpm. Torque: 280 lbs.-ft. at 1600 rpm. Five main bearings. Hydraulic valve lifters. Carburetor: Rochester Quadrajet.

TRANSMISSION

AUTOMATIC TRANSMISSION: A Turbo Hydra-Matic automatic transmission with floor-mounted gear shifter was standard equipment.

OPTIONAL MANUAL TRANSMISSION: A four-speed manual transmission with floor-mounted gear shifter was a no cost option.

CHASSIS FEATURES

Wheelbase: 98 inches. Overall length:

185.3 inches. Height: 48.1 inches. Width: 69 inches. Front tread: 58.7 inches. Rear tread: 59.5 inches. Wheel size: 15 x 8 inches. Standard tires: P225/70R-15/B SBR. Optional tires: P255/60R-15.

TECHNICAL FEATURES

Transmission: Four-speed manual transmission (floor shift) standard. Gear ratios: (1st) 2.88:1; (2nd) 1.91:1; (3rd) 1.33:1; (4th) 1.00:1; (Rev) 2.78:1. Three-speed Turbo Hydra-Matic optional: (1st) 2.52:1; (2nd) 1.52:1; (3rd) 1.00:1; (Rev) 1.93:1. Standard final drive ratio: 2.72:1 with four-speed manual transmission, 2.87:1 with automatic transmission. Steering: Recirculating ball. Front suspension: Control arms, coil springs and stabilizer bar. Rear suspension: Independent, with single transverse leaf spring and lateral struts. Brakes: Four-wheel disc (11.75-inch disc diameter). Ignition: Electronic. Body construction: Fiberglass, on separate frame. Fuel tank: 24 gallons.

OPTIONS

RPO AU3 Power door locks ($145). RPO A42 Power driver seat ($183). RPO CC1 Removable glass roof panels ($414). RPO C49 Rear window defogger ($119). RPO DG7 Electric sport mirrors ($117). RPO D84 Two-tone paint ($399). RPO FE7 Gymkhana suspension ($57). RPO F51 Heavy-duty shock absorbers ($37). RPO G92 Performance axle ratio ($20). RPO K35 Cruise control ($155). RPO MM4

Four-speed manual transmission (no cost option). RPO N90 Four aluminum wheels ($428). RPO QGR P255/70R-15 Raised-white-letter steel-belted radial tires ($72). RPO QXH P255/60R-15 Raised white-letter steel-belted radial tires ($491.92). RPO UL5 Radio delete ($118 credit). RPO UM4 AM-FM electronic tuning stereo radio with 8-track tape system ($386). RPO UM5 AM-FM electronic tuning stereo radio with 8-track tape and CB system ($712). RPO UM6 AM-FM electronic tuning stereo radio with cassette ($423). RPO UN5 AM-FM electronic tuning stereo radio with cassette and CB system ($750). RPO U58 AM-FM stereo radio ($95). RPO U75 Power antenna ($55). RPO V54 Roof panel carrier ($135). RPO YF5 California emissions certification ($46). RPO ZN1 Trailering package ($110).

HISTORICAL FOOTNOTES

Introduced: September 25, 1980. Model-year production: 40,606 (but Chevrolet first reported a total of 40,593 units). Calendar-year production: 27,990. Model-year sales by U.S. dealers: 33,414. Of the total output this model year, 8,995 Corvettes came out of the new plant at Bowling Green, Kentucky, which began production in June 1981. Despite some weak years in the industry, Corvette sales remained strong through this period.

1982

For the first time since 1955, no stick shift Corvettes were produced. Every Corvette had a new type of four-speed automatic transmission with lock-up function in every gear except first. Under the hood was a new kind of 350-cid V-8 with Cross-Fire fuel injection. Twin throttle-body injectors with computerized metering helped boost horsepower to 200 (10 more than in 1981) and cut emissions at the same time. This was the first fuel-injected Corvette in nearly two decades. It had a much different type of fuel-injection system since mini-computerization had arrived. In the gas tank was a new electric fuel pump. Externally, the final version of the "big" (Stingray-style) Corvette changed little, but the Collector Edition model displayed quite a few special features, highlighted by a frameless glass lift-up hatch in place of the customary fixed backlight. Its unique Silver-Beige metallic paint was accented by pin stripes and a "fading shadow" treatment on hood, fenders and doors . . . plus distinctive cloisonné emblems.

Special finned wheels were similar to the cast-aluminum wheels that dated back to 1967. The Collector Edition's removable glass roof panels had special bronze coloring and solar screening. The model's crossed-flags emblems read "Corvette Collector Edition" around the rim. Inside was a matching Silver-Beige metallic interior with multi-tone leather seats and door trim. Even the Collector Edition's hand-sewn leather-wrapped steering wheel kept the theme color and its leather-covered horn button had a cloisonné emblem. The tires were P255/60R-15 Goodyear SBR WLT Eagle GT. Standard equipment for other Corvettes included power brakes and steering, P225/70R-15/B SBR tires on steel wheels with center hub and trim rings, cornering lamps, front fender louvers, halogen high-beam retractable headlamps, dual remote sport mirrors, and tinted glass. The body-color front bumper had a built-in air dam. Also standard: Luggage security shade; air conditioning; push-button AM/FM radio; concealed wipers; power

THE 1982 CORVETTE COLLECTOR EDITION.

Jerry Heasley

Jerry Heasley

1982 CORVETTE COLLECTOR EDITION IN SILVER BEIGE PAINT UNIQUE TO THE MODEL.

windows; time-delay dome/courtesy lamps; headlamp-on reminder; a lighted visor vanity mirror; a leather wrapped tilt/telescoping steering wheel; a 7,000-rpm tachometer; an analog clock with sweep second hand; a day/night mirror; a lighter; and a trip odometer. Bucket seats could be trimmed in all-cloth or leather options. Standard body colors were: White; Silver; Black; Silver Blue; Dark Blue; Bright Blue; Charcoal; Silver Green; Gold; Silver Beige; Red; and Dark Claret. Four two-tones were available: White and Silver; Silver and Charcoal; Silver and Dark Claret; and Silver Blue and Dark Blue. Interiors came in Charcoal; Camel; Dark Blue; Dark Red; Silver Beige; Silver Green; and Silver Gray.

ENGINE

BASE ENGINE: [RPO L83] V-8. 90-degree overhead valve. Cast-iron block and head. Displacement: 350 cid (5.7 liters). Bore and stroke: 4.00 x 3.48 inches. Compression ratio: 9.0:1. Brake hp: 200 at 4200 rpm. Torque: 285 lbs.-ft. at 2800 rpm. Five main bearings. Hydraulic valve lifters. Induction: Cross-fire fuel injection (twin TBI).

TRANSMISSION

AUTOMATIC TRANSMISSION: A Turbo Hydra-Matic automatic transmission with floor-mounted gear shifter was standard equipment.

CHASSIS FEATURES

Wheelbase: 98 inches. Overall length: 185.3 inches. Height: 48.4 inches. Width: 69 inches. Front tread: 58.7 inches. Rear tread: 59.5 inches. Wheel size: 15 x 8 inches. Standard tires [Base Corvette]: P225/70R-15 SBR. Standard Tires [Collector Edition Corvette]: P255/60R-15.

TECHNICAL FEATURES

Transmission: THM 700-R4 four-speed overdrive automatic (floor shift). Gear ratios: (1st) 3.06:1; (2nd) 1.63:1; (3rd) 1.00:1; (4th) 0.70:1; (Rev) 2.29:1. Standard final drive ratio: 2.72:1 (except 2.87:1 with aluminum wheels). Steering: Recirculating ball (power assisted). Front suspension: Upper/lower A-arms, coil springs, stabilizer bar. Rear suspension: Fully independent with half-shafts, lateral struts, control arms, and transverse leaf springs. Brakes: Power four-wheel discs (11.75-inch disc diameter). Ignition: Electronic. Body construction: Separate fiberglass body and ladder-type steel frame. Fuel tank: 24 gallons.

OPTIONS

RPO AU3 Power door locks ($155). RPO A42 Power driver seat ($197). RPO CC1 Removable glass roof panels ($443). RPO C49 Rear window defogger ($129). RPO DG7 Electric sport mirrors ($125). RPO D84 Two-tone paint ($428). RPO FE7 Gymkhana suspension

Chevrolet

THE 1982 CORVETTE COLLECTOR EDITION, ONE OF 6,759 BUILT.

($61). RPO K35 Cruise control ($165). RPO N90 Four aluminum wheels ($458). RPO QGR P255/70R-15 Raised-white-letter steel-belted radial tires ($80). RPO QXH P255/60R-15 Raised-white-letter steel-belted radial tires ($542.52). RPO UL5 Radio delete ($124 credit). RPO UM4 AM-FM electronic tuning stereo radio with 8-track tape system ($386). RPO UM6 AM-FM electronic tuning stereo radio with cassette ($423). RPO UN5 AM-FM electronic tuning stereo radio with cassette and CB system ($755). RPO U58 AM-FM stereo radio ($101). RPO U75 Power antenna ($60). RPO V08 Heavy-duty cooling ($57). RPO V54 Roof panel carrier ($144). RPO YF5 California emissions certification ($46).

HISTORICAL FOOTNOTES

Introduced: December 12, 1981. Model-year production: 25,407. Calendar-year production: 22,838. Model-year sales by U.S. dealers: 22,086. All Corvettes now came from the factory at Bowling Green, Kentucky. Pro-duction fell dramatically this year, reaching the lowest total since 1967. The 1982 model was the last Corvette to employ the same basic body introduced in 1968. Its chassis dated back to even five years before that. No doubt, some buyers preferred to wait for the next genera-tion to arrive. Still, this was the end of the big 'Vette era: "An enthusiast's kind of Corvette. A most civilized one," according to the fac-tory catalog. *Road & Track* called it "truly the last of its series," though one with an all-new drive train. The Collector Edition earned the dubious distinction of being the first Corvette to cost more than $20,000. The Collector Edi-tion was built to order, rather than according to a predetermined schedule. It carried a spe-cial VIN code with a "0" in the sixth position (Body Code 07), but did not have a separate serial number sequence. The special VIN plates were used to prevent swindlers from turning an ordinary Corvette into a special edition (which had happened all too often with 1978 Indy Pace Car replicas).

1984

The eagerly awaited sixth-generation Corvette for the '80s missed the 1983 model year completely, but arrived in spring 1983 in an all-new form. An aerodynamic exterior featuring an "acute" windshield rake (64 degrees) covered a series of engineering improvements. A one-piece, full-width fiberglass roof (no T-bar) was removable. It had a transparent, acrylic lift-off panel with a solar screen optional. At the rear was a frameless glass back window or hatch above four round tail lamps. Hidden headlamps were featured, along with clear, integrated halogen fog lamps and front cornering lamps. The dual sport mirrors were electrically remote controlled. The unit body (with partial front frame) used a front-hinged "clam shell" hood with integral twin-duct air intake. The sole 1984 V-8 was L83 350-cid (5.7-liter) V-8 with cross-fire fuel injection. Stainless steel headers led into its exhaust system. The air cleaner and the valve train had cast magnesium covers. After being unavailable in 1982, a four-speed manual gearbox returned as the standard Corvette transmission (although not until January 1984). A four-plus-three-speed automatic with computer-activated overdrive in every gear except first, was offered at no extra cost. It used a hydraulic clutch. Overdrive was locked out during rigorous acceleration above specified speeds and when a console switch was activated. Under the chassis were an aluminum drive shaft, forged-aluminum suspension arms, and a fiberglass transverse leaf spring. Power rack-and-pinion steering and power four-wheel disc brakes were standard. Optional Goodyear 50-series "uni-directional" tires were designed for mounting on a specific wheel. Inside, an electronic instrument panel featured both analog and digital LCD readouts in either English or metric measure. A Driver Information System between the speedometer and tachometer gave a selection of switch-chosen readings. At the driver's left was the parking brake. Corvette's ample standard equipment list included an advanced (and very necessary) theft-prevention system

Jerry Heasley

A TOTAL OF 51,547 1984 CORVETTES COUPES WERE BUILT.

Jerry Heasley

THE 1984 CORVETTE COUPE IN BRIGHT SILVER METALLIC.

with starter-interrupt. Other standard equipment included: air conditioning; power windows; electronic-tuning seek/scan AM/FM stereo radio with digital clock; reclining bucket seats; leather-wrapped tilt/telescope steering wheel; luggage security shade; and side window defoggers. Body colors were White; Bright Silver Metallic; Medium Gray Metallic; Black; Light Blue Metallic; Medium Blue Metallic; Gold Metallic; Light Bronze Metallic; Dark Bronze Metallic; and Bright Red. Two-tone options were Silver and Medium Gray; Light Blue and Medium Blue; and Light Bronze and Dark Bronze. Interiors came in Carmine; Bronze; Graphite; Medium Blue; Medium Gray; and Saddle.

ENGINE

BASE ENGINE: [RPO L83] V-8. 90-degree overhead valve. Cast-iron block and head. Displacement: 350 cid (5.7 liters). Bore and stroke: 4.00 x 3.48 inches. Compression ratio: 9.0:1. Brake hp: 205 at 4200 rpm. Torque: 290 lbs.-ft. at 2800 rpm. Five main bearings. Hydraulic valve lifters. Induction: Cross-fire fuel injection (twin TBI).

TRANSMISSION

AUTOMATIC TRANSMISSION: A Turbo Hydra-Matic automatic transmission with floor-mounted gear shifter was standard equipment.

MANUAL TRANSMISSION: A four-speed manual transmission was available with overdrive capability to improve fuel efficiency.

CHASSIS FEATURES

Wheelbase: 96.2 inches. Overall length: 176.5 inches. Height: 46.7 inches. Width: 71 inches. Front tread: 59.6 inches. Rear tread: 60.4 inches. Wheel size: 15 x 7 inches. Standard tires: P215/65R-15. Optional tires: Eagle P255/50VR-16 on 16 x 8 inch wheels.

TECHNICAL FEATURES

Transmission: THM 700-R4 four-speed overdrive automatic (floor shift) standard. Gear ratios: (1st) 3.06:1; (2nd) 1.63:1; (3rd) 1.00:1; (4th) 0.70:1; (Rev) 2.29:1. Four-speed manual transmission optional: (1st) 2.88:1; (2nd) 1.91:1; (3rd) 1.33:1; (4th) 1.00:1; (overdrive) 0.67:1; (Rev) 2.78:1. Standard final drive ratio: 2.73:1 with automatic transmission, 3.07:1 with

Jerry Heasley

THE 1984 CORVETTE HAD THE 350-CID, 205-HP L83 V-8.

four-speed manual transmission; (3.31:1 optional). Steering: Rack and pinion (power-assisted). Front suspension: Single fiberglass composite monoleaf transverse spring with unequal-length aluminum control arms and stabilizer bar. Rear suspension: Fully independent five-link system with transverse fiberglass single-leaf springs, aluminum upper/lower trailing links and strut-rod tie-rod assembly. Brakes: Four-wheel power disc. Body construction: Unibody with partial front frame. Fuel tank: 20 gallons.

OPTIONS

RPO AG9 Power driver seat ($210). RPO AQ9 Sports cloth seats ($210). RPO AR9 Base leather seats ($400). RPO AU3 Power door locks ($165). RPO CC3 Removable transparent roof panel ($595). RPO D84 Two-tone paint ($428). RPO FG3 Delco-Bilstein shock absorbers ($189). RPO G92 Performance axle ratio ($22). RPO KC4 Engine oil cooler ($158). RPO K34 Cruise control ($185). RPO MM4 Four-speed manual transmission (no-cost option). RPO QZD P255/50VR-16 tires and 16-inch wheels ($561.20). RPO UL5 Radio delete ($331 credit). RPO UM6 AM-FM stereo radio with cassette ($153). RPO UN8 AM-FM stereo with Citizens Band ($153). RPO UU8 Delco-

Bose stereo system ($895). RPO V01 Heavy-duty radiator ($57). RPO YF5 California emissions certification ($75). RPO Z51 Performance handling package ($600.20). RPO Z6A Rear window and side mirror defoggers ($160).

HISTORICAL FOOTNOTES

Introduced: March 25, 1983. Model-year production: 51,547 (in extended model year). Calendar-year production: 35,661. Calendar-year sales by U.S. dealers: 30,424. Model-year sales by U.S. dealers: 53,877 (including 25,891 sold during the 1983 model year). Car and Driver called the new Corvette "the most advanced production car on the planet." Motor Trend described it as "the best-handling production car in the world, regardless of price." Heady praise indeed. During its year-and-a-half model run, orders poured in well ahead of schedule, even though the new edition cost over $5,000 more than the 1982 version. The body offered the lowest drag coefficient of any Corvette: just 0.341. Testing at GM's Proving Grounds revealed 0.95G lateral acceleration—the highest ever for a production car. Only 6,443 Corvettes had a four-speed manual transmission and only 410 came with a performance axle ratio, but 3,729 had Delco-Bilstein shock absorbers installed.

1985

Two details marked the 1985 Corvette as being different from its newly-restyled 1984 predecessor. The first detail was a new Tuned Port Injection nameplate on fender molding and the second was the straight tailpipes at the rear. That nameplate identified a new 350-cid (5.7-liter) V-8 under the hood. It had a tuned-port-fuel-injection (TPI) system and 230 hp. City fuel economy ratings went up. Otherwise, the only evident change was a slight strengthening in the intensity of the Red and Silver body colors. The Corvette's smoothly sloped nose, adorned by nothing other than a circular emblem, held retracting halogen headlamps. Wide parking and signal lamps nearly filled the space between license plate and outer body edge. Wide horizontal side marker lenses were just ahead of the front wheels. The large air cleaner of 1982 was replaced by an elongated plenum chamber with eight curved aluminum runners. Mounted ahead of the radiator, it ducted incoming air into the plenum through a Bosch hot-wire mass-airflow sensor. Those

tuned runners were meant to boost power at low to medium rpms, following a principle similar to that used for the tall intake stacks in racing engines. Electronic Spark Control (ESC) sensed knocking and adjusted timing to fit fuel octane. Under the chassis, the 1985 Corvette carried a reworked suspension (both standard and optional Z51) to soften the ride without losing control. The Z51 handling package now included 9.5-inch wheels all around, along with Delco-Bilstein gas-charged shock absorbers and a heavy-duty cooling system. The stabilizer bars in the Z51 package were thicker. Spring rates on both suspensions were reduced. Cast aluminum wheels held P255/50VR-16 Eagle GT tires. Brake master cylinders used a new large-capacity plastic booster. Manual gearboxes drove rear axles with 8.5-inch ring gears. The Corvette's instrument-cluster graphics had a bolder look and its roof panels added more solar screening. An optional leather-trimmed sport seat arrived at midyear. Corvette standard equipment included an electronic information

John Gunnell

THE 1985 CORVETTE COUPE HAD A TOP SPEED OF 150 MPH.

**THE 1985 CORVETTE COUPE FEATURED FUEL INJECTION
AS AN OPTION FOR THE FIRST TIME SINCE 1965.**

center; air conditioning; limited-slip differential; power four-wheel disc brakes; power steering; cornering lamps and a seek-and-scan AM/FM stereo radio with four speakers; and automatic power antenna. Also standard were a cigarette lighter; a digital clock; a tachometer; intermittent windshield wipers; halogen fog lamps; and side window defoggers. Corvettes had contour high-back cloth bucket seats; power windows; a trip odometer; a theft-deterrent system with starter interrupt; a compact spare tire; dual electric remote-control sport mirrors and tinted glass. Black belt, windshield, and body side moldings, plus color-keyed rocker panel moldings protected the bodies. A four-speed overdrive automatic transmission was standard, with a four-speed manual (with overdrive in three gears) available at no extra cost. Body colors were: Silver Metallic; Medium Gray Metallic; Light Blue Metallic; Medium Blue Metallic; White; Black; Gold Metallic; Light Bronze Metallic; Dark Bronze Metallic and Bright Red. Two-tone options were Silver and Gray; Light Blue and Medium Blue; and Light Bronze and Dark Bronze. Interiors came in Carmine; Bronze; Graphite; Medium Blue; Medium Gray; and Saddle.

ENGINE

BASE ENGINE: [RPO L98] V-8. 90-degree overhead valve. Cast iron block and head. Displacement: 350 cid (5.7 liters). Bore and stroke: 4.00 x 3.48 inches. Compression ratio: 9.0:1. Brake hp: 230 at 4000 rpm. Torque: 330 lbs.-ft. at 3200 rpm. Five main bearings. Hydraulic valve lifters. Induction: Tuned-port-induction (TPI) system.

TRANSMISSION

AUTOMATIC TRANSMISSION: A Turbo Hydra-Matic automatic transmission with floor-mounted gear shifter was standard equipment.

MANUAL TRANSMISSION: A four-speed manual transmission with overdrive capability was optional.

CHASSIS FEATURES

Wheelbase: 96.2 inches. Overall length: 176.5 inches. Height: 46.4 inches. Width: 71 inches. Front Tread: 59.6 inches. Rear Tread: 60.4 inches. Wheel Size: 16 x 8.5 inches. Standard Tires: P255/50VR-16 SBR.

Chevrolet

THE 1985 CORVETTE COUPE INTERIOR FEATURED IMPROVED INSTRUMENT GRAPHICS.

TECHNICAL FEATURES

Transmission: THM 700-R4 four-speed overdrive automatic (floor shift) standard. Gear ratios: (1st) 3.06:1; (2nd) 1.63:1; (3rd) 1.00:1; (4th) 0.70:1; (Rev) 2.29:1. Four-speed manual transmission optional: (1st) 2.88:1; (2nd) 1.91:1; (3rd) 1.33:1; (4th) 1.00:1; (overdrive) 0.67:1; (Rev) 2.78:1. Planetary overdrive ratios: (2nd) 1.28:1; (3rd) 0.89:1; (4th) 0.67:1. Standard final drive ratio: 2.73:1 with automatic transmission. Steering: Rack and pinion (power-assisted). Front suspension: Single fiberglass composite monoleaf transverse spring with unequal-length aluminum control arms and stabilizer bar. Rear suspension: Fully independent five-link system with transverse fiberglass single-leaf springs, aluminum upper/lower trailing links and strut-rod/tie-rod assembly. Brakes: Four-wheel power disc. Body construction: Unibody with partial front frame. Fuel tank: 20 gallons.

OPTIONS

RPO AG9 Power driver seat ($215). RPO AQ9 Sports leather seats ($1,025). RPO AR9 Base leather seats ($400). RPO Sports seats, cloth ($625). RPO AU3 Power door locks ($170). RPO CC3 Removable transparent roof panel ($595). RPO D84 Two-tone paint ($428). RPO FG3 Delco-Bilstein shock absorbers ($189). RPO G92 Performance axle ratio ($22). RPO K34 Cruise control ($185). RPO MM4 Four-speed manual transmission (no-cost option). RPO UL5 Radio delete ($256 credit). RPO UN8 AM-FM stereo with Citizens Band ($215). RPO UU8 Delco-Bose stereo system ($895). RPO V08 Heavy-duty cooling ($225). RPO Z51 Performance handling package ($470). RPO Z6A Rear window and side mirror defoggers ($160).

HISTORICAL FOOTNOTES

Chevrolet claimed a 17 percent reduction in 0-60 mph times with the TPI power plant. To save weight, Corvettes used not only the fiberglass leaf springs front and rear, but over 400 pounds of aluminum parts (including steering, suspension components and frame members). A total of 14,802 Corvettes had the Z51 performance handling package installed, 9,333 had Delco-Bilstein shocks were ordered separately and only 9,576 had a four-speed manual transmission. Only 16 Corvettes are listed as having a CB radio, and only 82 were sold with an economy rear axle ratio.

Chevrolet

THE 1986 CORVETTE COUPE IN DARK RED METALLIC.

1986

One new body style and an engineering development were the highlights of 1986. The Corvette line added a convertible during the model year, the first since 1975. A computerized anti-lock braking system (ABS) was made standard. It was based on a Bosch ABS II design. During hard braking, the system detected any wheel that was about to lock up, then altered braking pressure, in a pulsating action, to prevent lock up from happening. Drivers could feel the pulses in the pedal. This safety innovation helped the driver to maintain traction and keep the car under directional control without skidding, even on slick and slippery surfaces. Corvette's engine was the same 350-cid (5.7-liter) 230-hp tuned-port-injected V-8 as 1985, but with centrally-positioned copper-core spark plugs. New aluminum cylinder heads had sintered metal valve seats and increased intake port flow, plus a higher (9.5:1) compression ratio. The engine had an aluminum intake manifold with tuned runners, magnesium rocker covers and an outside-air induction system. Both four-plus-three manual and four-speed overdrive automatic transmissions were available, now with an upshift indicator light on the instrument cluster. Three monolith catalytic converters in a new dual-exhaust system kept emissions down during warm up. Cast alloy wheels gained a new raised hub emblem and a brushed-alumi-num look. The instrument cluster was tilted to cut glare. The sport seat from 1985 was made standard, with leather optional. Electronic air conditioning, announced earlier, arrived as a late option. Otherwise, standard equipment was similar to 1985. A new electronic Vehicle Anti-Theft System (VATS) was also made standard. A small electrically-coded pellet was embedded in the ignition key, while a decoder was hidden in the car. When the key was placed in the ignition, its resistance code was "read." Unless that code was compatible, the starter relay wouldn't close and the Electronic Control Module wouldn't activate the fuel injectors. Corvette's back end held four round recessed lenses, with 'Corvette' block letters in the center. The license plate sat in a recessed housing. Cloth seats had lateral support and back-angle adjustments. The new convertible (a.k.a. "roadster") had a manual top with a velour inner liner. The yellow console button that ordinarily controlled Corvette's hatch release instead opened a fiberglass panel behind the seats to reveal the top storage area. Size 16 x 8-1/2 inch cast-alloy aluminum wheels held uni-directional P255/50VR-16 Goodyear Eagle GT SBR tires. Corvettes came in Silver Metallic; Medium Gray Metallic; Medium Blue Metallic; Yellow; White; Black; Gold Metallic; Silver Beige Metallic; Copper Metallic; Medium Brown Metallic; Dark Red Metallic; and

Chevrolet

13,372 1986 CORVETTTES FEATURED LEATHER INTERIORS.

Bright Red. Two-tone combinations were Silver and Gray; Gray and Black; White and Silver; Silver Beige and Medium Brown; and Silver Beige and Black. Interior trims came win Blue; Black; Bronze; Graphite; Medium Gray; Red; Saddle; and White.

ENGINE

BASE ENGINE: [RPO L98] V-8. 90-degree overhead valve. Cast iron block and head. Displacement: 350 cid (5.7 liters). Bore and stroke: 4.00 x 3.48 inches. Compression ratio: 9.5:1. Brake hp: 230 at 4000 rpm. Torque: 330 lbs.-ft. at 3200 rpm. Five main bearings. Hydraulic valve lifters. Induction: Tuned-Port-Injection system.

TRANSMISSION

AUTOMATIC TRANSMISSION: A Turbo Hydra-Matic automatic transmission with floor-mounted gear shifter was standard equipment.

MANUAL TRANSMISSION: A four-speed manual transmission with overdrive was optional

CHASSIS FEATURES

Wheelbase: 96.2 inches. Overall length: 176.5 inches. Height: 46.4 inches. Width: 71 inches. Front tread: 59.6 inches. Rear tread: 60.4 inches. Wheel size: 16 x 8.5 inches. (9.5 inches. wide with optional Z51 suspension). Standard tires: P245/50VR-16 or P255/50VR-16 SBR.

TECHNICAL FEATURES

Transmission: THM 700-R4 four-speed overdrive automatic (floor shift) standard. Gear ratios: (1st) 3.06:1; (2nd) 1.63:1; (3rd) 1.00:1; (4th) 0.70:1; (Rev) 2.29:1. Four-speed manual transmission optional: (1st) 2.88:1; (2nd) 1.91:1; (3rd) 1.33:1; (4th) 1.00:1; (overdrive) 0.67:1; (Rev) 2.78:1. Standard final drive ratio: 2.59:1 or 3.07:1 with automatic transmission, 3.07:1 with four-speed manual transmission; (3.31:1 optional). Steering: Rack and pinion (power-assisted). Front suspension: Single fiberglass composite monoleaf transverse spring with unequal-length aluminum control arms and stabilizer bar. Rear suspension: Fully independent five-link system with transverse fiberglass single-leaf springs, aluminum upper/lower trailing links and strut-rod/tie-rod assembly. Brakes: Four-wheel power disc. Body construction: Unibody with partial front frame. Fuel

Chevrolet

THE 1986 CORVETTE CONSOLE WITH FOUR-SPEED MANUAL TRANSMISSION.

tank: 20 gallons.

OPTIONS

RPO AG9 Power driver seat ($225). RPO AQ9 Leather sports seats ($1,025). RPO AR9 Base leather seats ($400). RPO AU3 Power door locks ($175). RPO B4P Radiator boost fan ($75). RPO B4Z Custom feature package ($195). RPO C2L Dual removable roof panels for coupe ($895). RPO 24S Removable roof panels with blue tint for coupe ($595). RPO 64S Removable roof panels with bronze tint for coupe ($595). RPO C68 Electronic air conditioning control ($150). RPO D84 Two-tone paint ($428). RPO FG3 Delco-Bilstein shock absorbers ($189). RPO G92 Performance axle ratio 3.07:1 ($22). RPO KC4 Engine oil cooler ($110). RPO K34 Cruise control ($185). RPO MM4 Four-speed manual transmission (no-cost option). RPO NN5 California emissions requirements ($99). RPO UL5 Radio delete ($256 credit). RPO UM6 AM-FM stereo radio with cassette ($122). RPO UU8 Delco-Bose stereo system ($895). RPO V01 Heavy-duty radiator ($40). RPO Z51 Performance handling package for coupe ($470). RPO Z6A Rear window and side mirror defoggers for coupe ($165). RPO

4001ZA Malcolm Konner Chevrolet Special Edition paint option for coupe ($500).

HISTORICAL FOOTNOTES

Introduced: October 3, 1985. Model-year production: 35,109. Calendar-year production (U.S.): 28,410. Model-year sales by U.S. dealers: 35,969. Styled like the Corvette roadster that would serve as the 1986 Indianapolis 500 Pace Car, the new convertible went on sale late in the model year. The actual Indianapolis 500 Pace Car was Yellow, differing from showroom models only in its special track lights. Chevrolet considered its "Indy Pace Car" to be synonymous with "open top," so all convertibles were considered Indy Pace Car models. Special decals were packed in the car, but not installed. The Corvette was the only street-legal vehicle to pace the 500-mile race since the 1978 Corvette Indy Pace Car. Instead of a conversion by an outside company, as had become the practice for most 1980s ragtops, Corvette's roadster was built by Chevrolet right alongside the coupe. Problems with cracking of the new aluminum cylinder heads meant the first 1986 models had old cast-iron heads. The difficulties were soon remedied. It was estimated that

ABOVE AND BELOW, THE 1986 CORVETTE CONVERTIBLE

the new anti-theft system would require half an hour's work to overcome, which would dissuade thieves who are typically in a hurry. A total of 6,242 Corvettes had removable roof panels installed and 12,821 came with the Z51 performance handling package. Only 6,835 Corvettes carried the MM4 four-speed manual transmission.

1987

Except for the addition of roller hydraulic lifters to the Corvette's 350-cid (5.7-liter) V-8, little changed this year. Horsepower got a boost to 240 thanks to new friction-cutting roller-type valve lifters. The 1987 Corvettes also had a higher fuel-economy rating. Joining the option list was an electronic tire-pressure monitor that signaled a dashboard light to warn of low pressure in any tire. Two four-speed transmissions were available: manual or automatic. Standard equipment included power steering; power four-wheel disc brakes (with anti-locking); air conditioning; a theft-deterrent system; tinted glass; twin remote-control mirrors; power windows; intermittent wipers; tilt/telescope steering column; and an AM/FM seek/scan radio. Both the centers and slots of the wheels (unpainted in 1986) were now finished in Argent Gray.

Corvettes came in Silver Metallic; Medium Gray Metallic; Medium Blue Metallic; Yellow; White; Black; Gold Metallic; Silver Beige Metallic; Copper Metallic; Medium Brown Metallic; Dark Red Metallic; and Bright Red. Two-tone combinations were Silver and Gray; Gray and Black; White and Silver; and Silver Beige and Medium Brown. Interior trims came in Blue; Black; Bronze; Graphite; Medium Gray; Red; Saddle; and White. A removable body-colored roof panel for hatchbacks or body-colored convertible top were standard, along with cloth-upholstered seats.

ENGINE

BASE ENGINE: [RPO L98] V-8. 90-degree overhead valve. Cast iron block and head. Displacement: 350 cid (5.7 liters). Bore and stroke: 4.00 x 3.48 inches. Compression ratio: 9.5:1.

THE 1987 CORVETTE CONVERTIBLE.

Chevrolet

RAGTOPS WERE REINTRODUCED IN 1986 AND WERE AVAILABLE AGAIN IN 1987.

Brake hp: 240 at 4000 rpm. Torque: 345 lbs.-ft. at 3200 rpm. Five main bearings. Aluminum cylinder head. Hydraulic valve lifters. Induction: Tuned-Port-Injection system.

TRANSMISSION

AUTOMATIC TRANSMISSION: A Turbo Hydra-Matic automatic transmission with floor-mounted gear shifter was standard equipment.

MANUAL TRANSMISSION: A four-speed manual transmission was optional.

CHASSIS FEATURE

Wheelbase: 96.2 inches. Overall length: 176.5 inches. Height: (hatchback) 46.7 inches.; (convertible) 46.4 inches. Width: 71 inches. Front Tread: 59.6 inches. Rear Tread: 60.4 inches. Standard Tires: P245/60VR-15 Goodyear Eagle GT.

TECHNICAL FEATURES

Transmission: automatic or optional four-speed manual. Standard final drive ratio: 3.07:1 with manual transmission, 2.59:1 or 3.07:1 with automatic transmission. Steering: rack and pinion (power assisted). Front suspension: unequal-length control arms, single-leaf transverse spring and stabilizer bar. Rear suspension: upper/lower control arms with five links, single-leaf transverse springs, stabilizer bar. Brakes: Anti-lock; power four-wheel disc. Body construction: fiberglass; separate ladder frame with cross-members. Fuel tank: 20 gallons.

OPTIONS

RPO AC1 Power passenger seat ($240). RPO AC3 Power driver seat ($240). RPO AQ9 Leather sports seats ($1,025). RPO AR9 Base leather seats ($400). RPO AU3 Power door locks ($190). RPO B2K Callaway Twin Turbo installed by Callaway Engineering ($19,995). RPO B4P Radiator boost fan ($75). RPO C2L Dual removable roof panels for coupe ($915). RPO 24S Removable roof panels with blue tint for coupe ($615). RPO 64S Removable roof panels with bronze tint for coupe ($615). RPO C68 Electronic air conditioning control ($150). RPO DL8 Twin remote heated mirrors for convertible ($35). RPO D74 Illuminated driver vanity mirror ($58). RPO D84 Two-tone paint on hatchback ($428). RPO FG3 Delco-Bilstein shock absorbers ($189). RPO G92 Performance axle ratio 3.07:1 ($22). RPO KC4 Engine oil cooler ($110). RPO K34 Cruise control ($185). RPO MM4 Four-speed manual transmission (no-cost option). RPO NN5 California emissions requirements ($99). RPO UL5 Radio delete ($256 credit). RPO UM6 AM-FM stereo radio with cassette ($132). RPO UU8 Delco-Bose stereo system ($905). RPO V01 Heavy-duty radiator ($40). RPO Z51 Performance handling package for hatchback ($795). RPO Z52 Sport handling package ($470). RPO Z6A Rear window and side mirror defoggers for coupe ($165).

Jerry Heasley

THANKS IN PART TO A 240-HP V-8, CAR & DRIVER MAGAZINE PICKED THE 1987 CORVETTE AS ONE OF THE WORLD'S TOP 10 CARS.

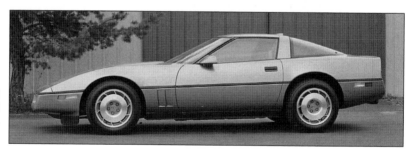

THE 1986 CORVETTE COUPE.

HISTORICAL FOOTNOTES

Introduced: October 9, 1986. Model-Year Production: 30,632. Calendar-year production (U.S.): 28,514. Model-year sales by U.S. dealers: 25,266. A $19,995 Callaway Twin-Turbo engine package could be ordered through specific Chevrolet dealers as RPO B2K. Cars that received this package were sent from Bowling Green, Kentucky, to the Callaway factory in Old Lyme, Connecticut, to receive engine modifications and other upgrades. A total of 184 Callaway Twin-Turbos were built (21 coupes and 63 convertibles). The 1987 Callaways had 345 hp and 465 lbs.-ft. of torque. All had manual transmissions and were not certified for sale in the state of California.

1988

By 1988, Chevrolet produced approximately 900,000 Corvettes in the 35 years since America's sports car bowed in 1953. Little changed in Corvette's appearance this year, except for restyled six-slot wheels. Optional 17-inch wheels looked similar to the standard 16-inch wheels, but held massive P275/40ZR-17 Goodyear Eagle GT tires. Suspension modifications were intended to improve control during hard braking, while brake components were toughened, including the use of thicker rotors. Under the hood, the standard 350-cid (5.7-liter) V-8 could breathe more easily with a pair of modified aluminum cylinder heads. Performance also got a boost via a new camshaft, though horsepower only rose by five. Both a convertible and a hatchback coupe were offered. Corvettes came in Silver Metallic; Medium Blue Metallic; Dark Blue Metallic; Yellow; White; Black; Dark Red Metallic; Bright Red; Gray Metallic and Charcoal Metallic. The only standard two-tone combination was White and Black. Interior trims came in Blue; Black; Gray; Red; Saddle; and White. A removable body-color roof panel for hatchbacks or body-color convertible top was standard, along with cloth-upholstered seats.

ENGINE

BASE ENGINE: [RPO L98] V-8. 90-degree overhead valve. Cast iron block and head. Displacement: 350 cid (5.7 liters). Bore and stroke: 4.00 x 3.48 inches. Compression ratio: 9.5:1. Brake hp: 240/245 (*) at 4000 rpm. Torque: 345 lbs.-ft. at 3200 rpm. Five main bearings. Aluminum cylinder head. Hydraulic valve lifters. Induction: Tuned-Port-Injection system.

(*) Engine rating is 245-hp for hatchbacks using 3.07:1 rear axle due to use of low-restriction mufflers with this option combination only.

TRANSMISSION

AUTOMATIC TRANSMISSION: A Turbo Hydra-Matic automatic transmission with floor-mounted gear shifter was standard equipment.

MANUAL TRANSMISSION: A four-speed manual transmission with overdrive was optional.

Chevrolet

THE 1988 CORVETTE COUPE.

Chevrolet

THE 1988 CORVETTE COUPE.

CHASSIS FEATURES

Wheelbase: 96.2 inches. Overall length: 176.5 inches. Height: (Hatchback) 46.7 inches; (Convertible) 46.4 inches. Width: 71.0 inches. Front tread: 59.6 inches. Rear tread: 60.4 inches. Standard tires: P255/50ZR-I6 Goodyear Eagle GT (Z-rated).

TECHNICAL FEATURES

Transmission: Automatic or optional four-speed manual. Steering: Rack and pinion (power assisted). Front suspension: Unequal-length control arms, single-leaf transverse springs and stabilizer bar. Rear suspension: Upper/lower control arms with five links, single-leaf transverse springs, stabilizer bar. Brakes: Anti-lock; power four-wheel disc. Body construction: Fiberglass; separate ladder frame with cross-members. Fuel tank: 20 gallons.

OPTIONS

RPO AC1 Power passenger seat ($240). RPO AC3 Power driver seat ($240). RPO AQ9 Leather sports seats ($1,025). RPO AR9 Base leather seats ($400). RPO B2K Callaway Twin Turbo installed by Callaway Engineering ($25,895). RPO B4P Radiator boost fan ($75). RPO C2L Dual removable roof panels for coupe ($915). RPO 24S Removable roof panels with blue tint for coupe ($615). RPO 64S Removable roof panels with bronze tint for coupe ($615). RPO C68 Electronic air conditioning control ($150). RPO DL8 Twin remote heated mirrors for convertible ($35). RPO D74 Illuminated driver vanity mirror ($58). RPO FG3 Delco-Bilstein shock absorbers ($189). RPO G92 Performance axle ratio 3.07:1 ($22). RPO KC4 Engine oil cooler ($110). RPO MM4 Four-speed manual transmission (no-cost option). RPO NN5 California emissions requirements ($99). RPO UL5 Radio delete ($297 credit). RPO UU8 Delco-Bose stereo system ($773). RPO V01 Heavy-duty radiator ($40). RPO Z01 35th Anniversary Special Edition package for hatchback ($4,795). RPO Z51 Performance handling package for hatchback ($1,295). RPO Z52 Sport handling package ($970). RPO Z6A Rear window and side mirror defoggers for coupe ($165).

HISTORICAL FOOTNOTES

Introduced: October 1, 1987. Model-year production: 22,789. Calendar-year production: 22,878. Model-year sales by U.S. dealers: 25,425. A $25,895 Callaway Twin-Turbo

Chevrolet photo

THE 1988 CORVETTE CONVERTIBLE LISTED AT $34,820.

Chevrolet photo

THE 1988 CORVETTE CONVERTIBLE WITH THE RAGTOP UP.

engine package could be ordered through specific Chevrolet dealers as RPO B2K. Cars that received this package were sent from Bowling Green, Kentucky, to the Callaway factory in Old Lyme, Connecticut, to receive engine modifications and other upgrades. The 1988 Callaways had 382 hp and 562 lbs.-ft. of torque. Callaway modified a Chevrolet truck-type Turbo Hydra-Matic transmission as a $6,500 option for Callaways. Chevrolet also built 56 Corvette race cars for use in the Sports Car Club of America's (SCCA) Corvette Challenge racing series. These "street-legal" track cars all had stock engines specially built at the Flint, Michigan, engine plant. They were matched for power and sealed to insure that all of the cars were as identical as possible in a technical sense. Protofab, an aftermarket race-car builder in Wixom, Michigan, installed race-car modifications and roll bars.

1989

Most of the Corvette publicity this year centered on the eagerly-awaited ZR-1 which was claimed to be the world's fastest production automobile. After several announcements proved premature, the ZR-1's introduction was delayed until the 1990 model year. Meanwhile, the "ordinary" Corvette added a new ZF six-speed manual gearbox with two overdrive ratios. To meet fuel-economy standards, the ingenious transmission was designed with a computer that sent a signal to prevent shifts from first to second gear unless the gas pedal hit the floor. Instead, a blocking pin forced the shifter directly into fourth gear for improved fuel economy during light-throttle operation. Joining the option list was a new FX3 Delco-Bilstein Selective Ride Control system with a switch to select the desired degree of shock absorber damping for touring, sport, or competition driving. Only hatchbacks with a manual transmission and the Z51 Performance Handling package could get the ride-control option. For the first time since 1975, a removable fiberglass hardtop became available for the convertible, but not until late in the model year. Corvettes came in White; Medium Blue Metallic; Dark Blue Metallic; Black; Dark Red Metallic; Bright Red; Gray Metallic; and Charcoal Metallic. Chevrolet also painted 33 cars in two non-standard colors. Six were done in Yellow and 27 were done in Arctic Pearl. Interior trims came in Blue; Black; Gray; Red; Saddle; and White. A removable body-color roof panel for hatchbacks or body-color convertible top were standard, along with cloth upholstery.

THIS 1989 CORVETTE ZR-1 WAS ONE OF ONLY 84 RELEASED.

Jerry Heasley

ENGINE DIFFICULTIES ULTIMATELY HELD BACK THE ZR-1 IN 1989.

ENGINE

BASE ENGINE: [RPO L98] V-8. 90-degree overhead valve. Cast iron block and head. Displacement: 350 cid (5.7 liters). Bore and stroke: 4.00 x 3.48 inches. Compression ratio: 9.5:1. Brake hp: 240/245 (*) at 4300 rpm. Torque: 340 lbs.-ft. at 3200 rpm. Five main bearings. Aluminum cylinder head. Hydraulic valve lifters. Induction: Tuned-Port-Injection system.

(*) Engine rating is 245-hp for hatchbacks using 3.07:1 rear axle due to use of low-restriction mufflers with this option combination only.

TRANSMISSION

AUTOMATIC TRANSMISSION: A Turbo Hydra-Matic automatic transmission with floor-mounted gear shifter was standard equipment.

MANUAL TRANSMISSION: A six-speed manual transmission was optional.

CHASSIS FEATURES

Wheelbase: 96.2 inches. Overall length: 176.5 inches. Height: (Hatchback) 46.7 inches.; (Convertible) 46.4 inches. Width: 71 inches. Front tread: 59.6 inches. Rear tread: 60:4 inch-

es. Standard tires: P275/40VR-17 Goodyear Eagle GT (Z-rated).

TECHNICAL FEATURES

Transmission: Automatic or six-speed manual. Steering: Rack and pinion (power assisted). Front suspension: Unequal-length control arms, single-leaf transverse springs and stabilizer bar. Rear suspension: Upper/lower control arms with five links, single-leaf transverse springs, stabilizer bar. Brakes: Anti-lock; power four-wheel disc. Body construction: fiberglass; separate ladder frame with cross-members. Fuel tank: 20 gallons.

OPTIONS

RPO AC1 Power passenger seat ($240). RPO AC3 Power driver seat ($240). RPO AQ9 Leather sports seats ($1,025). RPO AR9 Base leather seats ($400). RPO B2K Callaway Twin Turbo installed by Callaway Engineering ($25,895). RPO B4P Radiator boost fan ($75). RPO CC2 Auxiliary hardtop for convertible ($1,995). RPO C2L Dual removable roof panels for coupe ($915). RPO 24S Removable roof panels with blue tint for coupe ($615).

RPO 64S Removable roof panels with bronze tint for coupe ($615). RPO C68 Electronic air conditioning control ($150). RPO D74 Illuminated driver vanity mirror ($58). RPO FX3 Selective electronic Ride & Handling ($1,695). RPO G92 Performance axle ratio 3.07:1 ($22). RPO KO5 Engine block heater ($20). RPO KC4 Engine oil cooler ($110). RPO MN6 Six-speed manual transmission (no-cost option). RPO NN5 California emissions requirements ($100). RPO UJ6 Low tire pressure warning indicator ($325). RPO UU8 Delco-Bose stereo system ($773). RPO V01 Heavy-duty radiator ($40). RPO V56 Luggage rack for convertible ($140). RPO Z51 Performance handling package for hatchback ($575).

HISTORICAL FOOTNOTES

Model-year production: 26,412. Calendar-year production: 25,279. Model-year sales by U.S. dealers: 23,928. The $25,895 Callaway Twin-Turbo engine package could again be ordered through specific Chevrolet dealers as RPO B2K. Cars that received this package were sent from Bowling Green, Kentucky, to the Callaway factory in Old Lyme, Connecticut, to receive engine modifications and other upgrades. The 1989 Callaways had 382 hp and 562 lbs.-ft. of torque. Chevrolet built 60 Corvette Challenge cars with standard engines. Of these, 30 were shipped to Powell Development of America to receive race-modified engines and other competition modifications for the 1989 Sports Car Club of America (SCCA) Corvette Challenge racing series. At the end of the year, these cars had their original factory-numbered engines re-installed. Chevrolet built 84 ZR-1 type 1989 Corvettes for testing, but then said on April 19 that the ZR-1's introduction would be delayed until 1990.

THE 1989 CORVETTE COUPE.

1990

Finally, after months of hoopla and a few false starts, the super-performance ZR-1 Corvette arrived in 1990. Intended for production in limited quantity, with a price tag higher than any General Motors product, the ZR-1 became a collectible long before anyone ever saw one "in the flesh." Customers seemed eager to pay far above the suggested retail price for the few examples that became available. Under the ZR-1's hood was a Lotus-designed 32-valve, dual-overhead-cam, 350-cid (5.7-liter) V-8, built by Mercury Marine in Oklahoma. Although the displacement was identical to the standard Corvette V-8, this was an all-new power plant with different bore-and-stroke dimensions. Wider at the rear than a standard model, partly to contain huge 315/35ZR-17 rear tires, the ZR-1 was easy to spot because of its convex rear end and rectangular tail lamps. Ordinary Corvettes continued to display a concave rear end with round tail lamps. Standard ZR-1 equipment included an FX3 Selective Ride adjustable suspension,

which was also available on standard Corvettes with the six-speed manual gearbox. Four-speed overdrive automatic was available (at no cost) only on the regular Corvette. New standard equipment included an engine oil cooler, 17-inch alloy wheels, and improved ABS II-S anti-lock braking. The convertible added a new backlight made of flexible "Ultrashield" for improved scratch resistance and visibility. An air bag was installed in the new steering wheel on all Corvettes and a revised dashboard mixed digital and analog instruments. Corvettes came in White; Steel Blue Metallic; Black; Turquoise Metallic; Competition Yellow; Dark Red Metallic; Quasar Blue Metallic; Bright Red; Polo Green Metallic; and Charcoal Metallic. Interiors came in Blue; Black; Gray; Red; Saddle; and White. Standard features included a removable body-color roof panel for hatchbacks or a convertible top (Black, Saddle, or White top colors were available, but the choices you could order were determined by paint color). Cloth

Jerry Heasley

THE 1990 CORVETTE ZR-1 WAS A HIT WITH BUYERS.

Nicky Wright

A TOTAL OF 3,049 ZR-1 CORVETTES WERE BUILT FOR 1990.

Nicky Wright

THE 1990 CORVETTE ZR-1 IN BRIGHT RED.

upholstery was also standard.

ENGINES

BASE ENGINE: [RPO L98] V-8. 90-degree overhead valve. Cast iron block and head. Displacement: 350 cid (5.7 liters). Bore and stroke: 4.00 x 3.48 inches. Compression ratio: 9.5:1. Brake hp: 240/245 (*) at 4300 rpm. Torque: 340 lbs.-ft. at 3200 rpm. Five main bearings. Aluminum cylinder head. Hydraulic valve lifters. Induction: Tuned-Port-Injection system.

(*) Engine rating is 245-hp for hatchbacks using 3.07:1 rear axle due to use of low-restriction mufflers with this option combination only.

ZR-1 ENGINE: [RPO LT5] V-8. 90-degree

Nicky Wright

FAMED DESIGNER LARRY SHINODA PRODUCED A SPECIAL 1990 CORVETTE THAT FEATURED SUPERIOR AERODYNAMICS.

overhead valve with four valves per cylinder. Four overhead camshafts. Cast iron block and head. Displacement: 350 cid (5.7 liters). Bore and stroke: 4.00 x 3.48 inches. Compression ratio: 11.0:1. Brake hp: 375 at 5800 rpm. Torque: 370 lbs.-ft. at 5600 rpm. Five main bearings. Aluminum cylinder head. Hydraulic valve lifters. Induction: Tuned-Port-Injection system. LT5 engines were manufactured and assembled by Mercury Marine Corporation in Stillwater, Oklahoma, and shipped to the Corvette factory for installation in ZR-1 Corvettes.

TRANSMISSION

AUTOMATIC TRANSMISSION: An automatic transmission with floor-mounted gear shifter was standard equipment.

MANUAL TRANSMISSION: A six-speed manual transmission was optional.

CHASSIS FEATURES

Wheelbase: 96.2 inches. Overall length: (Base) 176.5 inches.; (ZR-1) 177.4 inches. Height: (Hatchback) 46.7 inches.; (Convertible) 46.4 inches. Width: (Base) 71 inches.; (ZR-1) 74 inches. Front tread: (All) 59.6 inches. Rear

tread: (Base) 60:4 inches.; (ZR-1) 61.9 inches. Standard tires: P275/40ZR-17 Goodyear Eagle GT (ZR-1 uses P315/35ZR-17 at rear).

TECHNICAL FEATURES

Transmission: Automatic or six-speed manual. Steering: Rack and pinion (power assisted). Front suspension: Unequal-length control arms, single-leaf transverse springs and stabilizer bar. Rear suspension: Upper/lower control arms with five links, single-leaf transverse springs, stabilizer bar. Brakes: Anti-lock; power four-wheel disc. Body construction: Fiberglass; separate ladder frame with cross-members. Fuel tank: 20 gallons.

OPTIONS

RPO AC1 Power passenger seat ($270). RPO AC3 Power driver seat ($270). RPO AQ9 Leather sports seats ($1,050). RPO AR9 Base leather seats ($425). RPO B2K Callaway Twin Turbo installed by Callaway Engineering ($26,895). RPO CC2 Auxiliary hardtop for convertible ($1,995). RPO C2L Dual removable roof panels for coupe ($915). RPO 24S Removable roof panels with blue tint for coupe ($615). RPO

Jerry Heasley

THE BODY KIT WAS EASY TO SPOT FROM ALL SIDES ON THE 1990 CORVETTES DESIGNED BY LARRY SHINODA.

64S Removable roof panels with bronze tint for coupe ($615). RPO C68 Electronic air conditioning control ($180). RPO FX3 Electronic Selective Ride & Handling system ($1,695). RPO G92 Performance axle ratio 3.07:1 ($22). RPO KO5 Engine block heater ($20). RPO KC4 Engine oil cooler ($110). RPO MN6 Six-speed manual transmission (no-cost option). RPO NN5 California emissions requirements ($100). RPO UJ6 Low tire pressure warning indicator ($325). RPO UU8 Delco-Bose stereo system ($823). RPO U1F Delco-Bose stereo system with compact disc changer ($1,219). RPO V56 Luggage rack for convertible ($140). RPO Z51 Performance handling package for hatchback ($460). RPO ZR-1 Special performance package for coupe ($27,016).

HISTORICAL FOOTNOTES

Model-year production: 23,646. Calendar-year production: 22,154. Model-year sales by U.S. dealers: 22,690. The $26,895 Callaway Twin-Turbo engine package could again be ordered through specific Chevrolet dealers as RPO B2K. Cars that received this package were sent from Bowling Green, Kentucky, to the Callaway factory in Old Lyme, Connecticut,

Nicky Wright

THE 1990 CORVETTE ZR-1 WITH THE LT5 375-HP V-8.

to receive engine modifications and other upgrades. For a limited time an RPO R9G option was offered through Chevrolet dealers for competition-minded Corvette buyers who wanted to participate in the new World Challenge racing series. Only 23 such cars were built. In 1990, Corvette chief engineer Dave McLellan was the annual recipient of the Society of Automotive Engineers' Edward N. Cole Award for automotive engineering innovation. McLellan was specifically recognized for his work on the ZR-1 package.

1991

Not a year of great change after the launch of the ZR-1 the previous year. Standard Corvettes were restyled at the rear to more closely resemble the ZR-1 with a convex rear fascia and two rectangular tail lamps on either side of the car. A new front end with wrap-around parking lamps was used on both models, along with new side-panel louvers and wider body-color body side moldings. Although more alike the standard Corvette in a visual sense, the ZR-1 again had different doors and a wider rear to accommodate its 11-inch wide rear wheels. Also the high-mounted stop lamp went on the roof of the ZR-1, instead of on the rear fascia, as on the YY Corvette. All models were again equipped with ABS II-S anti-lock braking and driver's side airbag as well as an anti-theft system. The ZR-1 was again powered by the 32-valve DOHC 5.7-liter V-8 matched with a six-speed transaxle. Corvette models used the 5.7-liter TPI V-8 fitted with the four-speed over-drive automatic or optional six-speed manual transmission. Corvettes came in White; Steel Blue Metallic; Yellow; Black; Turquoise Metallic; Dark Red Metallic; Quasar Blue Metallic; Bright Red; Polo Green Metallic; and Charcoal Metallic. Interiors came in Blue; Black; Gray; Red; Saddle; and White. Standard features included a removable body-color roof panel for hatchbacks or a convertible top. Black, Saddle, Red, White, and (late in the year) Blue top colors were available, but the choices were determined by body paint color. Cloth upholstery was also standard.

ENGINES

BASE ENGINE: [RPO L98] V-8. 90-degree overhead valve. Cast iron block and head. Displacement: 350 cid (5.7 liters). Bore and stroke: 4.00 x 3.48 inches. Compression ratio: 10.0:1. Brake hp: 245/250(*) at 4000 rpm. Torque: 340 lbs.-ft. at 3200 rpm. Five main bearings. Alu-

Jerry Heasley

THE 1991 CORVETTE ZR-1 FEATURED FOUR HORIZONTAL FENDER LOUVERS.

minum cylinder head. Hydraulic valve lifters. Induction: Tuned-Port-Injection system.

(*) Engine rating is 250-hp for hatchbacks using 3.07:1 rear axle due to use of low-restriction mufflers with this option combination only.

ZR-1 ENGINE: [RPO LT5] V-8. 90-degree overhead valve with four valves per cylinder. Four overhead camshafts. Cast iron block and head. Displacement: 350 cid (5.7 liters). Bore and stroke: 4.00 x 3.48 inches. Compression ratio: 11.0:1. Brake hp: 375 at 5800 rpm. Torque: 370 lbs.-ft. at 5600 rpm. Five main bearings. Aluminum cylinder head. Hydraulic valve lifters. Induction: Tuned-Port-Injection system.

TRANSMISSION

AUTOMATIC TRANSMISSION: An automatic transmission with floor-mounted gear shifter was standard equipment.

MANUAL TRANSMISSION: A six-speed manual transmission was optional.

CHASSIS FEATURES

Wheelbase: 96.2 inches. Overall length: (Base) 178.6 inches.; (ZR-1) 178.5 inches. Height: (Hatchback) 46.7 inches.; (Convertible) 46.4 inches. Width: (Base) 71 inches.; (ZR-1) 73.2 inches. Front tread: (All) 59.6 inches. Rear tread: (Base) 60:4 inches.; (ZR-1) 61.9 inches. Standard tires: P275/40ZR-17 Goodyear Eagle GT (ZR-1 uses P315/35ZR-17 at rear).

TECHNICAL FEATURES

Transmission: Automatic or six-speed manual. Steering: Rack and pinion (power assisted). Front suspension: Unequal-length control arms, single-leaf transverse springs and stabilizer bar. Rear suspension: Upper/lower control arms with five links, single-leaf transverse springs, and stabilizer bar. Brakes: Anti-lock; power four-wheel disc. Body construction: Fiberglass; separate ladder frame with cross-members. Fuel tank: 20 gallons.

OPTIONS

RPO AC1 Power passenger seat ($290). RPO AC3 Power driver seat ($290). RPO AQ9 Leather sports seats ($1,050). RPO AR9 Base leather seats ($425). RPO B2K Callaway Twin Turbo installed by Callaway Engineering ($33,000). RPO CC2 Auxiliary hardtop for convertible ($1,995). RPO C2L Dual removable roof panels for coupe ($915). RPO 24S Removable roof panels with blue tint for coupe ($615). RPO 64S Removable roof panels with bronze tint for coupe ($615). RPO C68 Electronic air conditioning control ($180). RPO FX3 Electronic Selective Ride & Handling system ($1,695). RPO G92 Performance axle ratio 3.07:1 ($22). RPO KC4 Engine oil cooler ($110). RPO MN6 Six-speed manual transmission (no-cost option). RPO NN5 California emissions requirements ($100). RPO UJ6 Low tire pressure warning indicator ($325). RPO UU8 Delco-Bose stereo system ($823). RPO U1F Delco-Bose stereo system with compact disc changer ($1,219). RPO V56 Luggage rack for convertible ($140). RPO ZR1 Special performance package for coupe ($31,683).

HISTORICAL FOOTNOTES

Model-year production: 20,639. Calendar-year sales: 17,472. The $33,000 Callaway Twin-Turbo engine package could again be ordered through specific Chevrolet dealers as RPO B2K. The 62 Cars that received this package were sent from Bowling Green, Kentucky to the Callaway factory in Old Lyme, Connecticut, to receive engine modifications and other upgrades. Callaway built its 500th conversion on September 26, 1991. Twin Turbos made after that were "Callway 500" editions with special features and a $600 higher price tag. Corvette buyers who wanted to participate in World Challenge Series racing had to buy a stock Corvette from Chevrolet and handle race-prep work themselves.

1992

Another year of little change in the makeup of the Corvette line. The ZR-1 was basically a carry-over from the year previous with new model badges above the rear fender vents. Standard Corvette models received an upgraded 300-hp 5.7-liter V-8 as well as Acceleration Slip Regulation. The ZR-1 was again powered by the 32-valve DOHC 5.7-liter V-8 matched with a six-speed transaxle. Corvette models used the aforementioned more powerful 5.7-liter V-8 fitted with the four-speed overdrive automatic or optional six-speed manual transmission. Both models had new rectangular exhausts. A new all-black dash treatment, relocated digital speedometer and improved instrument graphics were adopted. A Traction Control system became standard equipment along with new Goodyear GS-C tires. Corvettes came in White; Yellow; Black; Bright Aqua Metallic; Polo Green II Metallic; Black Rose Metallic; Dark Red Metallic; Quasar Blue Metallic; and Bright Red. Interiors came in Blue; Beige; Black; Light Beige; Light Gray; Red; and White. Standard features included a removable body-color roof panel for hatchbacks or a convertible top. All Corvette convertible buyers had a choice of Beige, Black, and White top colors and a Blue top was available with White Corvettes only. Also standard was Black cloth upholstery.

ENGINES

BASE ENGINE: [RPO LT1] V-8. 90-degree overhead valve. Cast iron block and head. Displacement: 350 cid (5.7 liters). Bore and stroke: 4.00 x 3.48 inches. Compression ratio: 10.3:1. Brake hp: 300 at 5000 rpm. Torque: 330 lbs.-ft. at 4000 rpm. Five main bearings. Aluminum cylinder head. Hydraulic valve lifters. Induction: Multiport Fuel Injection system.

Jerry Heasley

THE 350-CID V-8 PRODUCED 375 HORSES IN THE 1992 ZR-1.

THE 1992 CORVETTE CALLAWAY SPEEDSTER.

ZR-1 ENGINE: [RPO LT5] V-8. 90-degree overhead valve with four valves per cylinder. Four overhead camshafts. Cast iron block and head. Displacement: 350 cid (5.7 liters). Bore and stroke: 4.00 x 3.48 inches. Compression ratio: 11.0:1. Brake hp: 375 at 5800 rpm. Torque: 370 lbs.-ft. at 5600 rpm. Five main bearings. Aluminum cylinder head. Hydraulic valve lifters. Induction: Multiport Fuel Injection system.

TRANSMISSION

AUTOMATIC TRANSMISSION: An automatic transmission with floor-mounted gear shifter was standard equipment.

MANUAL TRANSMISSION: A six-speed manual transmission was optional.

CHASSIS FEATURES

Wheelbase: 96.2 inches. Overall length: (Base) 178.6 inches.; (ZR-1) 178.5 inches. Height: (Hatchback) 46.3 inches.; (Convertible) 47.3 inches. Width: (Base) 71.1 inches.; (ZR-1) 73.1 inches. Front tread: (All) 57.7 inches. Rear tread: (Base) 59 inches.; (ZR-1) 60.6 inches.

Standard tires: P275/40ZR-17 Goodyear Eagle GT (ZR-1 uses P315/35ZR-17 at rear).

TECHNICAL FEATURES

Transmission: Automatic or six-speed manual. Steering: Rack and pinion (power assisted). Front suspension: Unequal-length control arms, single-leaf transverse springs and stabilizer bar. Rear suspension: Upper/lower control arms with five links, single-leaf transverse springs, and stabilizer bar. Brakes: Anti-lock; power four-wheel disc. Body construction: Fiberglass; separate ladder frame with cross-members. Fuel tank: 20 gallons.

OPTIONS

RPO AC1 Power passenger seat ($305). RPO AC3 Power driver seat ($305). RPO AQ9 Leather sports seats ($1,100). RPO AQ9 White leather sports seats ($1,180). RPO AR9 Base leather seats ($425). RPO AR9 Base White leather seats ($555). RPO CC2 Auxiliary hardtop for convertible ($1,995). RPO C2L Dual removable roof panels for coupe ($950). RPO 24S Removable roof panels with blue tint for coupe ($650). RPO 64S Removable roof panels with bronze tint for coupe ($650). RPO C68 Electronic air conditioning control ($205). RPO FX3 Electronic Selective Ride & Handling system ($1,695). RPO G92 Performance axle ratio 3.07:1 ($50). RPO MN6 Six-speed manual transmission (no-cost option). RPO NN5 California emissions requirements ($100). RPO UJ6 Low tire pressure warning indicator ($325). RPO UU8 Delco-Bose stereo system ($823). RPO U1F Delco-Bose stereo system with compact disc changer ($1,219). RPO V56 Luggage rack for convertible ($140). RPO Z07 Adjustable suspension package for hatchback coupe ($2,045). RPO ZR-1 Special performance package for hatchback coupe ($31,683).

HISTORICAL FOOTNOTES

Model-year production: 20,479. Calendar-year sales: 19,819. The 1,000,000th Corvette was produced on July 2, 1992. It was a 1992 Corvette convertible and was posed for a factory publicity photograph alongside a first-year 1953 Corvette. With the introduction of the base LT1 V-8, the introduction of an Acceleration Slip Regulation (ASR) traction-control system as standard equipment and the standard use of Goodyear Eagle GS-C high-performance tires with directional and asymmetrical tread design, Chevrolet Motor Division could advertise that "The all-around performance of the Corvette has been raised to the highest point in the car's 39-year history." Eight major factors contributed to the increased power of the LT1 engine: 1) A reverse-flow cooling system; 2) Computer-controlled ignition timing; 3) A low-restriction exhaust system incorporating a two-piece converter and exhaust-runner as-

sembly for easier service access; 4) The use of high-compression-ratio pistons; 5) The use of a new camshaft profile; 6) The use of new free-flowing cylinder heads; 7) The use of four-bolt main bearing caps on the three center bearings and 8) The use of new synthetic 5W-30 engine oil (also eliminating the need for a separate engine-oil cooler). An LT1-powered Corvette with automatic transmission was tested for 0-to-60 mph in 5.26 seconds and did the quarter mile in 13.9 seconds at 102.2 mph. An LT1-powered Corvette with the six-speed manual transmission was tested for 0-to-60 mph in 4.92 seconds and did the quarter mile in 13.7 seconds at 103.5 mph. A 1992 Corvette ZR-1 with standard manual transmission was tested for 0-to-60 mph in 4.3 seconds and did the quarter mile in 12.9 seconds. This proved that the LT1 engine had dramatically narrowed the performance gap between the base Corvette and the much more expensive ZR-1 Corvette.

On August 28, 1992, Chevrolet Motor Division announced that David McLellan would be retiring as Corvette chief engineer. McLellan had taken over the Corvette program after the retirement of Zora Arkus-Duntov in 1975. Chevy's assistant manager of public relations Tom Hoxie said in 1992, "During McLellan's 18-year tenure he transformed the Corvette from an American muscle car into an internationally-acclaimed, high-performance sports car that runs rings around a host of more expensive European and Japanese models." Said McLellan, "I can't think of a better time for me to be leaving. No manufacturer has ever built one million sports cars and at the age of 40 the Corvette is stronger than it's ever been. Our all-new car is a few years old and it's time to let someone else put their stamp on it."

1993

Corvette for 1993 marked its 40th Anniversary with a special appearance package that included an exclusive "Ruby Red" exterior and interior with color-keyed wheel centers, headrest embroidery and bright emblems on the hood, deck and side-gills. This anniversary package was optional equipment on all models. The ZR-1's 5.7-liter LT5 V-8 was upgraded this year and featured significant power and torque increases. Improved air flow from cylinder head and valve train refinements boosted its rating from 375 hp to 405 hp! The 1993 Corvette also introduced GM's first Passive Keyless Entry system whereby simply leaving or approaching the Corvette automatically unlocked or locked the appropriate doors. The 1993 Corvette was also the first North American automobile to use recycled sheet-molded-compound body panels. The ZR-1 again used a six-speed transaxle. Standard Corvette models were again powered by the 5.7-liter LT1 V-8 connected to a four-speed overdrive automatic or optional six-speed

manual transmission. Corvettes came in Arctic White; Black; Bright Aqua Metallic; Polo Green II Metallic; Competition Yellow; Ruby Red; Torch Red; Black Rose Metallic; Dark Red Metallic and Quasar Blue Metallic. Interiors came in Black; Light Beige; Light Gray; Red; Ruby Red; and White. Standard features included a removable body-color roof panel for hatchbacks or a convertible top. All Corvette convertibles except those with the Z25 40th Anniversary Package could be ordered with a Beige, Black, or White cloth top. The 40th Anniversary ragtops came only with an exclusive Ruby Red cloth top. Black cloth upholstery was also standard.

TRANSMISSION

AUTOMATIC TRANSMISSION: An automatic transmission with floor-mounted gear shifter was standard equipment.

MANUAL TRANSMISSION: A six-speed manual transmission was optional.

Jerry Heasley

1,719 1993 CORVETTES FEATURED BLACK RAGTOPS.

Jerry Heasley

THE 1993 40TH ANNIVERSARY CORVETTE.

CHASSIS FEATURES

Wheelbase: 96.2 inches. Overall length: (Base) 178.5 inches.; (ZR-1) 178.5 inches. Height: (hatchback) 46.3 inches.; (convertible) 47.3 inches. Width: (Base) 70.1 inches.; (ZR-1) 73.1 inches. Front Tread: (All) 57.7 inches. Rear Tread: (Base) 59.1 inches.; (ZR-1) 60.6 inches. Standard Tires: (front) P255/45ZR-17 Goodyear Eagle GT/(rear) P285/40ZR-17 Goodyear Eagle GT; (ZR-1) P315/35ZR-17 inches rear.

TECHNICAL FEATURES

Transmission: automatic or six-speed manual. Steering: rack and pinion (power assisted). Front suspension: Unequal-length control arms, single-leaf transverse springs and stabilizer bar. Rear suspension: Upper/lower control arms with five links, single-leaf transverse springs, and stabilizer bar. Brakes: Anti-lock; power four-wheel disc. Body construction: fiberglass; separate ladder frame with cross-members. Fuel tank: 20 gallons.

OPTIONS

RPO AC1 Power passenger seat ($305). RPO AC3 Power driver seat ($305). RPO AQ9 Leather sports seats ($1,100). RPO AQ9 White leather sports seats ($1,180). RPO AR9 Base leather seats ($475). RPO AR9 Base White leather seats ($555). RPO CC2 Auxiliary hardtop for convertible ($1,995). RPO C2L Dual removable roof panels for coupe ($950). RPO 24S Removable roof panels with blue tint for coupe ($650). RPO 64S Removable roof panels with bronze tint for coupe ($650). RPO C68 Electronic air conditioning control ($205). RPO FX3 Electronic Selective Ride & Handling system ($1,695). RPO G92 Performance axle ratio 3.07:1 ($50). RPO MN6 Six-speed manual transmission (no-cost option). RPO NN5 California emissions requirements ($100). RPO UJ6 Low tire pressure warning indicator ($325). RPO UU8 Delco-Bose stereo system ($823). RPO U1F Delco-Bose stereo system with compact disc changer ($1,219). RPO V56 Luggage rack for convertible ($140). RPO Z07 Adjustable suspension package for hatchback coupe ($2,045). RPO Z25 40th Anniversary package ($1,455). RPO ZR1 Special

Jerry Heasley

A 1993 CORVETTE CONVERTIBLE.

Jerry Heasley

THE 1993 40TH ANNIVERSARY CORVETTE.

performance package for hatchback coupe ($31,683).

HISTORICAL FOOTNOTES

Calendar-year sales totaled 20,487 Corvettes. Model-year production totaled 21,590. Even Corvettes without the optional RPO Z25 40th Anniversary package had the special anniversary-style embroidered headrests. For the 1993 model year improvements in the LT5 engine's cylinder head and valve train included "blending" the valve heads and creating three-angle valve inserts, plus the use of a sleeve spacer to help maintain port alignment of the injector manifold. These added up to a 30-hp increase and higher torque rating. In addition, the LT5 was now equipped with four-bolt main bearings, platinum-tipped spark plugs and an electrical linear exhaust gas recirculating (EGR) system.

1994

Several refinements that focused on safety and smoother operation were the order for 1994 Corvettes. A passenger-side airbag was added and all Corvettes now offered dual airbags. In addition, other interior changes included new carpeting, new door-trim panels, new seats, a new steering wheel, a redesigned instrument panel and a restyled console. Other new equipment included an optional rear-axle ratio, revised spring rates, a convertible backlight with heated glass and new exterior colors. The ZR-1 also received new non-directional wheels for 1994. The 5.7-liter V-8 powering the standard Corvettes now used sequential fuel injection, which provided a smoother idle, better drivability and lower emissions. That engine was mated to a refined 4L60-E electronic four-speed automatic overdrive transmission that provided a more consistent shift feel. A brake-transmission shift interlock safety feature was also new for 1994. The ZR-1 again used the LT5 5.7-liter V-8. It was fitted with a six-speed manual transmission, which was again a no-cost option for LT1-powered Corvette models. Corvettes came in Arctic White; Admiral Blue; Black; Bright Aqua Metallic; Polo Green Metallic; Competi-

Chevrolet

THE 1994 CORVETTE COUPE.

Chevrolet

THE 1994 CORVETTE ZR-1 WITH FIVE-SPOKE WHEELS.

tion Yellow; Copper Metallic; Torch Red; Black Rose Metallic; and Dark Red Metallic. Interiors came in Black; Light Beige; Light Gray; and Red. Standard features included a removable body-color roof panel for hatchbacks or a convertible top. All Corvette convertibles except those with Polo Green Metallic finish could be ordered with one of three top colors: Beige, Black, or White cloth. The White convertible top was not available for Polo Green Metallic cars. Leather seats became standard upholstery.

ENGINES

BASE ENGINE: [RPO LT1] V-8. 90-degree overhead valve. Cast iron block and head. Displacement: 350 cid (5.7 liters). Bore and stroke: 4.00 x 3.48 inches. Compression ratio: 10.5:1. Brake hp: 300 at 5000 rpm. Torque: 340 lbs.-ft. at 3600 rpm. Five main bearings. Aluminum cylinder head. Hydraulic valve lifters. Induction: Sequential multiport-fuel injection.

ZR-1 ENGINE: [RPO LT5] V-8. 90-degree overhead valve with four valves per cylinder. Four overhead camshafts. Cast iron block and head. Displacement: 350 cid (5.7 liters). Bore and stroke: 4.00 x 3.48 inches. Compression ratio: 11.0:1. Brake hp: 405 at 5800 rpm. Torque: 385 lbs.-ft. at 5200 rpm. Five main bearings. Aluminum cylinder head. Hydraulic valve lifters. Induction: Sequential multiport-fuel-injection system.

TRANSMISSION

AUTOMATIC TRANSMISSION: An automatic transmission with floor-mounted gear shifter was standard equipment.

MANUAL TRANSMISSION: A six-speed manual transmission was optional.

CHASSIS FEATURES

Wheelbase: 96.2 inches. Overall length: (Base) 178.5 inches.; (ZR-1) 178.5 inches. Height: (Hatchback) 46.3 inches.; (Convertible) 47.3 inches. Width: (Base) 70.7 inches.; (ZR-1) 73.1 inches. Front tread: (All) 57.7 inches. Rear tread: (Base) 59.1 inches.; (ZR-1) 60.6 inches. Standard tires: (front) P255/45ZR-17 Goodyear Eagle GT/(rear) P285/40ZR-17 Goodyear Eagle GT; (ZR-1) P315/35ZR-17 inches rear.

Chevrolet

THE 1994 CORVETTE CONVERTIBLE WITH STANDARD LEATHER SEATS.

TECHNICAL FEATURES

Transmission: Automatic or six-speed manual.. Steering: Rack and pinion (power assisted). Front suspension: unequal-length control arms, single-leaf transverse springs and stabilizer bar. Rear suspension: upper/lower control arms with five links, single-leaf transverse springs, stabilizer bar. Brakes: Anti-lock; power four-wheel disc. Body construction: fiberglass; separate ladder frame with cross-members. Fuel tank: 20 gallons.

OPTIONS

RPO AC1 Power passenger seat ($305). RPO AC3 Power driver seat ($305). RPO AQ9 Sports seats ($625). RPO CC2 Auxiliary hardtop for convertible ($1,995). RPO C2L Dual removable roof panels for coupe ($950). RPO 24S Removable roof panels with blue tint for coupe ($650). RPO 64S Removable roof panels with bronze tint for coupe ($650). RPO FX3 Electronic Selective Ride & Handling system ($1,695). RPO G92 Performance axle ratio 3.07:1 ($50). RPO MN6 Six-speed manual transmission (no-cost option). RPO NG1 New York emission requirements ($100). RPO UJ6 Low tire pressure warning indicator ($325). RPO U1F Delco-Bose stereo system with compact disc changer ($396). RPO WY5 Extended-mobility run-flat tires ($70). RPO YF5 California emissions requirements ($100). RPO Z07 Adjustable suspension package for hatchback coupe ($2,045). RPO ZR1 Special performance package for hatchback coupe ($31,258).

HISTORICAL FOOTNOTES

Calendar-year sales totaled 21,839 Corvettes. Model-year production totaled 23,330.

1995

The big news of 1995 was the final appearance of the ZR-1 performance coupe after several years of availability. The ZR-1 was first announced in 1989, but not actually offered until 1990. Changes on the Corvette included the addition of heavy-duty brakes with larger front rotors as standard equipment, along with new low-rate springs (except ZR-1). DeCarbon gas-charged shock absorbers were used for improved ride quality. In addition to exterior color changes, Corvettes featured a new "gill" panel behind the front wheel openings to help quickly distinguish the 1995 models from predecessors. Other improvements included reinforced interior stitching and a quieter-running cooling fan. Engine and transmission offerings remained unchanged from the year previous. Corvettes came in Dark Purple Metallic; Dark Purple Metallic and Arctic White; Arctic White; Admiral Blue; Black; Bright Aqua Metallic; Polo Green Metallic; Competition Yellow; Torch Red; and Dark Red Metallic. Interiors came in Black; Light Beige; Light Gray; Red; and White. Standard features included a removable body-color roof panel for hatchbacks or a convertible top. All Corvette convertibles except those with Dark Purple Metallic, Arctic White, or Polo Green Metallic finish could be ordered with one of three top colors: Beige, Black, or White cloth top. The Dark Purple Metallic and Arctic White combination was available only with a White convertible top, which was again not available for Polo Green Metallic cars. Leather seats were standard equipment.

Jerry Heasley

THE 1995 CORVETTE ZR-1.

Jerry Heasley

1995 WAS THE LAST YEAR FOR THE GEN-4 ZR-1.

ENGINES

BASE ENGINE: [RPO LT1] V-8. 90-degree overhead valve. Cast iron block and head. Displacement: 350 cid (5.7 liters). Bore and stroke: 4.00 x 3.48 inches. Compression ratio: 10.5:1. Brake hp: 300 at 5000 rpm. Torque: 340 lbs.-ft. at 3600 rpm. Five main bearings. Aluminum cylinder head. Hydraulic valve lifters. Induction: Sequential multiport-fuel injection.

ZR-1 ENGINE: [RPO LT5] V-8. 90-degree overhead valve with four valves per cylinder. Four overhead camshafts. Cast iron block and head. Displacement: 350 cid (5.7 liters). Bore and stroke: 4.00 x 3.48 inches. Compression ratio: 11.0:1. Brake hp: 405 at 5800 rpm. Torque: 385 lbs.-ft. at 5200 rpm. Five main bearings. Aluminum cylinder head. Hydraulic valve lifters. Induction: Sequential multiport-fuel-injection system.

TRANSMISSION

AUTOMATIC TRANSMISSION: An automatic transmission with floor-mounted gear shifter was standard equipment.

MANUAL TRANSMISSION: A six-speed manual transmission was optional.

CHASSIS FEATURES

Wheelbase: 96.2 inches. Overall length: (Base) 178.5 inches.; (ZR-1) 178.5 inches. Height: (Hatchback) 46.3 inches.; (Convertible) 47.3 inches. Width: (Base) 70.7 inches.; (ZR-1) 73.1 inches. Front tread: (All) 57.7 inches. Rear tread: (Base) 59.1 inches.; (ZR-1) 60.6 inches. Standard tires: (front) P255/45ZR-17 Goodyear Eagle GT/(rear) P285/40ZR-17 Goodyear Eagle GT; (ZR-1) P275/40ZR-17 inches front.

TECHNICAL FEATURES

Transmission: Automatic or six-speed manual. Steering: Rack and pinion (power assisted). Front suspension: Unequal-length control arms, single-leaf transverse springs and stabilizer bar. Rear suspension: Upper/lower control arms with five links, single-leaf transverse springs, stabilizer bar. Brakes: Anti-lock; power four-wheel disc. Body construction: Fiberglass; separate ladder frame with cross-members. Fuel tank: 20 gallons.

Jerry Heasley

THE 1995 CORVETTE ZR-1.

OPTIONS

RPO AG1 Power driver seat ($305). RPO AG2 Power passenger seat ($305). RPO AQ9 Sports seats ($625). RPO CC2 Auxiliary hardtop for convertible ($1,995). RPO C2L Dual removable roof panels for coupe ($950). RPO 24S Removable roof panels with blue tint for coupe ($650). RPO 64S Removable roof panels with bronze tint for coupe ($650). RPO FX3 Electronic Selective Ride & Handling system ($1,695). RPO G92 Performance axle ratio 3.07:1 ($50). RPO MN6 Six-speed manual transmission (no-cost option). RPO NG1 New York emission requirements ($100). RPO UJ6 Low tire pressure warning indicator ($325). RPO U1F Delco-Bose stereo system with compact disc changer ($396). RPO WY5 Extended-mobility tires ($100). RPO YF5 California emissions requirements ($100). RPO Z07 Adjustable suspension package for hatchback coupe ($2,045). RPO Z4Z Indy 500 Pace Car Replica for convertibles only ($2,816). RPO ZR-1 Special Performance package for hatchback coupe ($31,258).

HISTORICAL FOOTNOTES

Calendar-year sales totaled 18,966 Corvettes. Model-year production totaled 20,742. For the third time in its existence (also 1978 and 1986), the Corvette was selected as the official pace car for the Indianapolis 500. The 1995 Dark Purple Metallic over Arctic White Corvette was driven by 1960 Indy 500 winner Jim Rathmann. Chevy built a total of 527 cars equipped with the RPO Z4Z Indy 500 Pace Car Replica package that sold for $2,816 over the price of a standard LT1-powered Corvette convertible.

1996

1996 was a landmark year for Corvette enthusiasts. With the demise of the ZR-1, Chevrolet offset the void by introducing two new special edition Corvettes, the Grand Sport and Collector Edition models. The Grand Sport evoked memories of its 1962-63 racing predecessors, sporting Admiral Blue Metallic Paint, a white stripe, red "hash" marks on the left front fender and black five-spoke aluminum wheels. Powering the Grand Sport and optional in all other Corvettes was a 330-hp 5.7-liter LT4 V-8 featuring a specially-prepared crankshaft, steel camshaft, and water pump gears driven by a roller chain. The LT4 was available only with the six-speed manual transmission. The Collector Edition Corvette was produced as a tribute to the final year of production of the fourth-generation Corvette (the fifth-generation model was to debut the following year). The 1996 Collector Edition Corvette featured exclusive Sebring Silver paint, Collector Edition emblems, silver five-spoke aluminum wheels and a 5.7-liter LT1 V-8. On all Corvettes, 1996 marked the introduction of the optional Selective Real Time Damping system that employed sensors at each wheel to measure movement. Data retrieved from each wheel and the Powertrain Control Module was processed by an electronic controller that calculated the damping mode to provide optimum control. Also optional was a Z51 Performance Handling Package available on the Corvette coupe, and tuned for autocross and Gymkhana competition. Standard Corvette models again used the 5.7-liter V-8 with sequential fuel injection and four-speed automatic transmission. Corvettes

Jerry Heasley

THE 1996 CORVETTE COLLECTOR EDITION. ALL CONVERTIBLE TOPS WERE BLACK.

THE 1996 CORVETTE COLLECTOR EDITION.

came in Dark Purple Metallic; Arctic White; Sebring Silver Metallic; Admiral Blue; Black; Bright Aqua Metallic; Polo Green Metallic; Competition Yellow; and Torch Red. Interiors came in Black; Light Beige; Light Gray; Red; and Red and Black. Standard features included a removable body-color roof panel for hatchbacks or a convertible top. All Corvette convertibles except those with code 13, 28, or 45 paint colors could be ordered with one of three cloth top colors: Beige, Black, or White.

Sebring Silver Metallic (code 13) cars came only with Black cloth tops. Admiral Blue (code 28) Grand Sports came only with White cloth tops. Polo Green Metallic (code 45) cars came with Beige or Black cloth tops, but not White. Leather seats were standard equipment.

ENGINES

BASE ENGINE: [RPO LT1] V-8. 90-degree overhead valve. Cast iron block and head. Displacement: 350 cid (5.7 liters). Bore and stroke:

THE 1996 CORVETTE CONVERTIBLE COLLECTOR EDITION.

Jerry Heasley

THE 1996 CORVETTE GRAND SPORT IN ADMIRAL BLUE WITH A WHITE STRIPE.

4.00 x 3.48 inches. Compression ratio: 10.4:1. Brake hp: 300 at 5000 rpm. Torque: 335 lbs.-ft. at 4000 rpm. Five main bearings. Aluminum cylinder head. Hydraulic valve lifters. Induction: Sequential multiport-fuel injection.

OPTIONAL ENGINE: [RPO LT4] V-8. 90-degree overhead valve with four valves per cylinder. Four overhead camshafts. Cast iron block and head. Displacement: 350 cid (5.7 liters). Bore and stroke: 4.00 x 3.48 inches. Compression ratio: 10.8:1. Brake hp: 330 at 5800 rpm. Torque: 340 lbs.-ft. at 4500 rpm. Five main bearings. Aluminum cylinder head. Hydraulic valve lifters. Induction: Sequential multiport-fuel-injection system.

TRANSMISSION

AUTOMATIC TRANSMISSION: An automatic transmission with floor-mounted gear shifter was standard equipment for the LT1.

MANUAL TRANSMISSION: A six-speed manual transmission was mandatory with the optional V-8.

CHASSIS FEATURES

Wheelbase: 96.2 inches. Overall length: (Base) 178.5 inches. Height: (hatchback) 46.3 inches.; (convertible) 47.3 inches. Width: (Hatchback) 70.7 inches.; (Convertible) 73.1 inches. Front tread: (All) 57.7 inches. Rear tread: (All) 59.1 inches. Standard tires: (front) P255/45ZR-17/(rear) P285/40ZR-17; (Grand Sport coupe) (front) P275/40ZR-17/(rear) P315/35ZR-17; (Grand Sport convertible) (front) P255/45ZR-17/(rear) P285/40ZR-17.

TECHNICAL FEATURES

Transmission: Four-speed automatic. Steering: Rack and pinion (power assisted). Front Suspension: Independent SLA forged-alumi-

THE 1996 CORVETTE GRAND SPORT – A TOTAL OF 1,000 CORVETTES HAD THIS OPTION.

num upper and lower control arms and steering knuckle, transverse monoleaf springs, steel stabilizer bar, and spindle offset. Rear suspension: Independent five-link design with tow and camber adjustment, forged-aluminum control links and steering knuckle, transverse monoleaf springs, steel tie rods, stabilizer bar, and tubular U-joint aluminum driveshaft. Brakes: Anti-lock: power four-wheel disc. Body construction: fiberglass; separate ladder frame with cross-members. Fuel tank: 20 gallons.

OPTIONS

RPO AG1 Power driver seat ($305). RPO AG2 Power passenger seat ($305). RPO AQ9 Sports seats ($625). RPO CC2 Auxiliary hardtop for convertible ($1,995). RPO C2L Dual removable roof panels for coupe ($950). RPO 24S Removable roof panels with blue tint for coupe ($650). RPO 64S Removable roof panels with bronze tint for coupe ($650). RPO F45 Electronic Selective Real Time Damping ($1,695). RPO G92 Performance axle ratio 3.07:1 ($50). RPO LT4 350-cid 330-hp V-8 ($1,450). RPO MN6 Six-speed manual transmission (no-cost option). RPO N84 Spare tire delete ($100 credit). RPO UJ6 Low tire pressure warning indicator ($325). RPO U1F Delco-Bose stereo system with compact disc changer ($396). RPO WY5 Extended-mobility tires ($70). RPO Z15 Collector Edition ($1,250). RPO Z16 Grand Sport package ($2,880 with convertible or $3,250). RPO Z51 Performance Handling package ($350).

HISTORICAL FOOTNOTES

Calendar-year sales totaled 17,805 Corvettes. Model-year production totaled 21,536.

1997

It was another landmark year for Corvette in that the 1997 C5 model was the first all-new Corvette in 13 years and only the fifth or sixth (depending upon your viewpoint) major change in the car's 44-year history. The "fifth-generation" Corvette was offered only as a coupe in its debut year. Among the equipment featured for the C5 was a new, more compact 5.7-liter LS1 V-8 that produced 350 hp and 345 lbs.-ft. of torque. A rear-mounted transaxle opened up more interior space and helped maintain a near 50/50 front-to-rear weight distribution. An Electronic Throttle Control system allowed engineers a limitless range of throttle progression. The 1997 Corvette's underbody structure was the stiffest in the car's history and consisted of two full-length, hydro-formed perimeter frame rails coupled to a backbone tunnel. The rails consisted of a single piece of tubular steel, replacing the 14 parts used previously. The cockpit of the all-new Corvette featured a twin-pod design reminiscent of the original 1953 Corvette. The instrument panel contained traditional backlit analog gauges and a digital Driver Information Center that comprised a display of 12 individual readouts in four languages. The new-design blunt tail section allowed for smoother airflow and resulting 0.29 coefficient of drag. The C5 Corvette was offered with a 4L60-E electronic four-speed overdrive automatic as the base transmission and an optional six-speed manual transmission. Corvettes came in Arctic White; Sebring Silver Metallic; Nassau Blue; Black; Light Carmine Red Metallic; Torch Red; and Fairway Green Metallic. Interiors came in Black; Light Gray; and Firethorn Red. Standard features included a removable body-color roof panel. Leather

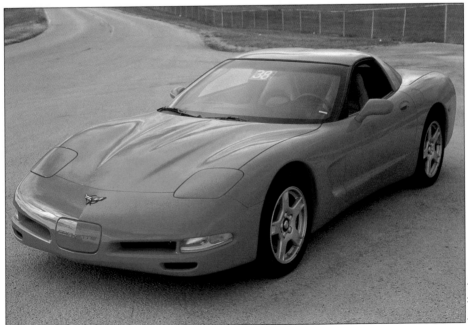

Jerry Heasley

THE 1997 CORVETTE IN TORCH RED.

Jerry Heasley

THE ALL-NEW 1997 C5.

seats were standard equipment.

ENGINE

BASE V-8: [RPO LS1] Overhead valve V-8. Cast aluminum block and head. Displacement: 346 cu. in. (5.7 liters). Bore & stroke: 3.90 x 3.62 in. Compression ratio: 10.1:1. Brake horsepower: 345 at 5600 RPM. Torque: 350 lb.-ft. at 4400 RPM. Hydraulic valve lifters. Sequential fuel injection.

TRANSMISSION

AUTOMATIC TRANSMISSION: A 4L60-E electronic overdrive transmission with floor-mounted gear shifter was standard equipment.

MANUAL TRANSMISSION: A six-speed manual transmission was optional.

CHASSIS FEATURES

Wheelbase: 104.5 in. Overall length: 179.7 in. Height: 47.7 in. Width: 73.6 in. Front tread: 62.0 in. Rear tread: 62.1 in. Standard tires:

(front) P245/45ZR-17, (rear) P275/40ZR-18.

TECHNICAL FEATURES

Transmission: AL60-E electronic four-speed automatic. Steering: Rack and pinion (power assisted). Front suspension: Independent SLA forged-aluminum upper and lower control arms and steering knuckle, transverse monoleaf springs, steel stabilizer bar, and spindle offset. Rear suspension: Independent five-link design with tow and camber adjustment, cast-aluminum upper and lower control arms and knuckle, transverse monoleaf springs, steel tie rods and stabilizer bar, and tubular U-jointed metal matrix composite driveshaft. Brakes: Anti-lock: power four-wheel disc. Body construction: Fiberglass; integral perimeter frame with center backbone/all-welded steel body frame construction. Fuel tank: 19.1 gallons.

OPTIONS

RPO CJ2 Dual-zone air conditioning

Jerry Heasley

THE 1997 CORVETTE.

($365). RPO AQ9 Adjustable leather bucket seats, requires six-way power passenger seat ($625). RPO G92 Performance axle ratio, not available with six-speed manual transmission ($100). RPO CYF California emission system ($170). RPO JL4 Active-handling System ($500). RPO Z51 Performance handling Package with Bilstein adjustable Ride-Control system ($350). RPO F45 Continuously Variable Real Time Damping, not available with RPO Z51 Pkg ($1,695). RPO AAB Memory package to recall settings for outside rearview mirrors, radio, power seats, and heating-ventilation and air-conditioning controls ($150). RPO U1S Remote CD changer ($600). RPO UN0 Delco/Bose music system ($100). RPO V49 Front license plate frame ($15). RPO T96 Fog lamps

($65). RPO D42 Luggage shade and cargo net ($50). RPO B34 Front floor mats ($25). RPO B84 Body side moldings ($75). RPO C2L Dual body color-keyed roof panel and blue transparent roof panel ($950). RPO CC3 Roof panel with blue tint ($650). RPO AG2 Power six-way passenger seat ($305).

HISTORICAL FOOTNOTES

The all-new C5 Corvette was designed under the direction of John Cafaro. *American Woman Motorscene* magazine named the 1997 Corvette its "Most likely to be immortalized" car. The C5 Corvette could do five second 0-to-60-mph runs and cover the quarter mile in 13.28 seconds at 107.6 mph according to Vette magazine.

1998

In its 45th year, the Corvette returned to offering convertible and coupe models with the debut of a "topless" version of the C5 Corvette. The convertible's glass rear window was heated and the top had an "express-down" feature that released the tonneau cover and automatically lowered the windows part way at the touch of a button. New-for-1998 was a magnesium wheel option featuring lightweight wheels with a unique bronze tone. Standard features included stainless steel exhaust system; Extended Mobility Tires capable of running for 200 miles with no air pressure; dual heated electric remote breakaway outside rearview mirrors; daytime running lamps; and five-mph front and rear bumpers. The LS1 V-8 and four-speed automatic transmission were again the standard offering, with the T56 six-speed manual transmission optional. Corvettes were available in Arctic White; Light Pewter Metallic; Sebring Silver Metallic; Radar Blue (Pace Car only); Nassau Blue Metallic; Navy Blue; Black; Light Carmine Red Metallic; Aztec Gold; Torch Red; and Fairway Green Metallic. Leather seats were standard and came in Black; Medium Pearl Purple Metallic; Light Oak; Light Gray; and Firethorn Red. Convertible tops came in Black, Light Oak, and White.

ENGINES

BASE V-8: [RPO LS1] V-8 Overhead valve. Cast aluminum block and head. Displacement: 346 cid. (5.7 liters). Bore and stroke: 3.90 x 3.62 inches. Compression ratio: 10.1:1. Brake horsepower: 345 at 5600 rpm. Torque: 350 lbs.-ft. at 4400 rpm. Cast aluminum block and heads. Hydraulic valve lifters, two valves per cylinder. Induction: Sequential fuel injection.

TRANSMISSION

AUTOMATIC TRANSMISSION: A Turbo Hydera-Matc automatic transmission with floor-mounted gear shifter was standard equipment..

MANUAL TRANSMISSION: A four-speed manual transmission was optional.

CHASSIS FEATURES

Wheelbase: 104.5 in. Overall length: 179.7

Jerry Heasley

THE 1998 CORVETTE CONVERTIBLE IN BLACK.

Chevrolet

THE 1998 CORVETTE INDIANAPOLIS 500 PACE CAR.

in. Height: 47.7 in. Width: 73.6 in. Front tread: 62.0 in. Rear tread: 62.1 in. Standard tires: (front) P245/45ZR-17, (rear) P275/40ZR-18.

TECHNICAL FEATURES

Transmission: Automatic or optional four-speed manual. Steering: Rack and pinion (power assisted). Front suspension: independent SLA forged-aluminum upper and lower control arms and steering knuckle, transverse monoleaf springs, steel stabilizer bar, and spindle offset. Rear suspension: Independent five-link design with tow and camber adjustment, cast-aluminum upper and lower control arms and knuckle, transverse monoleaf springs, steel tie rods and stabilizer bar, and tubular U-jointed metal matrix composite driveshaft. Brakes: Anti-lock; power four-wheel disc. Body construction: fiberglass; integral perimeter frame with center backbone. All-welded steel body frame construction. Fuel tank: 19.1 gallons.

OPTIONS

RPO AAB Memory package to recall settings for outside rearview mirrors, radio, power seats and heating-ventilation and air-conditioning controls ($150). RPO AG2 Power six-way passenger seat ($305). RPO AQ9 Sport seats ($625). RPO B34 Front floor mats ($25). RPO B84 Body side moldings ($75). RPO CC3 Roof panel with blue tint ($650). RPO C2L Dual body color-keyed roof panel and blue transparent roof panel ($950). RPO CJ2 Dual-zone air conditioning ($365). RPO D42 Luggage shade and cargo net ($50). RPO F45 Continuously Variable Real Time Damping, not available with RPO Z51 package ($1,695). RPO G92 Performance axle ratio, not available with six-speed manual transmission ($100). RPO JL4 Active-handling system ($500). RPO MN6 Six-speed manual transmission ($815). RPO NG1 Massachusetts/New York emissions requirements ($170). RPO N73 Custom magnesium wheels ($3,000). RPO T96 Fog lamps

Chevrolet

THE 1998 CORVETTE – 19,235 COUPES WERE BUILT THIS YEAR.

Chevrolet

11,849 RAGTOPS WERE BUILT FOR 1998.

($65). RPO UN0 Delco-Bose music system ($100). RPO U1S Remote CD changer ($600). RPO V49 Front license plate frame ($15). RPO CYF California emissions system ($170). RPO Z4Z Indy Pace Car package ($5,039 with automatic transmission or $5,804 with manual transmission). RPO Z51 Performance handling package with Bilstein adjustable Ride-Control system ($350).

HISTORICAL FOOTNOTES

Model-year production was 31,084 units. For the fourth time (1978, 1986, 1995, 1998), a Corvette was selected to pace the Indianapolis 500 with Indy 500 veteran Parnelli Jones driving the purple and yellow pace car. Corvette made its long-awaited return to Trans-Am racing successful by placing first in the 1998 season-opening event on the street circuit at Long Beach, California, in the No. 8 AutoLink Corvette driven by veteran road racer Paul Gentilozzi.

1999

The fifth-generation Corvette, in its third model year, added a fixed-roof hardtop to the lineup that already consisted of coupe and convertible body styles. The fixed-roof Corvette was the first offered since the legendary second-generation Sting Rays of 1963-1967. The new hardtop Corvette featured body lines unique to that model and they subtly set it apart from the coupe and convertible. Its standard equipment included the six-speed manual transmission (an automatic transmission was not available), limited-slip rear axle with 3.42:1 ratio and Z51 suspension with stiff springs, large stabilizer bars and large mono-tube shock absorbers. The Z51 suspension was also optional on coupes and convertibles. All 1999 Corvettes were powered by the 345-hp 5.7-liter LS1 V-8. The coupe and convertible used the 4L60-E electronically-controlled four-speed automatic overdrive transmission, with the six-speed manual unit optional. New optional features for 1999 Corvette coupe and convertible models included a Heads-Up Display (HUD) system which projected key instrumentation readouts onto the windshield

to allow drivers to view vehicle vitals without taking their eyes off the road; Twilight Sentinel, with delayed shutoff of headlamps, allowed for exterior illumination after the ignition was turned off; and they also featured a power telescoping steering column that allowed drivers to more accurately tailor the position of the steering wheel to their specific needs. Optional again on all 1999 Corvettes was the Active-Handling System (AHS). AHS operated in harmony with the anti-lock braking and traction-control systems to selectively apply any of the four brakes in an effort to help the driver counteract and diffuse dangerous handling characteristics such as oversteer and understeer. The Corvette's standard equipment list included next-generation dual airbags; air conditioning; leather seating; power door locks and windows; a PassKey II theft-deterrent system; electronic speed control; an electronic Driver Information Center; and Remote Function Actuation with Remote Keyless Entry. Colors for 1999 C5 Corvette coupes and convertibles were: Arctic White; Light Pewter Metallic; Sebring Silver Metallic; Nassau

Jerry Heasley

THE 1999 CORVETTE CONVERTIBLE.

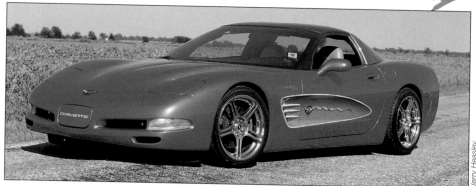

Jerry Heasley

THE 1999 CORVETTE COUPE.

Blue Metallic; Navy Blue; Black; Torch Red; and Magnetic Red II Clearcoat. The fixed-roof hardtop came only in five colors: Artic White; Light Pewter Metallic; Nassau Blue; Black; and Torch Red. Leather interiors were standard and came in Black; Light Oak; Light Gray; and Red. Convertible tops were available in White, Black, and Light Oak.

ENGINE

BASE ENGINE: [LS6] V-8 Overhead valve. Cast aluminum block and head. Displacement: 346 cid. (5.7 liters). Bore and stroke: 3.90 x 3.62 in. Compression ratio: 10.1:1. Brake horsepower: 345 at 5600 rpm. Torque: 350 lbs.-ft. at 4400 rpm. Hydraulic valve lifters. Induction: Sequential multiport fuel injection.

TRANSMISSION

AUTOMATIC TRANSMISSION: A Turbo Hydera-Matc automatic transmission with floor-mounted gear shifter was standard equipment.

MANUAL TRANSMISSION: A four-speed manual transmission was optional.

CHASSIS FEATURES

Wheelbase: 104.5 inches. Overall length: 179.7 inches. Height: 47.9 inches. Width: 73.6 inches. Front tread: 62 inches. Rear tread: 62.1 inches. Standard tires: (front) P245/45ZR-17, (rear) P275/40ZR-18.

TECHNICAL FEATURES

Transmission: [Coupe and Convertible] four-speed overdrive automatic; [Hardtop] six-speed manual. Steering: Rack and pinion (power assist-

Jerry Heasley

THE 1999 CORVETTE WITH 345-HP LS1 V-8 AND BLACK LEATHER INTERIOR.

Chevrolet

THE 1999 CORVETTE INTERIOR.

ed). Front suspension: Independent SLA forged-aluminum upper and pressure-cast aluminum lower control arms, forged aluminum steering knuckle, transverse monoleaf springs, steel stabilizer bar, and spindle offset. Rear suspension: Independent five-link design with toe and camber adjustment, cast-aluminum upper and lower control arms and knuckle, transverse monoleaf springs, steel tie rods and stabilizer bar, and tubular U-jointed metal matrix composite driveshafts. Brakes: Anti-lock; power four-wheel disc. Body construction: Fiberglass; integral perimeter frame with center backbone/all-welded steel body frame construction. Fuel tank: 19.1 gallons.

OPTIONS

RPO AAB Memory package to recall settings for outside rearview mirrors, radio, power seats and heating/ventilation and air-conditioning controls for coupe and convertible ($150). RPO AG1 Power six-way passenger seat, hardtop only ($305). RPO AP9 Parcel net, hardtop only ($15). RPO AQ9 Sport seats, coupe and convertible ($625). RPO B34 Front floor mats ($25). RPO B84 Body side moldings ($75). RPO CC3 Roof panel with blue tint ($650). RPO C2L Dual body color-keyed roof panel and blue transparent roof panel ($950). RPO CJ2 Dual-zone air conditioning ($365). RPO D42 Luggage shade and cargo net ($50). RPO F45 Continuously Variable Real Time Damping, not available with RPO Z51 package or hard top ($1,695). RPO G92 Perfor-

mance 3.15:1 axle ratio with automatic transmission, not available with six-speed manual transmission ($100). RPO JL4 Active-handling System ($500). RPO LS1 5.7-liter sequential fuel-injection aluminum V-8 (no-cost option). RPO MN6 Six-speed manual transmission, no charge in hardtop, in other models ($825). RPO N37 Tilt-telescope power steering column in coupe and convertible ($350). RPO N73 Custom magnesium wheels ($3,000). RPO R8C National Corvette Museum factory delivery option ($490). RPO T82 Twilight Sentinel for coupe or convertible ($60). RPO T96 Fog lamps ($69). RPO TR6 Lighting package, hardtop only ($95). RPO UN0 Delco-Bose music system ($100). RPO U1S Remote CD changer ($600). RPO UV6 Heads-up display ($375). RPO UZ6 Bose speaker and amplifier, hardtop only ($820). RPO V49 Front license plate frame ($15). RPO CYF California emission system ($170). RPO Z51 Performance handling Package ($350). RPO 86U Magnetic Red Metallic paint, coupe and convertible only ($500).

HISTORICAL FOOTNOTES

A fifth-generation Corvette C5 was the official pace car of the 67th running of the 24 Hours of LeMans in France. Additionally, Chevrolet introduced the Corvette C5-R, a General Motors-engineered and factory-backed GT2-classed sports car that competed in select U.S. and international sports car races.

2000

"Still eliciting the passion of bargain-minded speed fiends, the Chevrolet Corvette delivers power, handling and style at a relatively reasonable price," said Motor Trend in its October 1999 "Complete Buyer's Guide 2000 & 2001 New Cars" issue. As in 1999, the hardtop was the "loss leader" model from a pricing and marketing standpoint, but the stripped-for-high-performance model from the enthusiast's view. The Goodyear Eagle F1 tires and an upgraded version of the Z51 Performance Handling suspension package were offered with this model. A coupe and a convertible remained available. New exterior and interior color options were the main changes for 2000. A new five-spoke aluminum wheel design with an optional high-polish version was made available. The Corvette's standard equipment list again included next-generation dual airbags; air conditioning;

leather seating; power door locks and windows; a PassKey II theft-deterrent system; electronic speed control; an electronic Driver Information Center; and Remote Function Actuation with Remote Keyless Entry. Colors for 2000 Corvette C5 Coupes and Convertibles were: Arctic White; Light Pewter Metallic; Sebring Silver Metallic; Nassau Blue Metallic; Navy Blue Metallic; Black; Torch Red; Millennium Yellow Clear Coat; Magnetic Red II Clear Coat and Dark Bowling Green Metallic. Leather interiors were standard and came in Black; Light Oak; Torch Red; and Light Gray. Convertible tops were available in White, Black, and Light Oak.

ENGINE

BASE ENGINE: [LS6] V-8: Overhead valve V-8. Cast aluminum block and head. Displacement: 346 cid. (5.7 liters). Bore and stroke: 3.90 x 3.62 inches. Compression ratio: 10.1:1. Brake

THE 2000 CORVETTE FAMILY: HARDTOP, COUPE AND CONVERTIBLE.

Chevrolet

Chevrolet

THE 2000 CORVETTE COUPE IN TORCH RED.

horsepower: 345 at 5600 rpm. Torque: 350 lbs.-ft. at 4400 rpm. Hydraulic valve lifters. Sequential multiport fuel injection.

TRANSMISSION

AUTOMATIC TRANSMISSION: A Turbo Hydera-Matc automatic transmission with floor-mounted gear shifter was standard equipment..

MANUAL TRANSMISSION: A four-speed manual transmission was optional.

CHASSIS FEATURES

Wheelbase: 104.5 inches. Overall length: 179.7 inches. Height: [Coupe and Hardtop] 47.7 inches.; [Convertible] 47.8 inches. Width: 73.6 inches. Front tread: 62 inches. Rear tread: 62.1 inches. Standard tires: (front) P245/45ZR-17, (rear) P275/40ZR-18.

TECHNICAL FEATURES

Transmission: [Coupe and Convertible] four-speed overdrive automatic; [Hardtop] six-speed manual. Steering: Rack and pinion (power assisted). Front suspension: Independent SLA forged-aluminum upper and pressure-cast aluminum lower control arms, forged aluminum steering knuckle, transverse monoleaf springs, steel stabilizer bar, and spindle offset. Rear suspension: Independent five-link design with toe and camber adjustment, cast-aluminum upper and lower control arms and knuckle, transverse monoleaf springs, steel tie rods and stabilizer bar, and tubular U-jointed metal matrix composite driveshafts. Brakes: Anti-lock; power four-wheel disc. Body construction: Fiberglass; integral perimeter frame with center backbone; all-welded steel body frame construction. Fuel tank: 19.1 gallons.

OPTIONS

RPO 1SA coupe and convertible base equipment group (no-cost option). RPO AAB Memory package to recall settings for outside rearview mirrors, radio, power seats and heating/ventilation and air-conditioning controls for coupe and convertible ($150). RPO AG1 Power six-way passenger seat, hardtop only ($305). RPO AP9 Parcel net, hardtop only ($15). RPO AQ9 Sport seats, coupe and convertible, requires AG2 ($625). RPO B34 Front floor mats ($25). RPO B84 Body side moldings ($75). RPO CC3 Roof panel with blue tint ($650). RPO C2L Dual body color-keyed roof panel and blue transparent roof panel ($1,100). RPO CJ2 Dual-zone air conditioning ($365). RPO CV3 Mexico export (no-cost option).

Chevrolet

THE 2000 CORVETTE COUPE.

RPO D42 Luggage shade and cargo net for coupe ($50). RPO DD0 Electronic monochromatic mirrors (N/A). RPO EXP Export option (N/A). RPO FE1 Base suspension (N/A). RPO FE3 Sport suspension, included with Z51 (N/A). RPO FE9 Federal emissions (no-cost option). RPO F45 Selective Real Time Damping, not available with RPO Z06 package ($1,695). RPO G92 Performance 3.15:1 axle ratio, for automatic transmission only ($300). RPO GU2 2.73:1 standard axle ratio with M30 automatic transmission (N/A). RPO GU6 3.42:1 standard rear axle ratio with manual transmission (N/A). RPO JL4 Active-handling System ($500). RPO LS1 5.7-liter sequential fuel-injection aluminum V-8 (no-cost option). RPO MN6 Six-speed manual transmission, no charge in hardtop, in other models ($815). RPO MX0 M30 automatic transmission, included in G92 performance axle (no-cost option). RPO NB8 California and Northeast emissions requirements (no-cost option). RPO NC7 Emissions override. RPO NG1 Massachusetts and New York emissions requirements (no-cost option). RPO N37 Tilt-telescope power steering column in coupe and convertible ($350). RPO N73 Custom magnesium wheels ($2,000). RPO R8C National Corvette Museum factory delivery option ($490). RPO T82 Twilight Sentinel for coupe or convertible ($100). RPO T96 Fog lamps for coupe or convertible only ($69). RPO TR6 Lighting package, hardtop only ($95). RPO UN0 Delco-Bose music system with compact disc changer ($100). RPO U1S Remote 12-disc CD changer ($600). RPO UV6 Heads-up display ($375). RPO UZ6 Bose speaker and amplifier, hardtop only ($820). RPO V49 Front license plate frame ($15). RPO XGG Front tires P245/45ZR-17 (no-cost option). RPO CYF California emission system (no-cost option). RPO Z15 Gymkhana-Autocross package for hardtop, includes MN6, Z51, XGG, YGH, and GUG (no-cost option). RPO Z49 Canadian options (no-cost option). RPO Z51 Performance handling package ($350). RPO 79U Millennium Yellow paint with tint ($500). RPO 86U Magnetic Red Metallic Clear Coat paint, coupe and convertible only ($500).

HISTORICAL FOOTNOTES

Model-year production was 33,682 cars. A total of 3,578 of them left the factory with optional Millennium Yellow paint in honor of the Y2K year.

2001

The 2001 Corvette continued as a two-door, two-passenger performance sports car available in three trims ranging from a base coupe to a convertible to an all-new Z06 higher-performance edition. At new-model-introduction time the coupe was equipped with a standard 350-cid 350-hp Chevrolet LS1 V-8 and four-speed automatic transmission. A six-speed manual transmission was optional. The Corvette Z06 included a 350-cid 385-hp Chevrolet LS6 V-8 and a unique six-speed manual transmission with overdrive. This transmission featured more aggressive gearing for quicker acceleration and more usable torque at various speeds. A built-in temperature-sensing unit was designed to alert the driver when transmission oil temperature got too high. The Goodyear tires on the Z06 were made especially for it and were an inch wider than standard tires front and rear, but 23 pounds lighter. The Z06 also featured a windshield and backlight made of thinner glass and a titanium exhaust system to reduce its weight

by nearly 40 pounds. Standard on the C5 coupe was air conditioning; driver airbag; passenger airbag; alloy wheels; anti-lock brakes; anti-theft system; cruise control; rear defogger; keyless entry; power locks; power mirrors; heated side mirrors; power steering; power windows; AM/FM anti-theft radio with cassette; leather-trimmed power driver's seat; tachometer; tilt steering; automatic transmission; and Traction Control system. The C5 convertible came with all of the same standard equipment, plus a power antenna. The Z06 was basically equipped like the coupe, but with AM/FM cassette and radio optional and the automatic transmission was not available. Colors for 2001 Corvette Z06 Hardtops were: Quicksilver; Speedway White; Black; Torch Red; and Millennium Yellow Clear Coat. The standard Z06 Hardtop leather interiors came in Black; and Black with Torch Red inserts. Colors for 2001 Corvette C5 coupes and convertibles were: Light Pewter Metallic; Quicksilver Metallic; Navy Blue Metallic;

Jerry Heasley

THE 2001 Z06 CORVETTE.

Jerry Heasley

THE 2001 CORVETTE INTERIOR.

Jerry Heasley

THE 2001 CORVETTE COUPE.

Speedway White; Black; Torch Red; Millennium Yellow Clear Coat; Magnetic Red-II Clear Coat; and Dark Bowling Green Metallic. Leather interiors for Coupes and Convertibles came in Black; Light Oak; Firethorn Red; and Light Gray. Convertible Tops came in White, Black, and Light Oak.

ENGINES

BASE ENGINE: [LS1] V-8: Overhead valve V-8. Cast aluminum block and head. Displacement: 346 cid. (5.7 liters). Bore and stroke: 3.90 x 3.62 inches. Compression ratio: 10.1:1. Brake horsepower: 350 at 5600 rpm. Torque: 360 lbs.-ft. at 4000 rpm. Hydraulic valve lifters. Induction: Sequential multiport fuel injection.

OPTIONAL ENGINE: [LS6] V-8 Overhead valve. Cast aluminum block and head. Displacement: 346 cid. (5.7 liters). Bore and stroke: 3.90 x 3.62 inches. Compression ratio: 10.5:1. Brake

Jerry Hasley

FIVE GENERATIONS OF CORVETTES.

horsepower: 385 at 6000 rpm. Torque: 385 lbs.-ft. at 4800 rpm. Hydraulic valve lifters. Induction: Sequential multiport fuel injection.

TRANSMISSION

AUTOMATIC TRANSMISSION: A four-speed automatic transmission with floor-mounted gear shifter was standard equipment in coupes and convertibles.

MANUAL TRANSMISSION: A unique six-speed manual transmission with floor-mounted gear shifter was standard equipment in Z06. The MNG six-speed manual transmission was optional in coupes and convertibles.

CHASSIS FEATURES

Wheelbase: 104.5 inches. Overall length: 179.7 inches. Height: (coupe and hardtop) 47.7 inches.; (convertible) 47.8 inches. Width: 73.6 inches. Front tread: 62 inches. Rear tread: 62.1 inches. Standard tires coupe and convertible: (front) P245/45ZR-17, (rear) P275/40ZR-18. Standard tires Z06: (front) P265/40ZR-17, (rear) P295/35ZR-18.

TECHNICAL FEATURES

Transmission: (Coupe and Convertible) Four-speed overdrive automatic; (Hardtop) Six-speed manual. Steering: Rack and pinion (power assisted). Front suspension: Independent SLA forged-aluminum upper and pressure-cast aluminum lower control arms, forged aluminum steering knuckle, transverse monoleaf springs, steel stabilizer bar, and spindle offset. Rear suspension: Independent five-link design with toe and camber adjustment, cast-aluminum upper and lower control arms and knuckle, transverse monoleaf springs, steel tie rods and stabilizer bar, and tubular U-jointed metal matrix composite driveshafts. Brakes: Anti-lock; power four-wheel disc. Body construction: Fiberglass; integral perimeter frame with center backbone/all-welded steel body frame construction. Fuel tank: 19.1 gallons.

Z06 OPTIONS

RPO AAB Memory package to recall settings for outside rearview mirrors, radio, power seats, heating-ventilation, and air-conditioning controls for coupe and convertible ($150). RPO AG1 Power six-way driver seat, hardtop only ($305). RPO B34 Front floor mats ($25). RPO B84 Body side moldings ($75). RPO CJ2 Dual-zone air conditioning ($365). RPO CV3 Mexico export (no-cost option). RPO DD0 Electronic monochromatic mirrors ($120). RPO EXP Export option (N/A). RPO FE4 suspension, includes RPO M12 six-speed manual transmission unique to Z06 (N/A). RPO GU6 3.42:1 standard rear axle ratio with manual transmission (no-cost option). RPO NB8 California and Northeast emissions requirements (no-cost option). RPO NC7 Federal emissions override (no-cost option). RPO NG1 Massachusetts and New York emissions requirements (no-cost option). RPO N37 Tilt-telescope power steering column in coupe and convertible ($350). RPO R6M New Jersey surcharge, mandatory in New Jersey ($252). RPO R8C National Corvette Museum factory delivery option ($490). RPO V49 Front license plate frame ($15). RPO YF5 California emission system (no-cost option). RPO Z49 Canadian options (no-cost option). RPO 79U Millennium Yellow paint with tint ($500).

COUPE AND CONVERTIBLE OPTIONS

RPO 1SA Option package coupe and convertible base equipment group (no-cost option). RPO 1SB Option Package includes RPO 1SA ($1,700 on coupe and $1,800 for convertible). RPO 1SC Option Package includes RPO 1SB ($2,700 on coupe and $2,600 on convertible). RPO AAB Memory package to recall settings for outside rearview mirrors, radio, power seats, heating-ventilation, and air-conditioning controls, requires CJ2 ($150). RPO AG1 Power six-way driver seat, standard on Z06 ($305). RPO AN4 Child seat tether (N/A). RPO AP9 Luggage shade and parcel net ($50). RPO B34 Front floor mats ($25). RPO B84 Body side moldings ($75). RPO CC3 Transparent roof panel with blue tint ($750). RPO C2L Dual body color-keyed roof panel and blue transparent roof panel ($1,200). RPO CV3 Mexico export (no-cost option). RPO DD0 Electronic monochromatic mirrors ($120). RPO EXP Export option (N/A). RPO FE1 Base suspension (N/A). RPO FE3 Sport suspension, included with Z51 (N/A). RPO FE9 Federal emissions (no-cost option). RPO F45 Selective Real Time Damping, not available with Z06 ($1,695). RPO 79U Millennium Yellow paint with tint ($600). RPO G92 Performance 3.15:1 axle ratio, for automatic transmission only ($300). RPO GU2 2.73:1 standard axle ratio with M30 automatic transmission (N/A). RPO GU6 3.42:1 standard rear axle ratio with manual transmission (N/A). RPO LS1 5.7-liter sequential fuel-injection alumium V-8 (no-cost option). RPO MN6 Six-speed manual transmission, no charge in hardtop, in other models ($815). RPO MX0 M30 automatic transmission, included in G92 performance axle (no-cost option). RPO NB8 California and Northeast emissions requirements (no-cost option). RPO NC7 Emissions override (no-cost option). RPO NG1 Massachusetts and New York emissions requirements (no-cost option). RPO N37 Tilt-telescope power steering column ($350). RPO N73 Sport magnesium wheels ($2,000). RPO QD4 Domestic standard five-spoke wheels (no-cost option). RPO QF5 Deluxe high-polish wheels ($1,250). RPO R6M New Jersey surcharge, mandatory in New Jersey ($252). RPO R8C National Corvette Museum factory delivery option ($490). RPO UN0 Delco-Bose music system with compact disc changer ($100). RPO U1S Remote 12-disc CD changer ($600). RPO V49 Front license plate frame ($15). RPO XGG Front tires P245/45ZR-17 (no-cost option). RPO YGH Rear tire P275/40ZR-18 (no-cost option). RPO YF5 California emission system (no-cost option). RPO Z49 Canadian options (no-cost option). RPO Z51 Performance handling package ($350). RPO 86U Magnetic Red Metallic Clear Coat paint ($600).

HISTORICAL FOOTNOTES

Automobile Magazine awarded the 2001 Corvette Z06 "Automobile of the Year" honors. In its August 2000 issue, Road and Track said of the Z06 "The Empire has struck back in big numbers." That same month, a *Motor Trend* test driver tested a Z06 and reported, "I did things in the Corvette I wouldn't consider in the Cobra R, things that would result in an off-track excursion and maybe a big crash in the Dodge RT/10." The Automobile Journalists Association of Canada gave the Corvette Z06 its 2001 "Car of the Year Award" for best new sports and performance car.

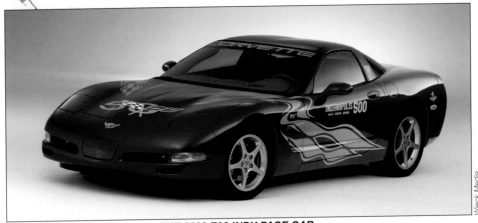

Wieck Media

THE 2002 Z06 INDY PACE CAR.

2002

In 2002, Chevrolet was looking forward to celebrating the Corvette's 50th anniversary. All 2002 Corvettes had a second-generation Active Handling system as standard equipment. This system featured dynamic rear brake proportioning to prevent rear wheel lockup, plus rear brake stability control to assist drivers in maintaining control under light braking and high-acceleration conditions. It also had integral traction control calibrated to allow better power and handling, while controlling excessive wheel spin. The system's on/off switch and "Competitive Mode" enabled drivers to disengage the traction control feature without giving up Active Handling's other benefits. The 2002 automatic transmission cooler case was constructed of lightweight cast aluminum, replacing stainless steel.

The Z06 Corvette, first introduced in 2001, was based on the former hardtop model and inspired by the legendary Z06 option of the '60s. It was aimed at true performance enthusiasts at the upper end of the high-performance market. For 2002, a 20-hp boost made the Z06 the quickest production Corvette ever. This improvement was the result of new hollow-stem valves, a higher-lift camshaft, a low-restriction mass air flow (MAF) sensor and a new low-restriction air cleaner.

Eliminating the PUP converter from the exhaust system enabled better flow of spent gasses and reduced vehicle weight without compromising the car's NLEV (National Low Emission Vehicle) status. The Z06-specific FE4 high-performance suspension system featured a larger front stabilizer bar, revised shock valving, a stiffer rear leaf spring and specific camber settings—all calibrated for maximum control during high-speed operation. The Z06 also had new rear shock valving for a more controlled ride. Although retaining the 2001 design and color, the unique aluminum Z06 wheels were now produced using a casting, rather than a forging, process. The magnesium wheel option for coupes and convertibles was no longer available. Hydroformed frame rails and a four-wheel independent front suspension with cast-aluminum upper and lower A-arms were other Z06 features. The Z06 (and C-5 Corvettes equipped with the Z51 package) now had aluminum front stabilizer bar links and reduced weight. The rear suspension had a transverse leaf spring system. Now standard on Z06s, the Head-Up Display (HUD) system projected the speedometer and many other gauges digitally on the windshield, ahead of the steering wheel, enabling the driver to keep his or her eyes on the road ahead.

A SPEEDWAY WHITE 2002 C5 CORVETTE.

Wieck Media

THE Z06 WAS LEAN AND MEAN FROM ALL ANGLES IN 2002.

Wieck Media

ENGINES

BASE ENGINE: [LS1] V-8: Overhead-valve V-8. Cast-aluminum block and head. Displacement: 346 cu. in. (5.7 liters). Bore & stroke: 3.90 x 3.62 in. Compression ratio: 10.1:1. Brake hp: 350 at 5600 rpm. Torque: (six-speed manual) 375 lbs.-ft. at 4400 rpm; (automatic) 360 lbs.-ft. at 4000 rpm. Hydraulic valve lifters. Sequential multiport fuel injection.

OPTIONAL ENGINE: [LS6] V-8: Overhead-valve V-8. Cast-aluminum block and head. Displacement: 346 cu. in. (5.7 liters). Bore & stroke: 3.90 x 3.62 in. Compression ratio: 10.5:1. Brake hp: 405 at 6000 rpm. Torque: 400 lbs.-ft. at 4800 rpm. Hydraulic valve lifters. Sequential multiport fuel injection.

TRANSMISSION

AUTOMATIC TRANSMISSION: A 4L60-E four-speed automatic transmission with floor-mounted gear shifter was standard equipment in coupes and convertibles.

MANUAL TRANSMISSION: A unique six-speed manual transmission with floor-mounted gear shifter was standard equipment in the Z06. A six-speed manual transmission was optional in coupes and convertibles.

CHASSIS DATA

Wheelbase: 104.5 in. Overall length: 179.7 in. Height: (coupe and hardtop) 47.7 in.; (convertible) 47.8 in. Width: 73.6 in. Front tread: 62.0 in. Rear tread: 62.1 in. Standard tires for coupe and convertible: (front) P245/45ZR17, (rear) P275/40ZR18. Standard tires for Z06: (front) P265/40ZR-17, (rear) P295/35ZR-18.

TECHNICAL

Transmission: (coupe and convertible) four-speed overdrive automatic; (hardtop) six-speed

Wieck Media

THE 2002 CORVETTE INSTRUMENT PANEL.

manual. Steering: speed sensitive power-assisted rack-and-pinion. Suspension (front): short/long arm (SLA) double wishbone, cast aluminum upper & lower control arms, transverse-mounted composite leaf spring, monotube shock absorber. Suspension (rear): short/long arm (SLA) double wishbone, cast aluminum upper & lower control arms, transverse-mounted composite leaf spring, monotube shock absorber. Brakes: Anti-lock: power four-wheel disc. Body construction: fiberglass; integral perimeter frame with center backbone/all-welded steel body frame construction. Fuel tank: 19.1 gallons.

COUPE AND CONVERTIBLE OPTIONS

RPO 1SA Option Package coupe and convertible base equipment group (N/A). RPO 1SB Option Package includes RPO 1SA ($1,750 on coupe and $1,850 for convertible). RPO AAB Memory Package to recall settings for outside rearview mirrors, radio, power seats and heating-ventilation and air-conditioning controls, requires CJ2 ($175). RPO AG1 Power six-way driver seat, standard on Z06 ($305). RPO AG2 Power passenger seat (N/A). RPO AN4 Child seat tether (N/A). RPO AP9 parcel net, coupe only ($15). RPO AQ9 Driver and passenger reclining bucket seats (N/A). AR9 Driver and passenger European bucket seats (N/A). RPO B34 Front floor mats ($25). RPO B84 Body side moldings ($150). RPO C2L dual roof package ($1,200). RPO C60 Basic climate control system (N/A). RPO CC3 Transparent roof panel with blue tint ($750). RPO CF7 Non-transparent roof panel (N/A). RPO CJ2 Auto Climate Control air conditioning (N/A). RPO CV3 Mexico export (N/A). RPO DD0 Electronic monochromatic mirrors ($120). RPO EXP Export option (N/A). RPO F45 Selective Real Time Damping, not available with Z06 ($1,695). RPO FE1 Base suspension (N/A). RPO FE3 Sport suspension, included with Z51 (N/A). RPO FE9 Federal emissions certificate (N/A). RPO G92 Performance axle ratio, 3.15:1 for automatic transmission only (N/A). RPO GU2 2.73:1 standard axle ratio with M30 automatic transmission (N/A). RPO GU6 3.42:1 standard rear axle ratio with manual transmission (N/A). RPO LS1 5.7-liter sequential fuel-injection aluminum V-8 (N/A). RPO M30 four-speed automatic transmission (N/A). RPO MM6 Six-speed manual transmission, no charge in hardtop, in other models ($915). RPO N37 Tilt-telescope power steering column ($350). RPO N73 Sport Magnesium Wheels (N/A). RPO NB8 California and Northeast emissions requirements (N/A). RPO NG1 Massachusetts and New York emissions requirements (N/A). RPO QD4 Domestic standard five-spoke wheels (N/A). RPO QF5 Deluxe high-polish wheels ($1,295). RPO R6M New Jersey surcharge, mandatory in New Jersey (N/A). RPO R8C National Corvette Museum factory delivery option ($490). RPO T96 fog lamps (N/A).

Wieck Media

THE 2002 CORVETTE Z06.

RPO U1S Remote 12-disc CD changer ($600). RPO UL0 AM/FM cassette stereo ($600). RPO UN0 Delco/Bose music system with compact disc changer (N/A). RPO UV6 heads-up display (N/A). RPO V49 Front license plate frame ($15). RPO XGG Front tires P245/45ZR17 (N/A). RPO YGH Rear tire P275/40ZR18 (N/A). RPO Z49 Canadian options (N/A). RPO Z51 Performance handling Package ($395).

Z06 OPTIONS

RPO 1SA Option Package coupe and convertible base equipment group (N/A). RPO AAB Memory Package to recall settings for outside rearview mirrors, radio, power seats and heating-ventilation and air-conditioning controls, requires CJ2 ($175). RPO AG1 Power six-way driver seat, standard on Z06 ($305). RPO AN4 Child seat tether (N/A). AR9 Driver and passenger European bucket seats (N/A). RPO B34 Front floor mats ($25). RPO B84 Body side moldings ($150). RPO CJ2 Auto Climate Control air conditioning (N/A). RPO CV3 Mexico export (N/A). RPO DD0 Electronic monochromatic mirrors ($120). RPO EXP Export option (N/A). RPO FE9 Federal emissions certificate (N/A). RPO GU6 3.42:1 Standard rear axle ratio with manual transmission (N/A). RPO LS1 5.7-liter sequential fuel-injection alumium V-8 (N/A). RPO NB8 California and Northeast emissions requirements (N/A). RPO NG1 Massa-chusetts and New York emissions requirements (N/A). RPO QD4 Domestic standard five-spoke wheels (N/A). RPO R6M New Jersey surcharge, mandatory in New Jersey (N/A). RPO R8C National Corvette Museum factory delivery option ($490). RPO UN0 Delco/Bose music system with compact disc changer (N/A). RPO V49 Front license plate frame ($15). RPO XGG Front tires P245/45ZR17 (N/A). RPO YGH Rear tire P275/40ZR18 (N/A). RPO Z49 Canadian options (N/A). RPO Z51 Performance handling Package ($395). NOTE: N/A = not applicable.

HISTORICAL FOOTNOTES

American Le Mans Series Road Racing returned to the downtown streets of Miami after a seven-year absence in October 2002. A pair of Chevrolet Corvette C5-Rs went up against a total of eight Ferrari 550 Maranello, Saleen S7 and Dodge Vipers to finish one-two in the production-based GTS class and ninth and 10th overall. Co-Drivers Ron Fellows and Johnny O'Connell, in the No. 3 GM Goodwrench car, scored its sixth win out of nine 2002 ALMS races. Corvette teammates Andy Pilgrim and Kelly Collins, with two wins in the No. 4 car, finished second. Corvette won its second consecutive J.D. Power IQS award. In the same study, the car's Bowling Green Assembly Plant earned the Silver Award as the industry's second-highest quality plant in North America.

2003

For 50 years, the Chevrolet Corvette has been carefully crafted from a precise blend of power, performance, style and comfort. For 2003, Chevrolet's image machine continued to reign as one of GM's technology and style bellwethers. Model-year highlights included a 50th Anniversary Edition package, more standard equipment on the coupe and convertible models and the availability of Magnetic Selective Ride Control. This feature used a revolutionary damper design that controlled wheel and body motion with Magneto-Rheological fluid in the shock absorbers. By controlling the current to an electromagnetic coil inside the piston of the damper, the MR fluid's consistency could be changed, resulting in continuously variable real time damping. Magnetic Selective Ride Control was optional on 2003 coupe and convertible models. New standard equipment for coupe and

convertible models included fog lamps, sport seats, a power passenger seat, dual-zone auto HVAC and a parcel net (and a luggage shade for the coupe). Also standard on the C5 coupe was air conditioning, a driver airbag, a passenger airbag, alloy wheels, anti-lock brakes, an anti-theft system, cruise control, a rear defogger, remote keyless entry, power locks, power mirrors, heated side mirrors, power steering, power windows, an AM/FM anti-theft radio with cassette, a leather-trimmed power driver's seat, a tachometer, tilt steering, an automatic transmission and the Traction Control system. The C5 convertible added a power antenna. The 2003 Corvette included Child Restraint Attachment System (CRAS) child seat hooks on the passenger seat to allow easier child seat connection. The air bag-"off" switch was used to disable the passenger-side air bag when a child seat was

Wieck Media

THE 50TH ANNIVERSARY CONVERTIBLE WAS ONLY SLIGHTLY MORE POPULAR THAN THE COUPE.

A TORCH RED 50TH ANNIVERSARY CORVETTE.

Wieck Media

installed. All 2003 Corvettes featured a special 50th anniversary emblem on the front and rear. The emblem wass Silver and featured the number "50" with the signature cross-flag design. In addition, Medium Spiral Gray Metallic exterior paint replaces Pewter for 2003.

C5 CORVETTE 50TH ANNIVERSARY (V-8) SERIES YY

The 50th Anniversary Edition package was available only during the 2003 model year on coupes and convertibles. It included special 50th Anniversary Red exterior paint, specific badging, a unique Shale interior (including color coordinated instrument panel and console) and champagne-painted anniversary wheels with special emblems. It also featured embroidered badges on the seats and floor mats, padded door armrests and grips and a Shale convertible top. The Anniversary Edition came with the standard Corvette LS1 engine, as well as Magnetic Selective Ride Control. A special 50th Anniversary Edition of the 2003 Corvette was the Official Pace Car of the Indianapolis 500 in May of 2003, marking the fifth time that a Corvette has paced the race.

C5 CORVETTE 50TH ANNIVERSARY INDY PACE CAR (V-8) SERIES YY

At the time of the Indianapolis 500, the three 2003 Corvettes provided to the Speedway for

Wieck Media

THE BASE LS1 GAVE THE 2003 'VETTE 350 HP.

Pace Car duties were the only 2003 models in existence. Motion picture star Jim Caviezel lead the field of Indy racing cars to the green flag as the Pace Car driver for "The Greatest Spectacle in Racing" on May 26, 2002. Caviezel played the lead role in "High Crimes," a 20th Century Fox film that told the story of an alleged military deserter charged with participating in a mass killing in El Salvador. Corvette brand manager Rick Baldick noted that the race signaled "the start of a year-long celebration leading up to Corvette's 50th anniversary in 2003." The Pace Car was virtually identical to the 50th Anniversary Edition Coupe made available at Chevrolet dealerships in the summer of 2002. It was equipped with a 350-hp 5.7-liter LS1 V-8. A few modifications were made to the 2003 Corvette

Wieck Media

THE 2003 CORVETTE 50TH ANNIVERSARY EDITION.

50th Anniversary Edition Pace Car to prepare it for pacing duties. They included special exterior graphics wrapped over the "Anniversary Red" exterior and a lower-restriction muffler system. A four-point racing-type safety belt setup and a safety strobe-light system were also required by the Indy Racing League. A special heavy-duty transmission and a power steering cooler were also added to the three pace cars.

Z06 CORVETTE (V-8) SERIES YY + Z06

The Z06 Corvette included a special engine, a unique six-speed manual gearbox, hollow-stem valves, a high-lift camshaft, a low-restriction mass air flow (MAF) sensor, a low-restriction air cleaner, a high-performance exhaust system, a Z06-specific FE4 high-performance suspension system, a fat front stabilizer, revised shock absorber valving, a stiffer rear leaf spring, specific camber settings, hydroformed frame rails, a four-wheel independent front suspension with cast-aluminum upper and lower A-arms, aluminum front stabilizer bar links, a transverse leaf spring system, the Head-Up Display (HUD) system and high-performance front brake pads. An AM/FM cassette/radio was op-

tional in the Z06 and no automatic transmission was offered.

ENGINES

BASE ENGINE: [LS1] V-8: Overhead-valve V-8. Cast-aluminum block and head. Displacement: 346 cid. (5.7 liters). Bore & stroke: 3.90 x 3.62 in. Compression ratio: 10.1:1. Brake hp: 350 at 5600 rpm. Torque: (Six-speed manual) 375 lb.-ft. at 4400 rpm; (automatic) 360 lb.-ft. at 4000 rpm. Hydraulic valve lifters. Sequential multiport fuel injection.

OPTIONAL ENGINE: [LS6] V-8: Overhead-valve V-8. Cast-aluminum block and head. Displacement: 346 cu. in. (5.7 liters). Bore & stroke: 3.90 x 3.62 in. Compression ratio: 10.5:1. Brake hp: 405 at 6000 rpm. Torque: 400 lbs.-ft. at 4800 rpm. Hydraulic valve lifters. Sequential multiport fuel injection.

TRANSMISSION

AUTOMATIC TRANSMISSION: A 4L60-E four-speed automatic transmission with floor-mounted gear shifter was standard equipment in coupes and convertibles.

MANUAL TRANSMISSION: A unique six-speed manual transmission with floor-mounted

Wieck Media

THE 2003 CHEVROLET CORVETTE.

gear shifter was standard equipment in Z06. A six-speed manual transmission was optional in coupes and convertibles.

CHASSIS DATA

Wheelbase: 104.5 in. Overall length: 179.7 in. Height: (coupe and hardtop) 47.7 in.; (convertible) 47.8 in. Width: 73.6 in. Front tread: 62 in. Rear tread: 62.1 in. Standard tires coupe and convertible: (front) P245/45ZR17, (rear) P275/40ZR18. Standard tires Z06: (front) P265/40ZR-17, (rear) P295/35ZR-18.

TECHNICAL

Transmission: (coupe and convertible) four-speed overdrive automatic; (hardtop) six-speed manual. Steering: rack and pinion (power assisted). Suspension (front): independent SLA forged-aluminum upper and pressure-cast aluminum lower control arms, forged aluminum steering knuckle, transverse monoleaf spring, steel stabilizer bar, spindle offset. Suspension (rear): independent five-link design with toe and camber adjustment, cast-aluminum upper and lower control arms and knuckle, transverse monoleaf spring, steel tie rods and stabilizer bar, tubular U-jointed metal matrix composite drive-

shafts. Brakes: Anti-lock: power four-wheel disc. Body construction: fiberglass; integral perimeter frame with center backbone/all-welded steel body frame construction. Fuel tank: 18.0 gallons.

HISTORICAL FOOTNOTES

Chevrolet Motor Division announced updated plans for a Corvette 50th Anniversary Celebration on January 16, 2003, at a media briefing prior to the start of the Nashville International Auto and Truck Show Media Preview Luncheon. The 50th Anniversary Special Edition 2003 Corvette was unveiled April 10, 2002 along with the news that it would be the Official Pace Car of the 86th Indianapolis 500. On April 24, Chevy announced a special Commemorative Edition 2004 Corvette to celebrate Corvette Racing's historic Le Mans victories and 2001-2002 GTS class championships at the famed Le Mans 24 Hours. The 2004 Commemorative Edition Z06 featured a new hood using carbon fiber material, new exterior graphics and unique Le Mans Blue paint. A Silver and Red center graphic designed for the 2003 Le Mans race car was also to be used on a limited number of 2004 Commemorative Edition Z06s.

2004

The C5 Corvette maintained its well-earned status as an American sports car icon that had been admired and sought after for a generation. Coming off two consecutive quality awards from J.D. Power and Associates, the C5 continued to earn accolades, in its final season, for providing surprising interior room, cargo space, comfort and fuel economy in a high-performance sports car. Only a handful of cars rivaled the Corvette's ability to capture the fancy of so many consumers and hold it for so long. Chevrolet continued to celebrate the nameplate's golden anniversary in 2004, with efforts to keep the car fresh and "cutting edge" with new designs and technologies such as those featured on the current line: Magnetic Selective Ride Control, Goodyear EMT "run-flat" tires (coupe and convertible), active handling and a rear transaxle. Standard equipment included a 5.7-liter V-8, a four-speed automatic transmission, rear-wheel drive with a limited-slip rear axle, 17 x 8.5-in. front and 18 x 9.5-in. rear alloy wheel rims, Goodyear Eagle F1 GS Extended Mobility run-flat tires, four-wheel independent suspension, front and rear stabilizer bars, front and rear ventilated disc ABS brakes, a passenger airbag de-activation switch, daytime running lights, dusk-sensing headlights, automatic-delay on/off headlights, front fog lights, variable intermittent windshield wipers, a rear window defogger, two-passenger seating with leather bucket seats, a 6-Way power height-adjustable driver's seat with adjustable lumbar support, remote power door locks, one-touch power windows, heated power mirrors, an AM/FM stereo cassette, four Bose premium radio speakers, an element antenna, speed-proportional power steering, air conditioning, front reading lights, dual illuminating visor-vanity mirrors, a leather-wrapped steering wheel, front floor mats, a cargo area light, a tachometer, a trip computer, a clock, and a low-fuel indicator. In addition to or in place of the above, the convertible featured a folding manual roof, a glass convertible rear window, a remote trunk release, and a trunk light.

C5 CORVETTE COUPE AND CONVERTIBLE COMMEMORATIVE EDITION (V-8) SERIES YY + Z15/Z167/Z18

The 2004 Corvettes Commemorative Edition packages recognized the success of the C5-R competition coupes campaigned by the

THE COMMEMORATIVE EDITION Z06 WAS DRESSED TO GO FAST.

Wieck Media

Wieck Media

THE CORVETTE PACED THE FIELD FOR THE SIXTH TIME AT INDY IN 2004.

Corvette Racing Team. The Commemorative Edition Coupe and Convertible included new Le Mans Blue paint with Shale interior, special badges, and polished wheels. The convertible's top also was Shale to match the interior. The Commemorative Edition package contents included a Code 19U LeMans Blue exterior, a Shale interior, special badges, special seat embroidery and RPO QF5 high-polished, five-spoke aluminum wheels with specific center caps. (The Commemorative Edition package was included with (and only available with) the 1SC package, which was a $3,700 option. It included a Shale convertible top with the convertible. The Z18 version of the Commemorative Edition package was for European market cars.

CORVETTE INDY PACE CAR (V-8) SERIES YY

A 2004 Corvette convertible was selected to serve as the Official Pace Car at the 2004 Indianapolis 500. Very few modifications were made to the Corvette to prepare it for this role. They included a heavy-duty transmission, power steering coolers, a lower-restriction muffler system, four-point racing-type safety belts and a safety strobe light system. A two-tone white-and-blue Indy Pace Car paint treatment incorporated Americana-themed graphics to tie into Chevrolet's new "An American Revolution" marketing theme. The theme highlighted Chevrolet's pride and passion for innovation and its success in motorsports,

Z06 CORVETTE (V-8) SERIES YY + Z06

The Z06 Corvette was a Corvette for the extreme performance enthusiast. All 2004 model Z06 Corvettes featured revised chassis tuning for quicker, smoother response in challenging environments. The chassis enhancements were subtle in terms of physical parts, but significant in terms of the car's performance and feel. GM engineers refined the Z06's shock-damping characteristics to provide improved handling in the most challenging conditions, while maintaining good ride control for the demands of daily driving. Continual analysis, development, and refinement of the shock valves in particular resulted in more damping control and force, delivered more smoothly. The new tuning was aimed at diminishing the impact of yaw and roll on the car, particularly in quick, transient ma-

Wieck Media

RACY POWER SEATS WERE ONLY PART OF THE 2004 INTERIOR PACKAGE.

neuvers such as "S-turns" or a series of tight corners. The refinements were the result of extensive testing and development, including several high-speed test sessions at Germany's famed Nurburgring circuit. The Corvette Z06 was one of a handful of cars to break the 8-minute barrier for lap times at Nurburgring.

Z06 CORVETTE COMMEMORATIVE EDITION (V-8) SERIES YY + Z06

The Commemorative Edition Z06 also is Le Mans Blue and also includes a C5-R Le Mans stripe scheme, special badges, polished Z06 wheels and a lightweight carbon fiber hood. For 2004, the regular Z06 was given two performance-enhancing upgrades. A lightweight, race-inspired carbon fiber hood was used on Z06s with the Commemorative Edition option and all Z06s had The carbon fiber hood (Commemorative Edition only) weighed 20.5 lbs. This was 10.6 lbs. less than the standard hood weighed and provided another means of saving

weight on a car that already enjoyed a potent power-to-weight ratio. Previously reserved for racing and exotic sports cars, the carbon fiber hood combined extremely high strength and low weight. The inside hood panel was a hybrid of carbon fiber and Sheet Molded Compound (SMC). Specifically developed for the Corvette, the Commemorative Edition Z06 hood achieved a higher level of exterior finish quality than previous automotive applications of carbon fiber. On most carbon fiber parts, the woven pattern of the material was easily seen beneath the exterior finish. To diminish that effect and preserve the rich LeMans Blue paint finish, on the Commemorative Edition Z06 the carbon fibers were aligned in a single direction.

ENGINES

BASE ENGINE: [LS1] V-8: Overhead-valve V-8. Cast-aluminum block and head. Displacement: 346 cid. (5.7 liters). Bore & stroke: 3.90 x 3.62 in. Compression ratio: 10.1:1. Brake hp: 350 at 5200 rpm. Torque: (six-speed manual)

Wieck Media

LEMANS BLUE WAS RESERVED FOR THE COMMEMORATIVE EDITION 2004 'VETTE.

375 lbs.-ft. at 4000 rpm; (automatic) 360 lbs.-ft. at 4000 rpm. Hydraulic valve lifters. Sequential multiport fuel injection.

OPTIONAL ENGINE: [LS6] V-8: Overhead-valve V-8. Cast-aluminum block and head. Displacement: 346 cid. (5.7 liters). Bore & stroke: 3.90 x 3.62 in. Compression ratio: 10.5:1. Brake hp: 405 at 6000 rpm. Torque: 400 lbs.-ft. at 4800 rpm. Hydraulic valve lifters. Sequential multiport fuel injection.

TRANSMISSION

AUTOMATIC TRANSMISSION: A 4L60-E four-speed automatic transmission with floor-mounted gear shifter was standard equipment in coupes and convertibles.

MANUAL TRANSMISSION: A unique Tremec T56 (M12) six-speed manual transmission with floor-mounted gear shifter was standard equipment in Z06. A Tremec T56 (MM6) six-speed manual transmission was optional in coupes and convertibles.

CHASSIS DATA

Wheelbase: 104.5 in. Overall length: 179.7 in. Height: (all) 47.7 in. Width: 73.6 in. Front tread: (coupe and convertible) 61.9 in.; (Z06) 62.4 in. Rear tread: (Ccoupe and convertible) 62.0 in.; (Z06) 62.6 in. Standard tires coupe and convertible: (front) P245/45ZR17 Goodyear Eagle F1 GS Extended Mobility, (rear) P275/40ZR18 Goodyear Eagle F1 SC Extended Mobility. Standard tires Z06: (front) P265/40ZR-17 Goodyear Eagle F1 SC Asymmetric Tread, (rear) P295/35ZR-18 Goodyear Eagle F1 SC Asymmetric Tread.

HISTORICAL FOOTNOTES

The Corvette performed Indy 500 pace car duties for a record sixth time. This also marked the third consecutive year and 15th time overall that a Chevrolet product had served as the official pace vehicle—the most appearances by any brand. "We're proud that this year's Memorial Day classic will showcase America's favorite sports car at the greatest spectacle in racing," said Brent Dewar, Chevrolet general manager. "As the 2004 model year is the last of Corvette's current design, pacing the Indy 500 acknowledges the significance the vehicle has played in American culture."

2005

On the outside, the all-new 2005 'Vette was a blend of form, function and emotion. The C6 had a new size that makes it a more agile machine, even though it is more powerful than its C5 predecessor. The C6 was 5.1 inches shorter and 1.1 inches narrower than the C5, but had a 1.1-inch-longer wheelbase, allowing it to maintain the same interior room and cargo space. The C6's overall dimensions produced a "tighter" package that was similar to a Porsche 911. "Designing the next Corvette was every designer's dream and a tremendous challenge," says Tom Peters, chief designer of the C6. "Everybody had their personal vision of what a Corvette should look like."

The 2005 Corvette's 6.0-liter LS2 V-8 was a fourth-generation Chevy small-block. GM Powertrain engineer Dave Muscaro described it as "a state-of-the-art engine that draws on a rich heritage of performance."

Three suspension setups were available, and it's important to note that not one single suspension part was carried over from the C5. In additon to the standard setup, the optional F55 Magnetic Selective Ride Control suspension adjusted the shock damping rates instantly in response to changing conditions. The Z51 package includedmore aggressive dampers and springs, larger stabilizer bars, shorter transmission gearing and larger cross-drilled brake rotors.

The new, traditional-looking center-mounted egg-crate grille was traditional, as well as functional, because the C6 switched from the C5's "bottom breathing" design to one that takes air in 60 percent from the front and 40 percent from the bottom. The C6 also used the first exposed headlights seen on a 'Vette since 1962.

The Corvette's traditional "fighter jet" side-profile wass continued in the C6. Viewed from

Wieck Media

THE LOW-SLUNG 2005 C6 CORVETTE WAS A MORE COMPACT DYNAMO, MEASURING 5.1 INCHES SHORTER AND 1.1 INCHES NARROWER THAN THE PREVIOUS GENERATION.

Wieck Media

RATED AT 400 HP, THE 2005 CORVETTE HAD FEW PEERS.

above, the "cockpit" styling was extended to the roof, with more defined dual blisters.

Major interior design elements included a flowing, wraparound upper feature line and a two-tone split between upper and lower instrument panel sections. An AM/FM radio with CD player and MP3 capability wass standard. A new-technology in-the-windshield antenna enhanced radio reception. A full-function On-Star system provided Virtual Advisor, Personal Calling, emergency notification, stolen vehicle tracking, routing assistance and automatic unlocking. Onboard navigation was optional for the first time. U

The new 6.0-liter LS2 V-8 motor was rated for 400 hp at 6000 rpm and 400 lb.-ft. of torque at 4400 rpm. That's 50 horses and 40 lbs.-ft. of torque over the previous LS1.

A Tremec T56 six-speed manual gearbox was standard, but a Hydra-Matic 4L65-E four-speed automatic was optional.

ENGINE

6.0L LS2 V-8; Displacement (liters/cu in/cc): 6.0/364 /5970; Bore & stroke (in / mm): 4 x 3.62 / 101.6 x 92; Block material: cast aluminum; Cylinder head material: cast aluminum; Valvetrain: OHV, 2 valves per cylinder; Fuel delivery: SFI (sequential fuel injection); Compression ratio: 10.9:1; Horsepower (hp / kw @ rpm): 400 / 298 @ 6000; Torque (lbs.-ft @ rpm): 400 @ 4400.

TRANSMISSIONS

Automatic: Hydra-Matic 4L65-E Tremec T56 ; Tremec T56.

Mamual: 6-speed manual, (optional w/Z51 Sport Package)

Wieck Media

THE C6 KEPT THE REMOVABLE ROOF PANEL, BUT WAS SLIGHTLY LARGER.

Wieck Media

CHASSIS

Wheelbase (in / mm): 105.7 / 2686; Overall length (in. / mm): 174.6 / 4435; Overall width (in / mm): 72.6 / 1844; Overall height (in / mm): 49.1/ 1246; Track (in / mm): front: 62.1 / 1577 rear: 60.7 / 1542; Curb weight (lb / kg): est. 3245 / 1470.

HISTORY

The 2005 Corvette Coupe was introduced at the North American International Auto Show in Detroit in January 2004. For the first time since 1968, a 350-cid (5.7 liter) oengine not offered under the Corvette's hood. The 6.0-liter "LS2" V8 was the C6's only engine choice.

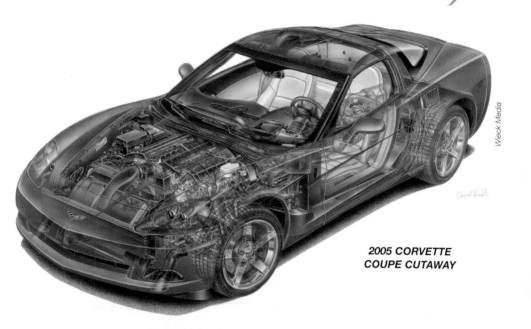

Wieck Media

**2005 CORVETTE
COUPE CUTAWAY**

Wieck Media

THERE WAS JUST ENOUGH ROOM IN THE HATCH TO STORE THE REMOVABLE TOP.

2006

With the debut of the all-new C6 (sixth-generation) Corvette in 2005, the 2006 model received few revisions. Topping the list of what was new was the return of the Z06 name to the Corvette lineup. Last seen as a C5 model in 2004, the new C6-based Z06 hatchback coupe featured power supplied by a 7.0-liter V-8 capable of delivering 505-hp and mated to the Tremec T56 six-speed manual transmission.

Also new for 2006 was the optional (except Z06) six-speed automatic transmission that fea-tured steering wheel paddles for manual opera-tion. It replaced the previously offered Hydra-Matic 4L65-E four-speed automatic.

Again, the Corvette was offered in both coupe and convertible formats. The base coupe had a lift-off roof panel while the ragtop fea-tured a manual-folding fabric top fitted with a heated glass rear window. A power-folding top was optional. The Z06 coupe featured a unique fixed roof panel that reduced overall weight and added structural rigidity.

THE 2006 CORVETTE Z06, FLANKED BY THE CORVETTE COUPE AND CONVERTIBLE.

THE 2006 Z06 HATCHBACK COUPE.

Z06

The return of the Corvette Z06 high-performance coupe was a more than $20,000 step up from the base coupe (original price: $64,890 vs. $43,690, respectively; base convertible cost $51,390). What you got for those extra dollars was what General Motors termed was its quickest and fastest production car ever produced. Chevrolet promoted the Z06 as capable of accelerating from 0 to 60 mph in under 4 seconds, running the quarter-mile in the mid-11-second range and topping out at 190 mph.

The C6 Z06 was powered by the LS7, a hand-assembled, dry-sump lubricated 7,000-rpm 7.0-liter (427-cid) normally aspirated small-block V-8. The all-aluminum engine was comprised of high-tech components such as titanium connecting rods and intake valves, sodium-filled exhaust valves, dry-sump oiling system, forged-steel crankshaft and computer-machined cylinder-head porting. Torque rating was 470 lb.-ft. at 4,800 rpm.

Other Z06 features included an aluminum body with a one-piece hydroformed frame and a magnesium engine cradle. Also included were carbon-fiber composite front fenders, front wheelhouses and floorboard.

Unique features of the Z06 were a larger grille, a cold-air scoop and lower air splitter, wide-body front and rear fenders, and a taller rear spoiler.

Exterior colors offered were Machine silver metallic, Victory red, Daytona sunset orange, Le Mans blue metallic, Velocity yellow tintcoat, and black.

Standard equipment included 18-inch front wheels with Goodyear Eagle 275/35ZR18 tires and 19-inch rear wheels with Goodyear Eagle 325/30ZR19 tires. Z06 brakes featured six-piston front calipers, four-piston rear calipers and used 20 brake pads total.

BASE ENGINE

LS2 6.0L V-8; Displacement (liters/cu. in.): 6.0/364 ; Bore & stroke (in.): 4 x 3.62; Block material: cast aluminum; Cylinder head materi-

al: cast aluminum; Valvetrain: OHV, two valves per cylinder; Fuel delivery: SFI (sequential fuel injection); Compression ratio: 10.9:1; Horsepower (hp at rpm): 400 at 6,000; Torque (lb.-ft. at rpm): 400 at 4,400.

TRANSMISSION

Automatic: six-speed w/overdrive (optional on base Corvette, N/A on Z06)

Manual: Tremec T56 six-speed manual (standard, optional w/Z51 Sport Package)

CHASSIS

Wheelbase (in.): 105.7; Overall length (in.): 174.6/Z06 175.6; Overall width (in.): 72.6/Z06 75.9; Overall height (in.): coupe (base and Z06) 49/convertible 49.2; Track (in.): front: 62.1, rear: 60.7; Curb weight (lbs.): est. 3,245.

HISTORICAL FOOTNOTES

The Z06 was hand-built at General Motors' new Performance Build Center near Detroit.

Lance Armstrong, seven-time Tour de France winner, drove a 2006 Chevrolet Corvette Z06 pace car to start the 90th Indianapolis 500 on May 28, 2006. It was the eighth time for a Corvette to pace the race. 2006 Corvette production figures: base coupe, 16,598 (49 percent); base convertible, 11,151 (33 percent); Z06 coupe, 6,272 (18 percent). Total: 34,021.

THE 2006 CORVETTE CONVERTIBLE.

THE 2006 CORVETTE COUPE.

THE 2006 ZO6.

THE Z06 HAD AN ALUMINUM BODY WITH A ONE-PIECE HYDROFORMED FRAME AND A MAGNESIUM ENGINE CRADLE.

THE CORVETTE WAS BACK AT DAYTONA WITH A PATRIOTIC PACE CAR.

THE 2007 CORVETTE Z06 INTERIOR.

2007

The Corvette's lineup of base coupe and convertible and Z06 was retained from the previous year, but a pair of special editions were added for 2007. These two new Corvettes were the Indianapolis 500 Pace Car edition convertible (that featured Atomic orange paint with gold ribbon stripes, split-spoke wheels and special seat embroidery) and the Z06 Ron Fellows Edition coupe, named after the victorious Corvette driver in the American Le Mans series. It featured red fender stripes on a white body along with a red and black two-tone cockpit.

Other upgrades focused mainly on interior function and included optional two-tone leather seating with embroidered accents, larger glove compartment space and steering wheel-mounted audio controls offered with Bose premium audio systems.

Additional optional equipment new for 2007 included cross-drilled brake rotors offered with the Magnetic Selective Ride Control technology, OnStar communications system available to Z06 buyers and a power top on the base convertible.

ENGINES

Base coupe and convertible (including the Indy 500 Pace Car softtop model) were again powered by the LS2 6.0-liter V-8, rated at 400 hp and 400 lbs.-ft. of torque. The Z06 (including the Ron Fellows Edition coupe) again used the LS7 7.0-liter V-8, rated at 505 hp and 470

THE 2007 CORVETTE SPORTING ATOMIC ORANGE METALLIC TINCOAT.

THE 2007 CORVETTE Z06 COUPE.

THE 2007 CORVETTE Z06 CONVERTIBLE.

AGOVE AND BELOW, THE INTERIOR OF THE 2007 Z06 CONVERTIBLE.

THE 2007 CORVETTE INDY 500 PACE CAR.

lb.-ft. of torque. The Tremec T56 six-speed manual transmission was again standard across the board, with the six-speed automatic listed as a no-charge option for the base coupe and convertible (and, again, N/A in Z06). The base Corvette equipped with an automatic ran the quarter-mile in 12.8 seconds, while the Z06 clocked a 12.2-second time.

SAFETY

Standard safety features again included four-wheel ventilated, antilock disc brakes and "Active Handling" stability control and traction control system (programmed to provide non-invasive assistance, while its performance driving mode gave the driver even more control at the track while maintaining a safety net). Side-impact airbags were optional.

BODY STYLES

Again listed as being available in two body styles, coupe and convertible, the 2007 Corvette in reality offered three: targa-roof coupe, fixed-roof coupe and convertible. The base coupe had a removable "targa" roof panel that allowed for an open-air experience similar to the convertible. The Z06 coupe's roof was fixed in place for additional structural rigidity.

FEATURES

The base coupe and convertible came standard with xenon headlamps, keyless entry and

THE RON FELLOWS EDITION Z06.

startup, tire-pressure monitor, leather seating, six-way power driver seat and dual-zone automatic climate control. Notable options included a navigation system, transparent roof panel for the coupe, head-up display (HUD), driver-seat memory and seven-speaker Bose audio system.

Suspension options available included the Magnetic Selective Ride Control that automatically firmed and softened the suspension in milliseconds according to how the car was being driven, and the Z51 performance handling package that added cooling capacity; stiffer springs, shocks and stabilizer bars; larger brakes with cross-drilled rotors; specific tires and specific gearing for the six-speed manual transmission.

The Z06 maintained most of the base coupe's features but added a lightweight aluminum frame, wider wheels and tires, a more stiffly tuned suspension, better brakes and unique sport seats.

HISTORICAL FOOTNOTES

Corvette pricing started at $42,503 for the base coupe, $52,590 for the base convertible and $69,175 for the Z06 coupe. A 2007 Chevrolet Corvette convertible driven by actor Patrick Dempsey paced the start of the 91st Indianapolis 500 on May 27, 2007. It marked the ninth time — and record fourth consecutive year — that Corvette has served as the official pace car of the Indy 500. 2007 Corvette production figures: base coupe, 21,484 (53 percent); base convertible, 10,918 (27 percent); Z06 coupe, 8,159 (20 percent). Total: 40,561.

2008

The biggest change to the 2008 Corvette was focused under the hood of the base coupe and convertible. A new, small-block LS3 6.2-liter V-8 replaced the LS2 V-8 that was introduced when the C6 debuted in the 2005 model year. The Tremec T56 six-speed manual transmission that was standard on previous C6 Corvettes was also replaced with the Tremec TR6060 six-speed manual.

Joining the pair of Corvette Indianapolis 500 Pace Car models (both a coupe and convertible) as a second 2008 special edition model was the Corvette 427 Limited Edition Z06 coupe. Only 505 were produced, with 427 of those offered for sale in North America.

Also new was the base coupe/convertible's split-spoke wheel design that debuted on the limited-edition 2007 Indianapolis 500 Pace Car edition models with a Sterling Silver finish. The standard 18-inch front wheels and 19-inch rear wheels featured a Sparkle Silver finish. Optional was a Competition Gray version.

Two new exterior colors became available in 2008: Jetstream Blue Metallic Tintcoat and Crystal Red Metallic Tintcoat (replacing Le Mans Blue Metallic and Monterey Red Metallic Tintcoat).

All Corvette models now came standard with features that were previously optional or part of equipment packages. These included: OnStar

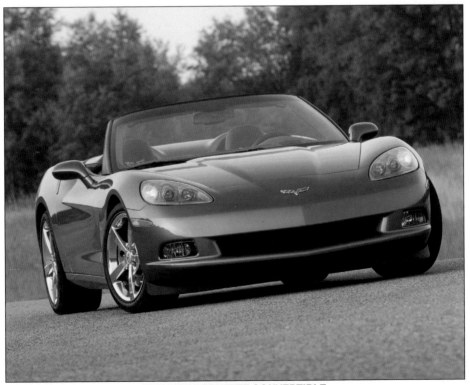

THE 2008 CORVETTE CONVERTIBLE.

THE BIG NEWS FOR THE 2008 'VETTE WAS A NEW SIX-SPEED MANUAL TRANSMISSION.

with available Turn-By-Turn Navigation, XM Satellite Radio, auto-dimming rearview mirrors (with compass) and audio input jack on all radio systems except navigation. Corvettes also came with a new Keyless Access fob, which featured the key and remote-function controls integrated in a single unit.

A new Custom Leather-Wrapped Interior Package was also offered across the board. It featured two-tone leather-appointed upper and lower instrument panel, door pads and seats; choice of new, exclusive colors: Linen or Sienna; padded door panel armrests; "Corvette" embroidered on passenger-side dash pad; embroidered crossed flags logo on headrests and a unique center trim plate with Bias pattern.

427 Z06

The Corvette 427 Limited Edition Z06 paid tribute to the big-block Stingray models of the mid-1960s. Its 427 designation referred to the cubic-inch displacement for the highest-performance engines Chevrolet offered between 1966 and '69 (as well as the cubic-inch equivalent of the Z06's LS7 7.0-liter small-block V-8).

The 427 Z06's unique features included: Crystal Red Metallic Tintcoat paint, chrome wheels, Dark Titanium leather-wrapped interior, chrome exterior badges, Z06 sill plates, special hood/fascia striping reminiscent of the "Stinger" design found on the '67 Corvette, 427 hood badges, 427 seat and floor mat embroidery, painted Z06 spoiler and body color door handles and certificate of authenticity.

Cost of the 427 Z06 was $84,195, approximately $13,000 more than the regular Z06.

ENGINES

The LS3 6.2-liter (376-cid) small-block V-8 became the standard engine in base coupe and convertible models. It was rated at 430 hp at 5,900 rpm and 424 lbs.-ft. of torque at 4,600 rpm with the standard exhaust system; with the optional two-mode exhaust system, power ratings increased to 436 hp and 428 lb.-ft. of torque. As a result, the Corvette was capable of 190 mph. The LS3, mated to the six-speed paddle-shift automatic transmission, was the

THE 2008 CORVETTE CONVERTIBLE.

fastest automatic-equipped Corvette ever, with 0-60 mph capability of 4.3 seconds.

The LS3 featured a larger-bore cylinder block (4.06-inch vs. the previous LS2's 4.00-inch bores, but the engine's stroke remained at 3.62 inches); high-flow, LS7/L92-style cylinder heads; larger-diameter pistons; revised camshaft and camshaft timing; revised valvetrain with offset intake rocker arms; high-flow intake manifold; high-flow fuel injectors from the Z06's LS7 engine; and an engine beauty cover.

HISTORICAL FOOTNOTES

Corvette pricing started at $42,503 for the base coupe, $52,590 for the base convertible and $69,175 for the Z06 coupe. History was made at the May 25, 2008, Indianapolis 500 when a pair of Corvettes served as the official pace cars. One was a customized Corvette Z06

E85 concept that ran on E85 ethanol fuel, and was driven by two-time Indianapolis 500 champion Emerson Fittipaldi. The other was a black-and-silver commemorative edition that marked the 30th anniversary of the celebrated 1978 pace car — the first Corvette to pace the Indianapolis 500. The 92nd Indianapolis 500 was the Corvette's 10th appearance — and fourth in-a-row — as the official pace car. A total of 500 2008 Corvette ZHZ coupes, fitted with the LS3 V-8 mated to the six-speed automatic transmission, were produced for Hertz Corporation's Fun Collection rental car fleet. All ZHZ models were painted yellow with black striping on the hood and roof. 2008 Corvette production figures: base coupe, 20,030 (57 percent); base convertible, 7,549 (21 percent); Z06 coupe, 7,731 (22 percent). Total: 35,310.

ABOVE AND BELOW, TWO VERSIONS OF THE 2008 INDY PACE CAR.
CHEVROLET PREPARED TWO OF THE SPECIAL GREEN CARS BELOW.

THE 2008 'VETTES GOT A NEW AVAILABLE LEATHER INTERIOR PACKAGE

THE LEATHER-WRAPPED INTERIOR GROUP INCLUDED A
TWO-TONE TREATMENT ON THE DOORS.

2009

As it did in 2006 with the Z06, Chevrolet again reached into its past to resurrect the ZR1 Corvette for 2009. Debuted late in the model year, the ZR1 was powered by a supercharged 6.2-liter V-8 that produced 638 horsepower. It was the most powerful and costliest (starting at $106,620) Corvette to date.

Also in tribute to its racing accomplishments, Chevrolet added a limited-production GT1 Championship Edition Corvette to the lineup for 2009.

The remainder of the Corvette lineup entered 2009 with minor revisions, the most significant of which was the availability of Bluetooth phone connectivity.

Two new exterior colors, Cyber Gray Metallic and Blade Silver Metallic were added, while Machine Silver Metallic was discontinued. The Corvette crossed flags emblem was also revised with a brighter surround.

Inside, two new leather-wrapped interiors, Dark Titanium and Ebony, were offered joining Sienna and Linen.

The Z06 also received several tweaks. These included: a "spider" design 10-spoke wheel offered in Sparkle Silver, Competition Gray or chrome; color-keyed door and instrument panels with red and titanium interiors; power-operated pull-down hatch now standard; door sill plates with the Z06 logo and an acoustic package now standard. The Z06 also received a larger-capacity dry-sump oiling system to replace the former eight-quart version. It was an upgrade to the 10.5-quart system of the new ZR1.

WITH A TOP SPEED OF 205 MPH, THE 2009 ZR1 WAS CERTAINLY AT HOME ON THE TRACK.

THE 2009 ZR1, WEARING VELOCITY YELLOW PAINT.

ZR1

The ZR1 name was previously used from 1990-'95 (then spelled ZR-1). The ZR1's LS9 engine was a modified version of the LS3 that featured 9.9:1 compression and produced 638 hp at 6,500 rpm and 604 lb.-ft. of torque. The LS9 employed a sixth-generation Eaton TVS R2300 roots four-lobe supercharger with intercoolers from Behr, utilizing an air-to-water, dual-brick design. The engine's connecting rods and inlet valve were titanium. Heads were made from a heat-resistant aluminum alloy. The camshaft lift was reduced from the LS7's to improve idle quality.

The ZR1 also featured a double-wishbone suspension system and Magnetic Selective Ride Control. This system adjusted shock-absorber damping in real time to either Tour or Sport mode.

The ZR1's chassis, similar to the 2008 Z06, was aluminum. To decrease overall weight, several of ZR1's body panels were carbon fiber. These included fenders, hood, roof, splitter and rocker extensions. The hood contained a polycarbonate window that allowed viewing of the intercooler. To prevent sun damage to the carbon fiber, panels received a special paint treatment.

Other ZR1 modifications included a strengthened Tremec TR6060 six-speed manual transmission, specialized wheels and tires and Brembo carbon-ceramic brakes. A larger spoiler than found on previous Corvettes topped the rear bumper and functional fender vents provided engine cooling. "LS9 Supercharged" graphics graced the plastic supercharger cover.

Curb weight of the ZR1 was 3,352 lbs., and its top speed was 205 mph. Production was limited to 2,000 units.

GT1

It was fitting that Chevrolet introduced its limited-production GT1 Championship Edition Corvettes at Sebring International Raceway. The GT1 Championship Edition (RPO GT1) commemorated the success of Corvette Racing and

THE 2009 ZR1 WAS BILLED AS THE FASTEST CAR EVER BUILT BY GENERAL MOTORS.

THE ZR1 FEATURED 20-INCH WHEELS IN BACK, 19-INCHERS IN FRONT.

**THE ZR1 HAD SPECIAL NAMEPLATES ON THE DOOR SILLS AND
A SPECIFIC GAUGE CLUSTER ON THE DASH.**

the Corvette C6.R. It was offered on the base coupe, convertible and Z06 models beginning in the spring of 2009.

Included in the GT1 Championship Edition package were graphics inspired by C6.R livery including Corvette Racing "Jake" mascot, ALMS championships and driver flags; ZR1-style body color full-width spoiler and chrome wheels; custom leather-wrapped ebony interior with exclusive yellow accent stitching; GT1 embroidery on leather seats, instrument panel and center console armrest; engine cover with carbon pattern and yellow Corvette lettering; windshield banner (owner installed)

The GT1 Championship Edition Corvette was available in Velocity Yellow (with black headlamps) or Black. Production was limited to 100 per each color and body style combination (600 total). The coupe and convertible versions also included the Z51 Performance Package and NPP Performance Exhaust, and the optional MX0 six-speed paddle-shift automatic transmission. The coupe also offered the optional dual-roof package.

HISTORICAL FOOTNOTES

ZR1 Corvettes were hand assembled in Bowling Green, Ky. Its engines were built at the General Motor Performance Build Center in Wixom, Mich. Adding to the 500 2008 coupes produced for Hertz Corporation's Fun Collection rental fleet, an additional 150 2009 Corvette ZHZ convertibles were built. They were again finished in yellow with black striping. 2009 Corvette production figures: base coupe, 8,737 (52 percent); base convertible, 3,343 (20 percent); Z06 coupe, 3,461 (20 percent); ZR1 coupe, 1,415 (8 percent). Total: 16,956.

THE LS3 ARRIVED IN 2008 AS THE CORVETTE'S BASE ENGINE, AND RETURNED FOR 2009.

THE EXOTIC AND ULTRA-FAST 2009 GT1.

2010

In keeping with previous recent introductions of models that recalled Corvette's glory years, Corvette re-launched the Grand Sport model for 2010. Planned well ahead of its model year launch, Corvette, nonetheless, needed this performance shot in the arm to help stem rapidly declining sales of America's sports car. (The alarming slide from 35,310 units produced in 2008 to 16,956 in '09 was partially due to the economic "recession" paralyzing both the United States and new car sales. Unfortunately, the economic woes and slide in sales continued for 2010, with Corvette production falling to 12,194 units.)

All manual-transmission 2010 Corvette models featured General Motors' new Launch Control that modulated engine speed to enhance grip during full-throttle launches. The ZR1 added a Performance Traction Management system that allowed drivers to select from five modes (Wet, Dry, Sport with Active Handling, Sport without Active Handling, Race), which optimized power delivery for specific conditions.

Also new were a Cashmere interior color option for the Z06, side airbags became standard and the convertible employed a Z06-style rear spoiler.

GRAND SPORT

Mimicking the base coupe and convertible, the Grand Sport was offered as both a two-door hatchback or convertible and was powered by the LS3 6.2-liter V-8. The optional dual-mode exhaust added another six hp and four lb.-ft. of torque. Grand Sport replaced the previous Z51 option package and included front fender stripes and vents, wider front and rear fenders with integrated Grand Sport badging up front, a Z06-style front splitter and tall rear spoiler, unique alloy wheels, Z06-size brakes and tires,

AS IT HAD DONE WITH THE ZR1 AND Z06 NAMEPLATES, CHEVROLET BROUGHT BACK THE GRAND SPORT NAME, DEBUTING THE NEW CAR FOR 2010.

THE STUNNING 2010 CORVETTE GRAND SPORT COUPE.

THE GRAND SPORT INTERIOR FEATURED SPECIALLY EMBROIDERED HEADRESTS.

THE SPECIAL LOUVERS WERE ONLY FOUND ON THE GRAND SPORTS FOR 2010.

specific manual-transmission gear ratios and a dry-sump oiling system for models fitted with the manual transmission and a specific rear axle ratio on automatic-equipped models.

With launch control, the Grand Sport was capable of a 0-60 mph time of four seconds.

HISTORICAL FOOTNOTES

Corvette pricing started at $48,930 for the base coupe, $53,580 for the base convertible, $54,770 for the Grand Sport coupe, $58.580 for the Grand Sport convertible, $74,285 for the Z06 coupe and $106,880 for the ZR1 coupe. 2010 Corvette production figures: base coupe, 3,054 (25 percent); base convertible, 1,003 (8 percent); Z06 coupe, 518 (4 percent); ZR1 coupe, 1,577 (13 percent); Grand Sport coupe, 3,707 (30 percent); Grand Sport convertible, 2,335 (19 percent). Total: 12,194.

THE 2010 CORVETTE CONVERTIBLE

THE 2010 CORVETTE COUPE

ABOVE AND BELOW, THE 2010 CORVETTE GRAND SPORT.

2011

Todd Schnitt, radio host of the nationally syndicated "Schnitt Show," inaugurated a program in August of 2010 that allowed Corvette buyers to help build their own car's V-8 engine. The option, which cost $5,800, was for customers who purchased either the 2011 ZR1's 6.2-liter supercharged V-8 or the 2011 Z06's 7.0-liter V-8. Both engines were hand-built at the General Motors Performance Build Center in Wixom, Mich. Customers signed up for the program when they ordered their Corvette, and typically built their V-8 in a few weeks.

THE 2011 CORVETTE CONVERTIBLE.

THE 2011 CORVETTE Z06.

THE 2011 CORVETTE GRAND SPORT

THE 2011 CORVETTE ZR1

THE 2011 CORVETTE ZR1 CARRIED A PAVEMENT-MELTING 638-HP LS9 ENGINE.

With the C6 version of the Corvette getting mature (see History), changes for 2011 models were minimal. The lineup of base coupe and convertible, Grand Sport coupe and convertible and Z06 coupe and ZR1 coupe carried over intact from 2010.

One new special edition, the Z06 Carbon coupe was launched in the summer of 2010. Only 500 were expected to be produced. The Carbon Special Edition was available in two colors: Inferno Orange and new-for-2011 Supersonic Blue. These two colors were also available on the 2011 Corvette ZR1.

The Carbon edition's exterior featured black headlamps and mirrors; ZR1-type spoiler; and carbon fiber hood, rockers and splitter. The interior featured Ebony leather and suede seats with body color-matching stitching. The Carbon coupe also included Magnetic Selective Ride Control, a carbon engine cover, 20-spoke black wheels (19-inch front and 20-inch rear) and ZR1's carbon ceramic Brembo brakes.

HISTORICAL FOOTNOTES

Corvette pricing started at $48,950 for the base coupe, $53,600 for the base convertible, $54,790 for the Grand Sport coupe, $58.600 for the Grand Sport convertible, $74,305 for the Z06 coupe and $111,100 for the ZR1 coupe. With the C6 (sixth generation) Corvette in its seventh year of production in 2011, the rumor mill concerning the design of the C7 was churning out-of-control. At press time for this book, General Motors confirmed that the C7 Corvette would begin production in April of 2012 as a 2013 model. The C7 Corvette will retain its front-engine layout, and one option would be a twin-turbo 3.6-liter DOHC V-6 capable of 400 horsepower. An extra-cost V-8 would most likely also be offered for those Corvette purists who shun change.

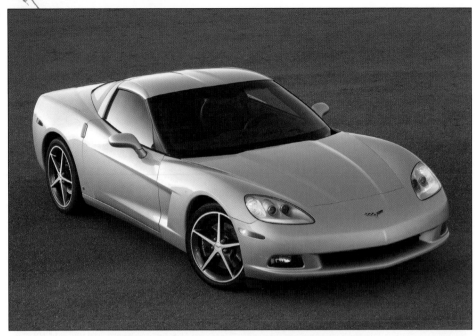

ABOVE AND BELOW, THE 2011 CORVETTE COUPE.

THE FENDER HASH STRIPES AND LOUVERS WERE BACK ON THE GRAND SPORT.

CHEVY PLANNED TO BUILD 500 COPIES OF A SPECIAL CARBON EDITION ZR1 FOR 2011.

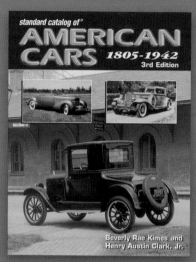
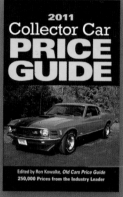
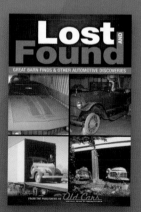
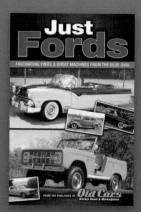
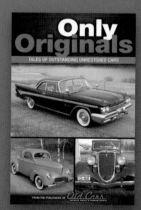

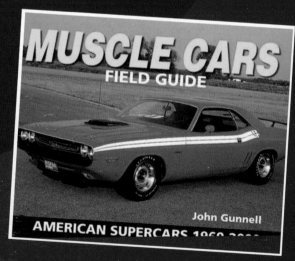